BARCODE IN BACK

T

Native American Performance and Representation

Native American Performance and Representation

S. E. WILMER, EDITOR

The University of Arizona Press Tucson

The University of Arizona Press
© 2009 The Arizona Board of Regents
All rights reserved

www.uapress.arizona.edu

Library of Congress Cataloging-in-Publication Data

Native American performance and representation / S. E. Wilmer,
editor.
    p. cm.
  Includes bibliographical references and index.
  ISBN 978-0-8165-2646-8 (cloth : alk. paper)
  1. American drama—Indian authors—History and criticism.
2. American drama—20th century—History and criticism.
3. Canadian drama—Indian authors—History and criticism.
4. Canadian drama—20th century—History and criticism.
5. Indian theater—United States—History—20th century.
6. Indian dance—North America.   7. Indians of North America—
Intellectual life.   8. Indians in literature.   9. Indians in motion
pictures.   I. Wilmer, S. E.
  PS153.I52N377 2009
  791.089'97–dc22   2008055274

Manufactured in the United States of America on acid-free, archival-
quality paper containing a minimum of 30% post-consumer waste
and processed chlorine free.

14   13   12   11   10   09   6   5   4   3   2   1

Contents

Preface

This book evolved out of a meeting of the 23rd American Indian Workshop on the theme of "Ritual and Performance" that I was asked to host at Trinity College Dublin in March 2002. Often papers from this conference are printed in the *European Review of Native American Studies* or *Acta Americana*, but I thought it would be appropriate to edit a collection of some of these papers into a book and commission additional ones, since so little has been published about modern Native performance. Although a non-Native, I have been encouraged by Native as well as non-Native scholars to pursue this project, and I would like to express my thanks to Christian Feest, Gerald Vizenor, and Ann Haugo for their advice in developing the material for this book. I also want to thank Denis Salter, Edward Little, and Ric Knowles for permission to reprint the essay by Monique Mojica, "Stories from the Body: Blood Memory and Organic Texts," which appeared in *alt. theatre: cultural diversity and the stage* 4, nos. 2 and 3 (May 2006): 16–20. Thanks also go to Holly Maples, Mary Caulfield, and Aoife Lucey for assistance in preparing the manuscript.

Native American Performance
and Representation

Introduction

THIS BOOK BEARS WITNESS to the traditional and modern forms of artistic expression among the Indigenous people of Canada and the United States. It is groundbreaking in its attempt to investigate a broad range of contemporary Native work from the viewpoint of Native scholars and practitioners who have engaged in these activities for most of their lives as well as from the perspective of non-Native scholars who have studied these practices with a theater, film, performance, or anthropological background. Applying diverse methodologies such as postcolonial discourse, feminism, literary and film theory, and autobiographical narrative, the essays consider the performance strategies of specific individual practitioners and groups, and they address a variety of current issues relating to the position of the Native in North America today. The book considers a variety of art forms in order to emphasize the importance of performance both historically and in the modern world as a means of preserving and reasserting cultural values amid Eurocentric incursions and globalized lifestyles. The aim of the book is not to investigate traditional performance practice from an anthropological point of view, as much ethnographic scholarship has done in the past. Neither is it to dwell on the tragedy of the inhuman treatment of the Indigenous people in North America and the demise of their earlier lifestyles, as some historical literature has done. Nor is it simply to glorify the ideologies implicit in Native belief and custom, as is prevalent in "new age" literature. The objective of the book is more to review and assess the changing nature of Native performance strategies in a multicultural society.

This is quite a new field, and it arises out of the proliferation since the Red Power movement of the 1960s and 1970s of Indigenous performance activity in such media as theater, dance, performance art, film, video, and multimedia. Theater and performance scholarship has been somewhat slow to tackle these new genres. The book reveals the ways in which Native culture and artistic expression have been controlled by non-Native culture, through Indian reservations and prohibitions on dance, ritual, and religious practices, and through the residential schools whereby Native children were taken from their parents and put in boarding schools so that they would be taught to forget their Native customs, values, and culture. This resulted in the suppression of Native languages and lifestyles and the gradual obliteration of Native identities. Thus many tribes have become dispersed and in some instances have recently sought outside help to re-educate themselves in their former practices. It is significant that during 2008, the prime minister of Canada apologized officially to the First Nations for their treatment in the past, and particularly for the residential schools.

The political and economic situation of Native North Americans has substantially improved in recent years, owing to successful campaigns for land rights and sovereignty that have been connected with a worldwide struggle since the 1960s for the legitimacy of the traditions, cultures, and lifestyles of Indigenous peoples. For example, the Canadian government made large political concessions to the Inuit population through the creation of the new territory of Nunavut in 1999, and in 2007 the United Nations adopted a Declaration on the Rights of Indigenous Peoples "to protect their lands and resources, and to maintain their unique cultures and traditions."[1] Commenting on the effectiveness of this political struggle, Simon Critchley has written, "indigenous political identity is that rare thing, a brand new political phenomenon. . . . What is fascinating about the example of Mexican indigenous political identity is the way in which a new political subject is formed against the repressive actions of the state through the articulation of a new universal name—the indigenous."[2] Often, Indigenous peoples have used performative strategies to further their visibility and achieve their political ambitions. For example, in 1972, Aboriginal activists erected an "Aboriginal Tent Embassy" outside the National Parliament in Australia to demand the restitution of Aboriginal land rights and a respect for their cultures. This "beach umbrella on a lawn in Canberra," according to Critchley, had "the effect of calling into question the entire legality of the state and calling for redress to a massive historical wrong."[3] The "Aboriginal Tent Embassy," which the Australian government has refused to recognize as the embassy of a sovereign nation, has been relocated or firebombed on several occasions, but since 1992 it has maintained a permanent presence, and the Australian government has gradually recognized the legitimacy of some of the Aboriginal claims. In 2008, the prime minister (like the

Canadian prime minister) officially apologized to the Indigenous peoples of Australia for their treatment in the past.

The prominence and success of these political campaigns internationally has also created a renewed energy in and enthusiasm for Indigenous cultural activities. The essays in this collection capture some of this passion, but not in an uncritical manner. Like the plays, films, and performances that they discuss, the authors do not shy away from controversy. They raise thorny issues, such as the relationship between authenticity and hybridity in Native performance; the response of different types of Native, non-Native, and mixed audiences to Native performance; the effect of miscegenation on traditional customs and lifestyles; the position of Native women in a multicultural society; and the problems that have affected modern Native life, such as racial discrimination, social exclusion, stereotyping, alcoholism, addiction, violence, rape, and child abuse. They also engage with some of the ongoing political debates over land rights and sovereignty and reveal the international scope of Indigenous activism. The book aims to create a greater understanding of the new forms of Native performance, to promote an appreciation of their rich diversity, and to instill a respect not only for traditional Native customs but also for contemporary cultural expression.

The contributors to the book examine not only how Native Americans and First Nations people have expressed and represented themselves, but also how they have been represented by non-Natives on stage, film, and television, in children's stories, and by the tourist industry. Their essays consider such issues as the authenticity of cultural forms and the processes by which they evolve, the tensions between traditional and modern values and ways of life, and the importance of the Red Power movement in the 1960s and 1970s as a watershed for the resurgence of Native cultural activity. They also discuss some of the patterns of cross-fertilization between disparate cultures, both Native and non-Native, and demonstrate the amalgamation of traditional and modern practices that have given rise to new methods and forms of narrative, performance, and cultural expression. Native cultural practices are not static. They change in response to many factors, not the least of which is influences from non-Native cultures. However, the question of authenticity has also been used as a means of control by both Natives and non-Natives. Native performers are often questioned about whether their work is authentic, as a way of validating or invalidating it. One of the issues lying behind some of the articles in this book is whether the notion of authenticity is a red herring or whether there is an important quality in Native cultural expression that can be deemed as authentic by contrast with, for example, a performance by a non-Native performing as Native. This question also relates to the definitional problem of what constitutes a Native performance and, more problematically, what is a Native or Indigenous person. For example, many of the Native performances are hybrid in their nature, and Native artists often have affiliations with more than one tribe. They have many cultural as well as genetic influences on their performance work and on their bodies. Full-blooded Indians from a particular tribe are rarer in North America today, and much of the performance work today mixes aspects from various tribes as well as from non-Native culture.

Traditional Native artistic expression has always been an integral part of Native life. Dance, music, costumes, masks, face painting, and storytelling are all part of the ceremonial practices of Native cultures. They vary enormously in form and appearance among different tribes, from the masked dances of the Kwakwaka'wakw on the Pacific Northwest Coast, to the kachina puppetry of the Hopi, to the Sun Dance of the Lakota. In his introduction to *Native American Expressive Culture*, Richard Hill observes that "Most Indian languages do not have words for 'art' or 'culture.' The idea that these concepts were separate from each other was unknown to the people of this land. Art and culture were integrated into the daily life of the people, as were religion and economy. This holistic way of being has been called a world view—the composite beliefs that stimulate the thinking, guide the actions, and inspire the creativity of a people."[4]

In the nineteenth and twentieth centuries, staged representations of Native Americans for non-Native commercial audiences became popular in Wild West Shows, circuses, fairs, exhibitions, vaudeville, and burlesque, as well as in museums and tourist venues. However, since the 1960s, Native artists have increasingly taken control of Native performances, molding them to conform with their own needs and values through various media such as drama, dance, performance art, and film.

In a book such as this, it would be impossible to present fully the vast field of Indigenous performance practices in North America, or the many ways in which Native Americans and First Nations people have been represented and continue to represent themselves. In recent years, we have seen the creation of many new theater and dance companies and venues, including the Native American Theatre Ensemble, Spider-woman, Native Earth, and Red Earth, as well as a huge increase in the number of Native playwrights, such as Hanay Geiogamah, Tomson Highway, Drew Hayden Taylor, Diane Glancy, and William S. Yellow Robe, and the work of performance artists such as James Luna, and dance artists such as Daystar, Belinda James, and Longboat. We have also witnessed the rise of Native media artists, including Sherman Alexie, Thomas King, Aaron Carr, Shelley Niro, Victor Masayesva, and George Burdeau, and the celebrated success of such writers as Leslie Marmon Silko, Louise Erdrich, Gerald Vizenor, Vine Deloria, and the Pulitzer Prize–winner N. Scott Momaday. Moreover, Native cultural infrastructure has expanded considerably with the development of radio and television programming like the Aboriginal People's Television Network in Canada, and with educational centers such as the Institute of American Indian Arts in Santa Fe and the Aboriginal Arts Programme at the Banff Centre for the Arts. Other art forms have also been growing at a rapid rate over the last decades, such as multimedia, puppetry, music, literature, sculpture, painting, embroidery, ceramics, jewelry, and weaving; and there are an increasing number of museums and art galleries in which Indigenous people have a dominant presence, such as the George Gustav Heye Center in New York, the National Museum of the American Indian in Washington, and the Pequot Museum in Mashantucket, Connecticut. Furthermore, there is now a proliferation of popular events that attract non-Natives as well as Natives, such as powwows and Sun Dances, as well as an ever-increasing number of Native-owned casinos that provide performance and other employment opportunities for Native artists. These casinos have also provided substantial economic subsidies to Native individuals, groups, and organizations. The most that one can hope to accomplish in this book is to introduce the variety and complexity of Indigenous performance traditions and current practices, and to analyze some of the related controversies and contradictions that have occurred. The book also ventures into somewhat less conventional territory by including essays on Chicano/a theater and nineteenth-century American melodrama, both of which have frequently employed Indigenous characters as part of their dramaturgy and have represented Native people from very different perspectives. Chicano/a theater, for example, has often represented Chicanos/as as having more in common with their

Native than their Spanish ancestors, while melodrama has tended to stereotype Native characters, though not always negatively.

The book is divided into four parts that deal with separate though overlapping themes. The first part considers the evolution of stories and performances over long periods of time and the ways that they have been transformed by Natives and non-Natives, and through Native and non-Native interaction. The second part stresses the role of the Native body and presence in performance, and how it affects the impact of the production on the audience. The third part focuses on written drama by Natives and non-Natives, and on how it represents the Native in society. The final part features discussions on Native media production and the new perspectives that they offer on Native customs and traditions.

One of the recurrent themes in the book is the tension between the traditional and the modern. The first part groups together four essays that focus on this topic with regard to dance, drama, and storytelling. Not static practices, Native stories and performances are shown to have been evolving over time, with or without the influence of non-Natives, thereby problematizing conventional notions of tradition and authenticity. Emerging from the community as a religious and ceremonial practice, dance has ventured into non-Native performance venues as a form of entertainment as well as a means of cultural expression, taking on both non-Native and Native attributes. Native artists have responded to new environments and contexts, altering and updating dance patterns, music, scenography, costumes, and storytelling, and availing themselves of modern technology (such as lighting and sound) to enhance and reappropriate performances and narratives for Native and non-Native audiences. These articles also record how younger generations, especially in the last forty years, have learned about traditional practices by engaging with new art forms.

The four essays are written from different perspectives and deal with various forms of performance. Daystar/Rosalie Jones provides a first-person narrative of her own involvement in the evolution of Native modern dance, showing how she has combined traditional and modern techniques to create new styles of dance for Native and non-Native audiences. Traditional Native dance is part of Native ceremonies that vary considerably from one tribe to another for both ceremonial and social purposes. Richard West argues that Native Americans dance "to assert cultural identity, to fulfill family and community obligations, to enjoy the sense of belonging to a group, to feel the sheer joy of movement. Whether it is ceremonial or social in nature, native dance is an essential part of being—it may be wonderfully entertaining, but it is never regarded as entertainment."[5]

Dance ceremonies, along with religious rituals, were generally frowned upon and often banned by colonial and national governments in North America up until the middle of the twentieth century. The second half of the twentieth century has seen a new appreciation of Native custom and tradition by both Natives and non-Natives that has encouraged a renaissance in many traditional as well as innovative forms of dance. From the position of an insider, Daystar/Rosalie Jones discusses the increased opportunities that have opened up for Native dance artists since the 1960s with the creation of the Institute of American Indian Arts in Santa Fe, New Mexico, the Center for Arts of Indian America, and the Native American Theatre Ensemble, as well as through funding from the U.S. government and cultural institutions such as the Ford and Rockefeller foundations. She proudly traces her career as one of the founders of Native modern dance, recalling how, with the assistance of tribal elders and non-Natives alike, she helped develop the concept and practice of Native modern dance, and reveals the evolving process of her own performances over the past forty years. Having grown up on a reservation in Montana, she shows how she has incorporated traditional storytelling and family history into her work, along with techniques acquired while training at Julliard. As a choreographer as well as a teacher and dancer, she has been responsible for some of the most innovative developments in Native modern dance and has worked with people of different tribes to create pieces that speak to audiences of all origins and backgrounds.

Sarah Bryant-Bertail reflects on the experience of visiting Tillicum Village, an enterprise outside Seattle, Washington, created forty years ago by a non-Native entrepreneur who hired Indigenous people to stage traditional masked performances. She examines the history of the masks and performance traditions of the Kwakwaka'wakw and other Northwestern tribes, and discusses the performances that originated from the community and are now staged in Tillicum Village. She also considers a number of complex cultural transactions that arose in her experience of visiting this tourist attraction.

Anne-Christine Hornborg documents the decline in interest among the Mi'kmaq in the traditional myth of Kluskap over the centuries and examines its subsequent revival from the 1960s. She reveals that the first ethnologists to record the story in the nineteenth century had already found a variety of forms of the story, many of which seem to have been affected by contact with Europeans. Moreover, ethnologists such as Rand, Leland, and Speck, who operated according to the "salvage paradigm," not only recorded the various versions of the story for posterity but also modified details in them as they felt appropriate. By the mid-twentieth century, ethnologists were regretting the disappearance of traditional stories about Kluskap from Mi'kmaq culture and its confusion with other non-Native cultural influences, such as Disney characters. Hornborg recounts how children's books and shows for Canadian television revitalized the myth. In the late 1960s and 1970s, interest in Native traditions arose amongst the Native as well as the non-Native populations in Canada, and Hornborg notes that a non-Native theater performance about the Kluskap story excited the younger Mi'kmaq generation about using theater for preserving traditional culture. Like the resurgence of Native theater and dance described by Daystar/Rosalie Jones, Native artists in Nova Scotia sought to research the disappearing traditions of folk stories—particularly the Kluskap stories—and often relied on non-Native research for guidance. Moreover, Hornborg shows how the Mi'kmaq invoked traditional stories for political purposes in a land dispute on Cape Breton Island, and discloses the process by which the tribe incorporated the scholarly work of non-Natives to reinforce their own traditions. The political dispute over the proposed quarry in Kluskap's mountain resulted in the need to invoke the research of non-Native ethnographers to verify the mountain as a sacred place and authenticate Mi'kmaq traditions that had been partly lost.

In contrast to Hornborg, Maria Lyytinen focuses on a historical Native character, Pocahontas, who was turned into a legendary figure by non-Native writers as a means of justifying their occupation of Native lands and assuaging their guilt after killing off the original inhabitants of the United States. Through histories, plays, novels, and films written by non-Natives (including the recent Disney films), Pocahontas was constructed as a virtuous and virginal figure who fell in love with a white man, adopted the values of his culture, and helped him overcome the hostile Native population. She has been portrayed as the savior and protector of European immigrants and as having assimilated European culture as part of a non-Native discourse that implies that the "good Indian" is one who rejects her own people. By contrast, many Native Americans have regarded Pocahontas as a traitor to her people, similar to Malinche, the mistress of the conquistador Hernán Cortés. However, Lyytinen proceeds to show

how recent Native artists have reappropriated Pocahontas for their own purposes, often parodying non-Native representations of her. In particular, the playwright and performer Monique Mojica characterizes her as a ridiculous figure conjured up as a subject of the white man's gaze. In her play *Princess Pocahontas and the Blue Spots*, Mojica satirizes her, as well as a series of other stereotyped women, by way of reclaiming those figures of colonial discourse for the empowerment of Native women today.

One of the common issues that the authors confront in this part is the way in which traditional practices have been transformed and updated in recent times, and they question the extent to which it is meaningful to speak about cultural authenticity. On the one hand, the notion of authenticity can be seen as misleading, since culture is always in the process of evolving as a result of changing circumstances, contact with other (Native and non-Native) cultures, and spontaneous improvisation and invention. Thus, the idea that traditional values and customs remain static seems misguided. However, the attempt by non-Native commercial enterprises to package and sell Native authenticity as a commodity—even when it is clearly presented in a consciously inauthentic manner—can be differentiated from the work of Native artists such as Daystar/Rosalie Jones who create performances that have evolved from the community and, despite modernization, retain traditional features and values.

All of the authors in the first part trace a long historical process in their essays, showing the changing nature of narrative and performance practices over centuries. They also focus on the watershed of the 1960s as a turning point for developing new forms of Native artistic expression and recuperating lost traditions, histories, and identities. They indicate that Native artists have not only survived threats to their cultures but also countered demeaning colonial discourse by using performance and storytelling as a means of positive self-expression and representation. They demonstrate that, in spite of confusing juxtapositions with contrasting cultural forms and ways of life, Native traditions and values will continue to be perpetuated in new and complex forms.

The second part of the book focuses on staged productions and on the importance of the Native body in performance, both as a site of presence and memory and as a means of conveying "acts of transfer." The performance of Native plays and one-person shows has increased enormously in the last forty years. Many new Native-run venues and production companies have been established in both Canada and the United States.[6]

The opportunities for Native artists to tell stories and perform traditional dances and newly written plays seem to be increasing all the time. The importance of the Native bodily presence in these performances is the subject of this part.

Monique Mojica recalls the childhood memories and experiences, both sensory and historical, that feed into her artistic process and provide material for her performances. She reveals how her connections with the "show Indians" in her extended family and the wider Native community have given her a rich heritage to tap for such pieces as *The Only Good Indian* and *Princess Pocahontas and the Blue Spots*. She recounts the ways in which knowledge of the tragedies of Native peoples throughout the Americas—from a massacre in Chiapas, Mexico, to the disappearance of the Manhattan Indians—wounds her emotionally and informs her work. She conveys how her body, as a site of memory and heritage, reflects those experiences and affects the impact of her performance on an audience.

Julie Pearson-Little Thunder discusses the origins of the Red Earth Performing Arts Company and their first two productions of *Raven* and *Body Indian* in the 1970s. She argues that the presence of Indian performers and directors raised an awareness of Native customs, values, and physical behavior that informed the scenography and choreography as well as the characterization, gestures, physical presence, and vocal patterns of the actors. Like Mojica, she indicates that the bodies of Indians onstage provided a visual message to the audience, as well as transferring knowledge about Native ways of life. The two productions discussed differed considerably, in that one recounted a series of fanciful folktales of animal creatures, whereas the other presented a realistic, though at times expressionistic, portrayal of binge drinking in an extended Kiowa family. However, both productions benefited from the Native actors' and directors' intimate knowledge of Native customs, traditions, and use of the body.

Likewise, Shelley Scott identifies the importance of the Native body onstage as a "signifier of authenticity and the site of lived experience" in her analysis of monologues by Native artists. Focusing on the work of three practitioners—Shirley Cheechoo, Daystar/Rosalie Jones, and Monique Mojica—she reveals the autobiographical nature of their work and the ways in which they and other Native female artists use their bodies and personal memories in performance to convey a visceral experience to the audience. Shirley Cheechoo acts out different moments of her own life, while Daystar/Rosalie Jones inhabits the bodies of her ancestors as well as her own, and Monique Mojica embodies the characters of historical and mythical women from five hundred years of contact history. All of these performers present their material in a somewhat metatheatrical way, acting as storytellers as well as embodying the characters they present. As Shelley Scott suggests, "the acknowledgment of the performer *as* performer is crucial to the meaning of the performance, embodied in her physical presence as a self-identified Aboriginal woman." Specifically, the performer acts out her own traumas from the past, enabling a healing process both for herself and for the members of the audience.[7]

Like Mojica, Pearson-Little Thunder, and Scott, Ric Knowles comments on the importance of the Native body in recent performances. He reviews the large number of Native plays that have featured the theme of rape and sexual violence against Native women, arguing that in plays written by Native women, it displays material consequences for the characters in the here and now, whereas it is frequently used as a metaphor in plays written by Native and non-Native men. He demonstrates how myths of racial purity have been used against Native women, who have been implicated in the transformation of the population through mixed-race alliances, and he argues that by re-membering their heritage and legacy (and here the body of the performer can become critical), Native women can recover their past and resist colonization and assimilation. Reviewing a range of plays and performances by Native women artists, including Shirley Cheechoo and Monique Mojica, Knowles shows, as does Scott, the significance of the embodied practice of these performers who speak autobiographically about their and their ancestors' experiences. He further points to the similarity in performance styles of Mojica and her mother, Gloria Miguel of Spiderwoman, both of whom employ memory and history to embody the characters of their ancestors, and he examines how Mojica, like Gloria Anzaldúa, has redeemed the characters of sexually abused Native women for posterity.

In these four essays, one can appreciate the visceral impact of Native bodies on the stage both for Native and non-Native spectators. Pearson-Little Thunder calls the Native body a "living link between past and present," and, similarly, Scott suggests that the "scars of history are worn on the body, and made visible by a kind of storytelling that is a mixture of public testimonial and personal healing."

The third part concerns the dramaturgy in plays by Native and non-

Native authors that depict Native characters, lifestyles, and behaviors. The number of published Native plays has grown from only a handful in the 1960s to over two hundred by 2007,[8] some of which, like those by Hanay Geiogamah, Tomson Highway, and Drew Hayden Taylor, have achieved international acclaim. Furthermore, seven major play antholo- gies,[9] as well as volumes of single and multiple texts by individual authors, have been published. In addition, there is increasing scholarly interest (both in North America and Europe) in Native plays.

In this part, Jaye T. Darby discusses the work of one of the best-known Native playwrights, Hanay Geiogamah, who has written hard-hitting dramas about dysfunctional families and self-destructive lifestyles. She shows that his aim is, ultimately, to strengthen a sense of Native identity and self-esteem. Darby, who has worked closely with Geiogamah, ana- lyzes his early works *Body Indian* and *49*, emphasizing their "communit- ist" (community and activist) function. Despite portraying members of a dysfunctional extended family whose abuse of alcohol leads them to abuse one another, *Body Indian*, in Darby's view, provides a redemptive message for the Native community, encouraging it to recognize the evils of this type of self-destructive behavior and to return to traditional values of community responsibility. Likewise, in Geiogamah's play *49*, com- munal Native values and traditional responsibilities have been disrupted by modern life. However, the intercession of Night Walker, the timeless spiritual leader of the tribe, who engages in a vision quest to redeem the Native community, causes a positive outcome for the younger generation, influencing a "cultural and spiritual metamorphosis . . . from their earlier self-destructive behavior and selfish individualism [to] the restoration of kinship ties and the sacred power of communitarianism."

David Krasner compares William S. Yellow Robe's play *The Inde- pendence of Eddie Rose* to a bildungsroman, arguing that the play depicts sixteen-year-old Eddie in a moment of transformation, as he decides to take on the responsibility of his family at an early age. Tempted to flee his dysfunctional family, he resolves by the end of the play to stay and change the domestic situation. Like Bobby in Geiogamah's *Body Indian*, Eddie Rose suffers from a family damaged by alcohol abuse. But unlike Bobby, Eddie takes control and makes a responsible, though difficult, decision for the good of his family. Reminiscent of the final action taken by the characters in *49*, Eddie's decision is enabled by the restoration of traditional customs and values, and it works for the good of the community. Thus, as the *Bildung* dimension of the play (with Eddie's maturation influenced partly as a result of the support of his aunt and the spirit of his dead grandmother) is similar to the spiritual effect of Night Walker on the youth in *49*, one might also consider the similarity between "communitism" and *Bildungseffekt*.

Jorge Huerta provides a different perspective by discussing the work of two Chicano/a playwrights, Estela Portillo and Luis Valdez, who have posited Native characters and myths as important aspects of their dramaturgy. He reveals that many Chicano/a playwrights have used Indigenous myths and characters of the Americas in their work, such as Cherríe Moraga, Edit Villareal, Octavio Solís, and Josefina Lopez. As Huerta suggests, Chicanas/os, living in the "borderlands" between North America and Latin America, are a people "with a fractured, postmodern identity that is more Mexican than Anglo and more Indio than Spanish." Like Jaye Darby, Jorge Huerta also examines the dramaturgy of two recent plays—in this case written by Chicana/o playwrights and portraying Chicana/o characters identifying with their Indigenous roots. He investigates the representation of Native traditions and cultures in *Day of the Swallows* by Estela Portillo, which he considers to be a "poetic realist" play, and *The Mummified Deer* by Luis Valdez, which he terms a "poetic fantasy." Portillo's *Day of the Swallows*, which is set in the nineteenth century, features a protagonist who, ashamed at being seen kissing another woman, cuts out the tongue of the witness and later commits suicide, confident that, in accordance with Indigenous beliefs, she will live on in spirit. Luis Valdez, who used Aztec and Mayan imagery in his early myth plays (*mitos*) of the 1970s, employed images from his own Yaqui heritage to convey a sense of Indigenous culture in his recent play *Mummified Deer*. The central character is an eighty-four-year-old Yaqui woman who carries a sixty-year-year-old fetus in her womb, a metaphor for the Chicana/o's stifled Indio heritage. Set at the end of the 1960s, at the time of the awakening of political consciousness amongst the Chicanas/os (as well as Native North Americans), the play features a Yaqui deer dancer as a symbol of the mummified fetus, and at the same time as someone that the grandmother identifies as a rebel figure in Mexican political history. As in *Day of the Swallows*, the protagonist of *Mummified Deer* dies at the end of the play, but she also finds redemption in an Indigenous afterworld.

Bruce McConachie considers yet another historical era and genre of playwriting relevant to Native life: nineteenth-century melodrama written by non-Natives. The subject of Native Americans was common in the United States in the 1800s, and, after sketching out some of this terrain, McConachie focuses on one particular play and the scholarly debate that has arisen about its highly successful reception: John Augustus Stone's *Metamora, or the Last of the Wampanoags*. McConachie sees the play as important because it fostered a number of imitations in its wake, creating a precedent for the "stage Indian" in North American theater. He reviews the debate as to whether or not the play was racist and legitimated the Jacksonian policy of Indian removal. He concludes that the role of the Native chief, Metamora, was a vehicle through which the actor Edwin Forrest could show his talent, and that the play's ideological subtext was, for the audience, not one of racism but of class and national consciousness, as well as "scorn for the emerging norms of Victorian respectability and domesticity." Edwin Forrest played a number of similarly charismatic roles in which he represented the common man acting against the aristocratic oppressor. As in real life, when a riot occurred in New York because an English actor had insulted Forrest's dignity, the audience identified with Forrest (in the role of Metamora) as an American superhero taking justifiable revenge against those who had wronged him. Rather than seeing him as an Indian (despite Forrest having lived with the Choctaw tribe as a young man and having adopted some of their mannerisms and speech patterns in his performance), the audience saw the character of Metamora as an American oppressed by the English. For the working-class audiences watching *Metamora* in the 1840s and 1850s, in McConachie's interpretation, the "Indians are the American people of the Revolutionary era, yearning for freedom from English tyranny."

The chapters in this part analyze individual plays written by Native, Chicana/o and non-Native playwrights, and focus on the dramaturgy of the works as well as their effects on the audience. Despite discussing very different kinds of plays, all four chapters conclude that, in general, the dramas exhibit a redemptive quality that provides positive reinforcement for Indigenous custom and tradition.

The last part focuses on video and film work by Native American artists, which has mushroomed in the last thirty years. As Jacquelyn Kilpatrick has argued in her book *Celluloid Indians: Native Americans and Film*, "the history and cultures of Native Americans have been miscommunicated in films, and the distortions have been accepted as truth, with sometimes disastrous results."[10] Stereotypical characters such as the noble savage, the bloodthirsty, war-mongering heathen, the virginal Indian Princess, and the sexually promiscuous squaw filled cinema and television screens in the United States for much of the twentieth century.

Since the Red Power movement, as Kristin Dowell observes, Native artists have reclaimed the screen from Hollywood producers, using the media "to document cultural practices, recuperate community narratives, and sustain cultural memory," as well as to "challenge the power hierarchy of dominant society to represent Native communities." Increasing opportunities have opened up for Native filmmakers, through the establishment of various media organizations. By contrast with the stereotypes of the "cowboy and Indian" films of the twentieth century, Native screenwriters and documentary makers such as Gerald Vizenor, Thomas King, Aaron Carr, Shelly Niro, Victor Masayesva, George Burdeau, and Drew Hayden Taylor have transformed how Native lifestyles are portrayed in the media, privileging Native audiences.

In the first of the two essays in this part, Kristin Dowell reviews the work of documentary makers and other Native artists who have undermined Hollywood stereotypes of Native Americans on film and developed a "medium through which Native filmmakers resignify cultural traditions and practices of representation in the borderlands between dominant and Indigenous forms of film/video practice." In particular, she applies border theory and notions of trickster discourse and embedded aesthetics to her analysis of the work of Mohawk filmmaker and photographer Shelley Niro, who employs film to "critique dominant perceptions of Native peoples while celebrating the resilience of Native women." Dowell demonstrates the humor in several of Niro's works that "destabilize stereotypes of Native people." She interprets Niro's parodic film *Honey Moccasin* as an example of trickster discourse, which playfully shows the inventiveness of Native people in responding to a crisis when their powwow costumes are stolen. Like Daystar/Rosalie Jones and Sarah Bryant-Bertail, Dowell remarks how the constant changes in Native culture have helped it survive. The powwow is a particularly good example of this, being a Native festival where members of many different tribes come together and exchange cultural customs. As Dowell writes, "Native cultural survival has always involved a sense of constant innovation and improvisation." Moreover, as in Shelley Scott's chapter, Dowell attests to the importance of Native embodiment in performance, describing a moment in the film when a Native performance artist projects archival images of atrocities onto her body.

Annie Kirby-Singh's chapter concludes the book with an examination of two additional Native filmmakers, Victor Masayesva and George Burdeau, who have sought to use film for the purpose of celebrating Native culture and challenging its portrayal by the dominant society. She comments on the sense of moral responsibility that these Native filmmakers share in their concern about what to show and what not to show about their Native cultures, and in questioning "how best to express their knowledge so that it will not be misused or misinterpreted." Kirby-Singh demonstrates that Masayesva has preferred to focus exclusively on Hopi culture and orientate his films toward a Hopi audience, as a result of which non-Natives have found them hard to understand. By contrast, Burdeau has filmed various tribes for a broader audience, with an interest in passing on traditional stories, and his film *Backbone of the World* emphasizes not only the narrative but also the art of the storyteller. As in Hornborg's discussion of Mi'kmaq storytelling practices, Kirby-Singh comments on the authorless nature of Blackfeet storytelling that is revealed in Burdeau's film, whereby the teller relays a story that has been told to him/her, thus passing on communal knowledge. As a common trait of Native storytelling, "they are all conveyors but not originators of the story, which forms part of the body of Blackfeet oral tradition."

Both Dowell and Kirby-Singh reveal the political awareness and activism involved in Native filmmaking. Similar to Jaye Darby's discussion of Hanay Geiogamah's texts as examples of communitism (activist and community), Dowell and Kirby-Singh observe that the filmmaking of Niro, Masayesva, and Burdeau are concerned with preserving community values. They take their social responsibility as filmmakers seriously. For example, as Kirby-Singh points out, Masayesva regards film as a medium for "radical empowerment" and as a means to "subvert the colonizer's indoctrination and champion Indigenous expression in the political landscape." Like drama, storytelling, and dance, Native film is being used to challenge the dominant discourse and ensure cultural survival.

These chapters show that issues of authenticity, intercultural/bicultural experiences, transnational identifications, and multicultural reception continue to trouble Native performance and representation. However, through self-representation in a wide range of cultural forms, including the use of the Native body onstage and in the media, Native peoples have reclaimed control over their heritage and sought to belie the stereotypes of non-Native image makers. In so doing, they have also worked to heal the traumas of the past and to reassert their own sense of identity.

Part I

Reframing Dance, Performance,
and Traditional Stories for a Postmodern Era

CHAPTER 1

Inventing Native Modern Dance
A *Tough Trip through Paradise*

DAYSTAR/ROSALIE JONES

A View from the Mountain: A Journey Begins

I was born in the United States on the Blackfeet Reservation in the state of Montana. My ancestry is of the mixed bloods of Blackfeet, Pembina Chippewa, French-Cree, and, on my father's side, Welsh. Growing up on the reservation, we all knew that it was a Blackfeet chief who contributed a portion of the tribe's traditional territory to the United States so that Glacier National Park could be created. Glacier is actually an alpine ecological system, the only one of its kind in the lower forty-eight states. My ancestors knew that terrain—they lived near its lakes and rivers, hunted in its forests, gathered its berries and roots, and endured its winters. Although Glacier is one of the most beautiful spots on earth, its dangers can be subtle, and for that reason, the area can be frightening, overwhelming, and unforgiving.

I have vivid recollections of being camped out there with my parents and grandparents. It could be a bright sunny day, green grass, sparkling mountain streams, birds singing. Then you notice a few soft white flakes drifting down ever so quietly—at that moment, an alarm goes off! Everyone shifts into double time—sleeping mats are rolled up, the tent comes down, pots and pans are thrown in the trunk, and the car is on the road, bumping down the mountain, just as fast as you can go. It could be September, or May, or June, or August. It doesn't matter—a storm can boil up at any time. You don't want to take the chance of taking a "tough trip through paradise"!

Yet, despite the record number of fatal bear attacks and drownings in various glacial lakes over the years, people continue to flock to Glacier National Park. Why? It must be the sheer pristine beauty and mystery of the place. Once you are standing on the "backbone of the world"—the

Continental Divide—you crane your neck to look up at the surrounding mountains that rise even higher from where you are, into the "big sky," where mountains that are engulfed in clouds and mist can only be described as the *ladder to the Creator's House.*

Entering the realm of Native performing arts has a similar beauty and austerity. The very existence of Native people and their land, the dances they dance, and the songs they sing, beckons to many individuals. Some see the beautiful and the eclectic, and others recognize the tradition from which it comes; still others want to dissect the whole into its components in an effort to find the metaphoric root of the blossoming tree. The long-standing question, looking "in" from the outside, is: What is American Indian ritual and performance? My question, looking from the inside out, is: What does dance and dance performance mean to the American Indian? What does it mean to dance traditional or to dance "modern," and how do these two seemingly contradictory forms coexist for the Native person?

It is in this spirit that I compile this document: to create a record of a first-person experience from within the practice of *Native modern dance.* I do not present myself as a scholar, but rather as an artist with a history in the field as I have known it over the past forty years. I will tell this story through my experiences, and the experiences of other Native and non-Native people who had a vision, climbed some mountains, survived both squalls and whiteouts in the journey to the summit; a journey still ongoing. We begin our tough trip through paradise in the foothills—green, rolling, and gentle.

It is best to view the field of Native modern dance within a broader context, that of Native North American performing arts. In the Native worldview, one cannot speak of dance without speaking of the drum and the song. In actuality, one cannot dance without the song. In the Native world, ceremony is often referred to as "dance." In the Native worldview, dance and song are intimately fused to the ceremonials, and the ceremonials are tied to the cosmologies, and the cosmologies are tied to the life and being of the Creator. It is because of the Creator that we are able to sing and dance and, therefore, to give thanks for his many gifts to us. Giving thanks is one of the most important reasons for traditional song and dance. Equally important reasons to dance in a traditional manner are to cry out for assistance, to fulfill a spiritually inspired vow or ceremonial cycle, for social interaction, and to maintain a healthy body and mind.

First of all, what is *Native modern dance*? The term was coined by Dr. Charlotte Heth, Cherokee ethnomusicologist, when she titled the chapter that I was to write for an article to be published in the 1992 Smithsonian publication *Native American Dance: Ceremonies and Social Traditions.*[1] That book became the first official publication of the new National Museum of the American Indian in Washington, D.C. Dr. Heth, in asking me to write the essay, wanted me to formulate a written impression of what was being done by Native peoples in the performing arts, especially dance, in the latter half of the twentieth century. Dr. Heth suggested the title "Native Modern Dance: Beyond Tribe and Tradition." This gave me pause. It was the first time I had heard a Native person admit that there was such a performing art form in the United States, that Native peoples were evolving it and practicing it, and that the art form was actually moving "beyond tribe and tradition."

From the beginning of my professional career I have asked myself the question, Should we be doing such a thing? It can be agreed that, because of governmental or personal relocation in America over the past five hundred years, many Native peoples no longer live with their tribes, at least not on an ongoing physical basis. But does this mean that we are also moving beyond tradition? And more importantly, if that is happening, where will it lead? Because Native modern dance has been brought into being primarily by the younger generations of Native peoples, and because my career in teaching young Native people existed and still exists in tandem with Native communities, much of my material will be drawn as well from their contribution to this developing art form.

Institute of American Indian Arts, 1966

My actual work in this aspect of the field began as I was working on a master's degree in dance at the University of Utah in 1966. The call came from Ronald Meinholtz, then director of theater at the Institute of American Indian Arts (IAIA) in Santa Fe, New Mexico. He was looking for someone to choreograph a mainstage production using Native performers—dancers, actors, singers, and musicians—that would be performed at the Carter Barron Amphitheatre in Washington, D.C. The

secretary of the interior, Stewart Udall, and his wife, Lee, were very interested in having IAIA showcase their student talent before a Washington
audience of Congressional cabinet members. Funding for the school was
the end purpose of the project. The superintendent of the institute later
told me that they had approached Agnes de Mille to choreograph, but she
declined with the phrase, "I wouldn't touch that with a forty-foot pole!" I
give her credit for that—she realized that there was more to choreograph-
ing an "Indian," that is, Native, production than beads and feathers. I was
honored to step in for Ms. de Mille.

IAIA was founded in 1962, in large part through the vision and political lobbying of the late Lloyd Kiva New, a well-known Native textile artist
of Scottsdale, Arizona. The main thrust of the school was the visual arts,
but the theater program was also well organized. The school was known
for its innovative use of Native cultural material and perspective in developing the usual courses such as acting, voice and movement training,
costuming, set design, and performance. The school also encouraged
original student playwriting. The Carter Barron production, however, had
to be seen as a special instance; it needed spectacle—a certain largeness
and authenticity that would get IAIA the funding it needed to continue to
pursue its vision as the only national school of its kind for Native artists.

Sipapu: A Drama of Authentic Dance and Chants of Indian America
was based on Coyote trickster stories of the Southwest, with a core acting
ensemble created with the IAIA theater students. Dr. Louis Ballard, internationally known Cherokee/Quapaw composer, pianist, and teacher on
the IAIA faculty, would write an original symphonic and choral score, to be
performed by the IAIA Chorus and the Washington Symphony Orchestra.
Once in Washington, the core group was joined by almost two hundred
Native traditional dancers and singers from tribes across America.

The script had been conceived in such a way as to utilize various tribal,
intertribal, and social dances that would contribute to the dramatic line of
action. The amalgam of the two hundred traditional dancers represented
dancers and dance styles from all regions in the United States, including
Oklahoma plains dancers, Seminole stomp dancers, Alaskan Northwest
Coast Haida and Tlingit dancers, and Iroquois and Pueblo dancers. For
the first time on stage in America, the Hopi Butterfly Dance appeared in
full regalia during the final scene. And what of the modern dance? The
dance elements were treated as an integral part of the dramatic elements.

Character movements were provided for Coyote, the Skookum Hags, and other characters, and dance was seen as a means of illustrating the action-based scenes, such as "the building of the pueblo."

This was 1966, and the production *Sipapu* was a complete success, both culturally and financially. IAIA did get its funding, but the money was not given to the theater program alone, as is often the case in funding strategies. Rather, the performing arts had been used as a vehicle to garner funds for the school as a whole. The trek through paradise just got tougher. Later I would realize how often this particular stratagem is employed in the larger world. Native performing artists are, on a regular basis, asked to bring out their talents, hard-won by discipline, cultural integrity, and creativity, in the support of others not of their field, albeit for very worthy causes.

In my next few years of teaching at IAIA, I was to see a caring faculty with a good curriculum who were training talented students to ask the question, Can there be a Native theater and dance form, and if so, what could it, and should it, be? These young people were drawing from both tribe and tradition and from the experience of their own lives. Their generation was making a solid beginning in the process of creating their own theater. This is no small matter. The performing arts program, as it was being developed in the 1960s at the Institute of American Indian Arts, *was* the beginning of theater and dance training for Native people in North America. The fact that IAIA has not been able to fulfill the scope of professional training in the performing arts arena, as it did in the visual arts arena, is one of the tragic chapters in American Native performing arts. This storm cloud would gather, not suddenly, but slowly and deliberately, over the years.

Juilliard School, 1969

Meanwhile, the alpine sun graciously continued to shine for me, as I pursued my own development, largely thanks to the interest and support of one woman, Lee Udall. As wife of the secretary of the interior, she had taken a special interest in the training of the Native youth in the performing arts and created an organization called the Center for Arts of Indian America. Under those auspices she developed a regimen of sending two people each year—for almost ten years—to New York City, for further training. I was chosen for such a scholarship in 1969 and spent a year at the Juilliard School, studying with José Limón, Betty Jones, and Erick Hawkins—all exponents of the José Limón and Martha Graham techniques, and pioneers of the American modern dance movement.

José Limón became both a mentor and friend to the Native modern dance movement. He had transformed himself from a newly Americanized immigrant from Mexico in the early 1940s into a painter, dancer, choreographer, assistant, and, finally, the artistic director to Doris Humphrey, herself an early modern dance pioneer. Being of mixed blood himself— Spanish and Indian—he had a blood rapport with those of us who were struggling with the issues of how to handle the choreographic material for Native expression. The experience of living in New York was another influential aspect of my year at Juilliard. We were told to see everything we could, from off-Broadway to Broadway to opera to modern dance to ballet, and the tickets were gratis, courtesy of the Udall project budget. We studied and observed, and we began the upward climb in earnest.

Flandreau Indian School, 1970

My work with Native young people began that next fall, when I was sent to teach at Flandreau Indian High School in South Dakota. "Center" scholarship recipients were to spend one year teaching out in the field, and through her contacts in Indian country, Mrs. Udall arranged for Flandreau Indian High School to engage a Native dance teacher and choreographer to work with their students. We would see where the experiment would take us.

I came to know the story of the White Buffalo Calf Pipe Woman at Flandreau Indian High School in South Dakota. Originating from the Lakota oral tradition, the highly respected and almost ceremonial story relates how the gift of the Pipe was given by the Creator to the Lakota people. Seven gifts were given in all, and those gifts were candidly described by holy man Ben Black Elk in his book *The Sacred Pipe*, recorded and edited by Joseph Epes Brown for the 1953 publication of the same name. It was significant to me, upon this first invitation to introduce modern dance into a Native school, that one of the most traditional and sacred stories would be brought out for interpretation and, furthermore, that it would be performed by the younger generation of the Lakota, who were my students.

Because the story was not spoken of in everyday conversation, or spoken of casually, those unfamiliar with tribal behaviors would assume, therefore, that the story was of little meaning or consequence. Just the opposite was true. In the process of the work, I realized that here was a story that most of the Lakota students knew intimately. As if of one voice, they were able to realize a strong, poetic, and respectful presence onstage. I also found that I had almost equal numbers of boys and girls in the class—not at all what one would find in a conventional dance class of the Western world. To this day, this attribute remains one of the consistent elements of Native modern dance—that men dance, and always with great spirit, pride, and finesse. I also discovered two elements that allowed inexperienced students to feel secure in the theatrical process: wearing masks and not having to memorize lines. To this end, we settled on a format of storyteller and dancer/actor. An elder or a teaching adult became the storyteller, while students took the role of dancers; some were masked for character work, and others were without mask. In addition, there would be a contingent of traditional dancers of all ages who were ready to dance, and who could be called upon to provide the musical framework. And, as is always the case, a drum group, along with singers, was available to create traditional drum and song for either the traditional or the modern dancers.

As we worked on the project, certain priorities established themselves. The elders would work with us as we prepared the material. They would be our guides as to which portions of the story could be told and which portions were inappropriate and restricted from the general public. By the close of a semester's work, these Lakota students created and performed, in a theatrical modern dance context, the work we called *The Sacred Pipe*, based on a script written specifically for the project by Cordell Morsette, a young Lakota writer and teacher (fig. 1). This initial Native modern dance project taught me an important paradigm in the teaching of Native students: What other story should they do? What other material would work as well for them as the material from the ancestry and beliefs of their own cultural heritage? I realized that such work reinforces tribal and personal identity, and this in turn instills confidence and belonging. On another level, such work can be seen as a contemporary vehicle for reinforcing the art of storytelling and its place in the culture.

Martha Hill, director of dance at the Juilliard School in New York City at that time, and José Limón, one of two stellar dancers (along with

FIGURE 1. *The Sacred Pipe*, 1969. Performance group at Flandreau Indian High School. Lakota students Eagle Horse as White Buffalo Calf Pipe Woman (front), Charles Wall as Chief Two Bears (center back). Choreographer: Rosalie Jones. (Photographer unknown)

Martha Graham) who were teaching at Juilliard, arrived at the high school as special guests for the buildup to the performance. The visitation was a direct outcome of the training program for Native dancers at Juilliard, to assess the program thus far realized. An unprecedented moment was about to take place: José Limón, world-renowned pioneer of modern dance in America, would lead the final rehearsal of fledgling Native dancer/actors as they presented a staging of one of the most sacred stories from their oral tradition. In the audience sat Martha Hill, former Graham dancer. It was a moment to remember. Mr. Limón addressed the student body at the close of the performance. I paraphrase his remarks: "You are being held in reserve for the contributions that you can make to the future of your people." What none of us knew at the time was that José Limón was dying of cancer. He had taken the train from New York City, gaining some extra hours of sleep before rejoining the José Limón Company on tour in California. We would not see him again. Cancer would overtake a chore-ographer and teacher of truly exceptional poetry and humanity.

Professional Developments, 1972

In the meantime, other Native theater and dance hopefuls were start-ing their climb to the summit. The year was 1972, and a young Kiowa playwright named Hanay Geiogamah managed to pull the Native theater rabbit out of the reservation hat! The first professional Native theater com-pany in American was being created, with the assistance of that great lady of New York theater, Ellen Stewart, founder and director of the La MaMa Experimental Theatre Club in New York City. It was she who helped Mr. Geiogamah secure the necessary start-up money from the NEA, and the Rockefeller and Ford Foundations, to create NATE—the Native American Theater Ensemble.[2]

Out of a pool of two hundred audition hopefuls, Mr. Geiogamah selected sixteen Native actors. Some of those are well established today as professionals: playwrights Bruce King (Oneida) and Gerald Bruce Miller (Skokomish), comedian-actor Charlie Hill (Oneida), poet, novelist, and musician Joy Harjo, and writer Debbie Finley Snyder. Out of the sixteen, only one was already a working New York actress—Marie Antoinette Rogers. It was of special interest to Native theater development that seven from the list of the chosen sixteen were graduates of the Institute of American Indian Arts and had performed in the Carter Barron produc-tion. One individual, Jane Lind (Aleut) went on to become a seasoned New York professional, doing both theater and film. Geraldine Keams and Timothy Clashin went on to teach and establish a theater troupe at Navaho Community College and to work in the Los Angeles film indus-try. Bernadette Track returned to the Taos Pueblo to teach children's per-forming arts and, in the 1990s, to perform with my company, DAYSTAR. And of special note was Navajo Robert Shorty, also a fine sculptor, who had created the original Coyote character for *Sipapu*. Until disbanding in the 1980s, NATE performed extensively in the United States and Europe. Mr. Geiogamah has since become a full professor of theater and Native American studies at the University of California, Los Angeles.[3]

DAYSTAR: Contemporary Dance-Drama
of Indian America, 1980

Flash forward ten years. The experiences at Flandreau Indian School in South Dakota and at the Institute of American Indian Arts implanted in me a desire to share with Native people the possibilities of modern dance and theater both in education and as a profession. I now had some ideas about Native modern performing art, some experience, and the youthful energy to pursue it.

I traveled to every school interested, from South Dakota to North Dakota to Wisconsin to Minnesota to Montana to Colorado to New Mexico. I conducted workshops, held residencies, and performed a one-woman production that I called *DAYSTAR: An American Indian Woman Dances* (fig. 2). On stage, I became Napi, the Blackfeet trickster in stories such as "The Creation of the World," "The Origin of Death," "Napi and the Rock," and "Napi Tries to Get Married." I found that I was also writing original short scripts utilizing recorded voice-overs, simulating the story-teller's position. Character work was expanded as I wove masks, costuming, set design, and music together to create a world with which I now felt familiar—the mythic theatrical world of Native oral tradition.

Traditional, that is, intertribal, dance had always been a part of my life. Now I began to entertain the idea of interfacing Native dance movement with a modern context. I asked myself obvious but crucial questions: In the use of space and time, is it necessary to always dance in a circle, clockwise from left to right, to always start with the song, and to always end with the song? In the use of movement quality and shape, how would a character in this story, at this moment, move, and with what quality and for what purpose? During this period, I was dancing primarily for Indian audiences. As Native communities began to see a Native person performing Native stories *as theater* in a stage space, audience members began to sense the elements of universality within their stories. "Oh, we have a story like that," many would say. "Oh, I'd like to perform this kind of dance," said a young girl. "Where can I go to learn to do this?" from yet another. The conceptual elements of Native modern dance were finding recognition and acceptance, and at the same time I was finding a form, a style, and a process that would continue, ultimately, into the work that I would create for my own company.

FIGURE 2. *Napi: Tales of Old Man*, 1975. Dancer/Choreographer: Daystar/ Rosalie Jones. Masked dance derived from Blackfeet oral tradition of Old Man Napi. (Photographer unknown)

In Wisconsin Dells, Wisconsin, the time and place presented itself. I found a mentor. Thomas Davis was not Native, but he resided on the Menominee Reservation and had worked with Native people for a considerable number of years. He assisted me in gathering a first board of directors, and the company was incorporated in 1980. It was named DAYSTAR: Contemporary Dance-Drama of Indian America to reflect the scope that I hoped would become self-fulfilling—a theatrical dance company shining light on some of the vast possibilities for the future of Native modern dance (fig. 3).

Over the following twenty years, cast members would change as young people were trained to perform with Daystar, with new members taking their places as people moved on to more training or other companies, or into teaching. With few exceptions, the company performers are Native

FIGURE 3. Daystar Dance Company poster, 1982. Three figures of Daystar/ Rosalie Jones as the masked dancer, the traditional Native American dancer, and the modern dancer. (Photograph by Norman A. Regnier @ Photo-Imagery)

North American, from a wide variety of tribal affiliations—Cherokee, Creek, Blackfeet, Lakota, Pueblo, Umatilla, and Apache, amongst others. Many have been of mixed heritage, including Spanish and Métis. Some have also been trained in other disciplines such as ballet, the martial arts, and gymnastics. Whenever possible, Daystar productions are enhanced by the work of Native musicians, set designers, and costumers.

The touchstone of Daystar performance is storytelling, manifested within such theatrical devices as persona, movement, and mask. Performance material, in the beginning, was drawn largely from the oral tradition of Native peoples. Almost always the dance-dramas were developed in association with the community of their origin, with their elders or consultants. In some cases, stories were reinterpreted from written and published narratives. At other times, Daystar has gone beyond oral tradition, into personal and tribal histories, even anecdotes. The Daystar

FIGURE 4. *Wolf: A Transformation*, 1995. Dancer: John Silversmith (Navajo). Choreographer: Daystar/Rosalie Jones. (IAIA Studio Portrait. Photographer: Murrae Haynes)

repertoire includes *Napi: Tales of Old Man* (Blackfeet), *Sacred Woman, Sacred Earth* (Lakota), *The Corn Mother* (Eastern Cherokee), *Malinche: The Woman with Three Names* (Aztec/Mayan/historical), *Wolf: A Transformation* (Anishinabe) (fig. 4), and *Prayer of the First Dancer* (intertribal fancy, hoop dance/shawl dance, and modern dance).

The most recent production of Daystar is *No Home but the Heart*. The process through which this work evolved is a departure for the Daystar Company, as the material did not come strictly from tribal oral tradition. Rather than referencing material from an ancient story now existing as oral tradition, I turned to stories and memories passed down within my own family. From an early age, I was intrigued by the stories my mother told me about growing up on the Blackfeet reservation. The stories were random, intense revelations about family and tribal life on the reservation, from the smallpox epidemic of 1837, through the turn of the century,

FIGURE 5. "The Spirits Dance," *No Home but the Heart*, 2000. Daystar Company performers (left to right): Shawl Dancer Santee Smith (Mohawk), Jingle Dancer Daystar/Rosalie Jones, Shawl Dancer Rose Stella (Tarahumara/Italian). Center panel is a photograph of Jones's great-grandmother. SUNY-Brockport. (Photographer: Jim Dusen)

and into the modern day. In developing the script, I drew from selected events in the lives of my great-grandmother, grandmother, and mother, and tied these episodes to historical events that affected the settlement of Native peoples in the Northern Plains of the United States and Canada (fig 5.). In the dance-drama, the Daughter (myself), living in the present day, passes through scenes from the past in which embodiments of the ancestors play out selected events in their lives.

The play has twelve short scenes, to be performed continuously without an intermission, with a storyteller and three dancer/actresses. Because my family's ancestry stems from the displaced French-Cree/Chippewa peoples from the "north," I feel that this work acknowledges our common search for identity, family, and homeland. The script has been published in an anthology of plays under the title *Keepers of the Morning Star: An Anthology of Native Women's Theater* (UCLA American Indian Publication, 2003). The inclusion of *No Home but the Heart* in this publication speaks volumes for Native theater: the editors allowed choreographed segments to be written as a "suggested text," thereby handling such sequences as an essential element of the written script.

A New Beginning: Aboriginal Arts Program, 1993

If *Native modern dance* is acknowledged as existing among the Native peoples of North America, then one must also recognize the work being done in Canada. The Aboriginal Arts Program at the Banff Centre for the Arts began as the result of a partnership negotiated between the Aboriginal Film and Video Art Alliance and the Banff Centre for the Arts in 1993. Its objective was to create a cultural space for Aboriginal artists in Banff, allowing them to explore several art forms, including dance, song, music, theater, and scriptwriting in a contemporary and Aboriginal context. In 1995, the remarkable Marrie Mumford, a Canadian Métis, became the program's executive director. By 1998, *Indian Artist* magazine was saying that the effort was "perhaps the most active and creative dance study and performance program for Natives in the hemisphere."[4]

Although located in a somewhat remote area of western Canada (directly west of Calgary, Alberta), and operating primarily as a summer intensive, the program draws master teachers and students from all parts of Canada and the United States, as well as from Nunavut, Greenland, and Central and South America. In 2001, the program also attracted students from Australia and New Zealand. Until 2004 two programs ran concurrently: the Apprentice Program and the Professional Section. Course sessions varied from Song Processing to Choreography Symposiums to Masking to Professional Production.

The Aboriginal Arts Program in Banff was unique in many respects. First of all, it paid definitive respect to the Native worldview. The Apprenticeship Program, "Chinook Winds," took as its paradigm an acknowledgment of the ways in which Native people approach the world: how they relate to the world, how stories are told, and how songs and dances are created. Elders were involved on a regular basis, teaching through their artistic knowledge and therefore sharing the culture and its vision. At the

FIGURE 6. "Neighbours," *Light and Shadow,* 1997. Dancers: Siobhan Arnatsiq-Murphy (Inuit) and Jonathan Fisher (Ojibway/Odawa). Choreographer: Alexandro Ronceria. Chinook Winds Aboriginal Dance Program. Banff Centre for the Arts. (Photographer: Donald Lee)

same time, students were given rigorous physical training, but not always in the conventional systems of modern dance. Rather, guest dancers and choreographers were invited in to show their work and to do extended workshops. I count myself as one among many who were invited to lecture, teach, supervise, and perform.

Native storytellers were invited to share their stories and styles of storytelling. Musicians would look at traditional forms and find relevant connections to modern, pop, and classical music and jazz. Little by little, a reservoir of form and meaning, both traditional and modern, would be accumulated over the course of a three-year program. Only then would students be asked to choreograph within a contemporary milieu, drawing from their own Native stories and customs, a knowledge accompanied by its own intuitive perceptions, and filtered through their own abilities as artists and teachers. The resulting performance work reflected an unexpected richness of particular human beings steeped in tradition but living very much in the contemporary world. The resulting work was, at once, traditional and contemporary, personal and communal, real and mythic (fig. 6).

Beyond the art are the social implications, which cannot be ignored. The Canadian government has now apologized, in a historic legal document, for its treatment of Aboriginal populations, and has spelled out what it would do to rectify the situation. Sizable amounts of money were made available for expanded medical, educational, and economic opportunities, in an effort to right past wrongs against native Canadians. The Aboriginal Arts Program was a project receiving such funding. Marrie Mumford has commented that in the year 2000, 50 percent of Canada's Native population was under the age of twenty-five and in need of supportive leadership that would in turn stimulate their own abilities to become leaders of a new generation of First Nations peoples. "One of the things that colonization has created is a divisiveness amongst our communities and nations. . . . I believe that our arts work is part of our healing. Our hope is by providing that training, that people then take it back to their home communities."[5] *Indian Country Today*, a well-known newspaper on Indian affairs in the United States, summed up the work: "the Aboriginal Arts Program is a prime example of what can happen when people really strive for excellence and partnership in the arts."[6]

A View from the Prairie: The Journey Revealed

I have a vivid recollection of my own first performance in the genre that is now being called *Native modern dance*. It was the mid-1970s, and I was teaching and working in the state of Wisconsin, in and near the many reservations there. In a dance work entitled *The Dispossessed*, my scenario followed a line of action—a story—familiar to many Native peoples who lived through the mid-twentieth century. A young girl is raised in a traditional manner but is soon "scooped up" from her family and raised in the boarding school. Upon graduation, she moves to the city to seek employment as a secretary. She soon discovers the city's underbelly—crime, alcohol, and drugs. A series of episodes culminate in the girl's rape, and we see her in the final scene alone in a jail cell. There, in a moment of overwhelming loneliness and desperation, a personal awakening pushes her to reconnect with the truth and beauty of her ancestors, a revelation that the audience knows will be her key to renewed self-respect and to her future.

The Dispossessed was not a great piece of choreography, but it was my first public performance of such material. I was frightened to death as to how a largely Native audience would respond to it. I told myself that this audience was not a "theater-going" audience by any means. When the curtain rang down, the audience gave a light sprinkling of polite applause. I changed, packed up, and walked up the theater aisle, now strangely silent. Just as I stepped out the theater door, I found a solitary figure standing in the lobby. She was a small, somewhat thin, elderly Indian lady in a winter coat and flowered head scarf. She seemed to be waiting for me. We shook hands. Quietly, she said: "Was that your *vision?*" On reflection, I wonder if she detected my dumbfounded expression at her question. After agonizing over whether I would be accepted, it was this eloquent, still presence who made the connection between the old and the new, between traditionalism and modernism. She reminded me of the original intent of storytelling and dance and song and ceremony. *It is to recount your vision.*

Perhaps we have not *invented* Native modern dance so much as we have *evolved* it through our own sensibilities as Native people. Perhaps we are not so much on a path "beyond tribe and tradition," as on a path of *vision* and vision-seeking, wherever that may take us. The possibilities are endless; the results might well be astonishing. It will remain for the new generation of Native dancers, musicians, singers, actors, screenwriters, and filmmakers to seek their own visions and to create their own new methods of vision-making.

One thing is certain: we are all on that tough trip through paradise. And we are all craning our necks, looking up toward the surrounding mountains that rise even higher from where we are, to the mountains engulfed in clouds. We are climbing the *ladder to the Creator's House*. We are crying and singing and dancing for the visions of our future.

Postscript 2008: Coming Full Circle

As of this writing, I am preparing to speak at two major international conferences this summer. In doing so, I have cause to reflect on my first writing about Native modern dance in the M.S. thesis completed in 1968 at the University of Utah. I posed for myself, and for the dance community of the time, a challenge. "The use of Indian dance as a base upon which to build meaningful technique and a significant style of movement, however, has not been fully explored. . . . American Indian cultures contain a wealth of material that could serve as the basis for new compositions. Young Indian people who know the traditional dances could become the main core of a company which would endeavor to develop a dance idiom appropriate to, and expressive of, the unique qualities of the American Indian."[7]

In the short six-year span since the 2002 Dublin 23rd Annual Conference of the American Indian Workshop, the number of practitioners of what is now being called (in Canada) *Indigenous contemporary dance*, has burst upon the Western stages of North America as if to say in one cultural voice: See! Here we are! In 2006, Native dancers, choreographers, and company directors basked in the astonishment of not one, but two, major international dance conference/festivals. The first took place at the Banff Centre for the Arts, Alberta, which hosted the annual conference of the Society for Dance History Scholars—"Grounding Moves: Landscapes for Dance." From an international arena, scholars assembled to listen to and learn from Indigenous contemporary and traditional dancers, choreographers, writers, and teachers, all professionals in their fields. This author presented an illustrated survey of current work under the title "Indigenous

Contemporary Dance: The State of the Art." Jacqueline Shea Murphy announced the publication of her new book, *The People Never Stopped Dancing: Native American and Modern Dance History*. It is a landmark study on the subject and sorely needed. Perhaps this is the beginning of vigorous research in and visibility for the field of Native modern dance.

Moreover, in July 2006, Toronto was the site of a conference called "Living Ritual: World Indigenous Dance Festival," which preceded but folded naturally into the prestigious "World Dance Alliance Global Assembly," hosted by York University. The "Living Ritual: World Indigenous Dance Festival," organized by Canadian Indigenous dancer Santee Smith, further elucidated the world of Indigenous dance by bringing the delegates to the Woodland Cultural Centre, Brantford—Haudenosaunee country—on the first day of the conference.

The lineup of performance and lecture for the conference was impressive and presented work from the full scope of the Americas, including Mexico and South America. Over two nights, the program of dancers and dance companies featured Kaha:wi Dance Theatre (Canada) performing *Here on Earth*—choreographer Santee Smith (Haudenosaunee); Dancing Earth (USA) performing *The Naming*—choreographer Rulan Tangen (Lakota); Gaeton Gingras (Mohawk), 1998 winner of the Clifford E. Lee Choreography Award 1998, performing *My Father Told Me*; Norma Araiza of Tolmec Dance Theatre performing *Dear Deer Dance* (Mexico); and Living Roots Foundation presenting *Yetina: Origin of the Spirit of Water*—directed and choreographed by Floresmiro Rodriguez with codirection by Alejandro Ronceria (Colombia, South America). The preservation of tradition was represented by the Le-la-la Northwest Coast dancers (under the direction of George "Me'las" Taylor), in masked dances entitled, *The Spirit of the Mask*, and the Tewa Singers and Dancers from the North (under the direction of Andrew Garcia, Tewa), presenting the dances of his pueblo in New Mexico.

Since 2005, I have had the good fortune to work closely with Marrie Mumford in creating the curriculum in Indigenous Performance Studies at Trent University in Ontario, Canada. We have together created a two-year program of study that integrates such courses as Indigenous Contemporary Dance and Music, Masked Dance and Storytelling, Indigenous Theatre, and Indigenous Dance Theatre into the stable environment of a thirty-year-old Indigenous Studies Department. In a very real sense, we have integrated the most durable aspects of her work at the Banff Center for the Arts with my work at the Institute of American Indian Art. Presently, the Indigenous Performance Studies is a significant "stream" of study within the department. When Indigenous Performance Studies achieves degree status, it will be the first of its kind in North America.

Where will the Native modern dance movement go from here? Be assured it will not be in a straight line, as in western thinking, a projectile speeding into the vast unknown. As in all things cyclical, the "dance of the people" will continue naturally to circle, as ripples in a pond, filtering through history and ancestry and sacred story and back again, moving ever outward but taking meaning and substance in remembering the original source. By whatever name—*Native modern dance, Indigenous contemporary dance*—its source, the "dance of the people," will be a song and dance of welcoming. Perhaps those who witness the warmth and beauty of it will allow themselves to be drawn into the timeless circle that is the dancing community of the Indigenous peoples of our holy Mother Earth.[8]

CHAPTER 2

Old Spirits in a New World

Pacific Northwest Performance:
Identity, Authenticity, Theatricality

SARAH BRYANT-BERTAIL

The masks of the indigenous peoples of the Pacific Northwest
Coast are powerful objects that assist us in defining our place in the
cosmos. In a world of endless change and complexity, masks offer a
continuum for Native people to acknowledge our connection to the
universe.
—Chief Robert Joseph, Kwakw*aka*'wakw Nation[1]

An unshakable core of tradition, a self-definition that resists change:
this is an ahistorical concept of identity. All avowed Indians emerged
from the same historical maelstrom with self-definitions their
ancestors would not recognize. Yet all define themselves as Indians
and distinguish themselves from people who are not Indians largely
on the basis of history.
—Alexandra Harmon[2]

If you look Indian, you don't have to act so Indian. But if you don't
look very Indian, then you have to act more Indian. It's like a scale. If
your hair is blond, you have to wear a lot of turquoise. I pass as being
Indian, so I don't have to follow some prescribed behavior of what a
real Indian does.
—Ned Blackhawk, quoted by Sherman Alexie[3]

IN THE OPENING CHAPTER of his 1975 study *The Way of the Masks*,
Claude Lévi-Strauss quotes words he had written in 1943, describing his
first encounter with the Northwest Coast dance masks and house posts
in an exhibit of the Museum of Natural History in New York City. The
masks and posts were made of red cedar carved into animal and human

figures, embodying a cosmos where all living forms are interconnected with each other: Frog within Raven within Human within Orca Whale or Thunderbird, their curved shapes deeply carved and painted boldly in red, black, cobalt blue, and white, colors and shapes accented by strong black form lines. Lévi-Strauss already recognizes this spiritual cosmology embodied by the masks, as well as their theatrical artifice:

> For the spectator at initiation rites, the dance masks (which opened sud-denly like two shutters to reveal a second face, and sometimes a third . . .) were proofs of the omnipresence of the supernatural and the prolifera-tion of myths. Upsetting the peace of everyday life, the masks' primal message retains so much power that even today the . . . insulation of the showcases fails to muffle its communication. . . . [The dance masks] are not so much things as living beings "with friendly eyes." . . . One would have to make an effort to remain deaf to their voices; just as it would be difficult not to perceive, . . . behind the showcase glass, a sombre face, the "Cannibal Raven" clapping its beak-like wings, or the "Master of the Tides" summoning forth the ebb and flow with a wink of its ingeniously articulated eyes.
>
> For nearly all these masks are simultaneously naïve and ferocious mechanical contraptions. A system of ropes, pulleys, and hinges. . . . This unique art . . . blends the . . . serenity of the statues in the cathedral at Chartres . . . with the artifices of the carnival.[4]

Three decades later, Lévi-Strauss would travel to the Pacific Northwest coast of British Columbia to study firsthand these masks that he aptly called the "forest of symbols." This "forest" had grown dense and, for the outsider, almost impenetrable, with the meaning of the masks embedded within numerous tribal and family histories and mythical stories that each mask carries. As the translator, Sylvia Modelski, explains, the book's origi-nal title contains a pun that expresses Lévi-Strauss's encounter with the masks: "*Voie*, the French word for 'way,' is a homophone of *voix*, meaning 'voice.' Thus, the original title, *La Voie des masques*, is polysemous and not fully translatable into English."[5]

Origin and Aims of the Study

The present study has its origin in a graduate seminar entitled "Theater and Anthropology" taught at the University of Washington in the spring of 1995. Many of the basic questions framing our inquiry then are still being explored in the research presented here: how have white Europeans and their American and Canadian descendants approached the performance traditions of the Pacific Northwest Native Americans, especially the masked dances and the masks themselves? With what effects? What cultural assumptions shape the masked dances as a performance event experienced by Natives and non-Natives? How have these assumptions changed over time for both groups? And finally, what are the stakes and responsibilities for non-Indian researchers? The first and last sites we visited during the eleven-week course are bookends for the class as well as for this essay. In the first week, we visited the Burke Museum of Natural History and Culture on the university campus, particularly its reconstructed interior of a Pacific Northwest cedar longhouse, with clothing, cooking utensils, blankets, woven straw hats, masks, and carved storage boxes in their supposedly everyday places. For the last week, I had written on the syllabus: "Plan on a field trip to Tillicum Village."

This seemed a somewhat dubious research venue at first, compared to the widely respected Burke Museum, because, as everyone in Seattle knows, Tillicum Village is a tourist attraction that purports to offer a taste of Northwest Coast Native tradition condensed into a four-hour package: cruise, culture, and cuisine. And yet this field trip to what we expected to be an "inauthentic" venue has had a lasting effect on all who were present: a desire to learn more about what we saw and did not see, and a decision to not assume that we understand the interchange between cultures or appreciate the positions of all the parties involved, including our own.

The Quest for Authenticity

In addition to the questions listed above, the present study will also address the issues of how the dance mask, as both sacred spirit and theatrical artifice, has related to the cultural identity of Native people in the past, and how this seeming paradox plays out in the contemporary era, when many masks and dances have also been recruited into the ever-growing, worldwide industry of cultural tourism. In short, how has the dominant culture's touristic appropriation of the dance masks affected the cultural identity of present-day Indians, and how does the sense of ambivalent identity in both Native and white people relate to the quest for authenticity?

Authenticity, according to the Marxist-oriented existentialist philosophy of Jean-Paul Sartre, is the conscious self coming to terms with being in a material and materialistic world, and meeting outside pressures and influences different from the self. Authenticity is the degree to which one is true to one's character, despite these pressures.[6] Dean MacCannell, in his 1976 book, *The Tourist: A New Theory of the Leisure Class*, builds on this concept of authenticity as a resistance to the material world, which is inauthentic. He explains that modern people feel "inauthentic" and "shallow" in their own materialist culture and are attracted to "the sacred in primitive society," because, being spiritualist rather than materialist, it seems more authentic than modernity.[7] James Clifford calls this attraction to "sacred" and "primitive" cultures a "quest for authenticity" that involves the "salvage paradigm," which is the mission of a dominant culture to rescue the authenticity of a subordinate culture rather than seeing that culture's ongoing destruction in the present: "The salvage paradigm, reflecting a desire to rescue 'authenticity' out of destructive historical change, is alive and well."[8]

Focusing on the masks and dances as a register of the uneven social and economic struggle between Indian and white cultures, which is waged in terms of authenticity and identity, a few key moments from past and present performance sites will be described, including the cultural exposition, the world's fair, the natural history museum, an early "ethnic" film, and a visit to the present-day site of Tillicum Village, which exemplifies the cultural tourist industry and its main business: the buying and selling of authenticity.

History of the Masks: Native and Non-Native Stories

> In the interior, a forest of symbols, both human and non-human, rise up in a hundred different, sometimes amiable, sometimes tragic forms.
> —Lévi-Strauss[9]

Lévi-Strauss built his work on that of the anthropologist Franz Boas (1858–1942), whose many volumes contain decades of recorded observations and photographs of the languages, mythologies, religion, social organization, art, and dance of the Northwest Coast Natives of Canada and the United States in the late nineteenth and early twentieth centuries.[10] His contemporary Edward S. Curtis (1868–1952), whose published photographs of Native Americans number in the thousands, had a similar motive for his own work.[11] Both Boas and Curtis were desperately racing to record Native lives and culture at a time when whole tribes were dying of disease and rapidly becoming extinct. Also, both were dedicated to what James Clifford calls the "salvage paradigm," a desire to record and save what they saw as a vanishing culture whose precontact purity—later equated with authenticity—they attempted to restore.[12]

Because the masks in performance seldom mimetically represent specific individuals or historical events, they are not artifacts in the same way as those used for realistic Western art and theater. And yet from the arrival in 1778 of Captain James Cook, the first European to amass collections of Indian artifacts, the Europeans and their descendants long regarded the dance masks and other ceremonial "paraphernalia" as exotically attractive but primitive products of an equally primitive culture, that is, a culture that was not "advancing," but frozen in a prehistoric time. These first collectors had an ambivalent attitude toward Northwest Native art in general: they recognized the hypnotic power of the bold colors, carved shapes, and strong form lines but saw the stylized depiction of animals and humans as evidence of a naïve, childlike intellect and an art inferior to the realistic European art produced by a more advanced "adult" civilization.

Not until the latter part of the nineteenth century did Europeans and white Americans try to understand what the masks meant to the West Coast Natives themselves. For this, it was necessary to hear the many stories, songs, and myths that the masks embodied, and to learn to interpret the dance ceremonies in which all these came to life. The complex relationship of the masks to the dance performances, and the performances to the stories, make it impossible to trace the history of Native Americans through the physical artifacts alone. In addition, even when painstaking ethnographic information about them is gathered, the masks themselves, especially pre-twentieth-century masks, resist attempts to date them and to decipher their messages. Their power to evoke and define Native culture lies partly in the fact that they have probably not changed in basic symbolic design principles for at least a thousand years, even though new materials—including commercial paint, buttons, and wool from Hudson

Bay blankets—were quickly substituted for the original materials that had involved the labor of gathering and processing.[13]

The masks belong to both the material culture and the performance culture of the Northwest Coast people, from the Tlingets on the northern coast of Alaska to the Chinook at the mouth of the Columbia River, hundreds of miles to the south. In these two cultural functions, as object and performer, the masks have traditionally led a dual life akin to that of those creatures that lie dormant and secret until they awaken one day, metamorphose, and emerge into the open. In single-family or communal houses today where the sacred dances are still performed, the masks are carefully hidden and protected for most of the year, then literally come to life in sacred celebrations, worn by dancers who have spent weeks or months in secret rehearsals not witnessed by others. The masks have a central role in cultures whose most important ceremony is the dance that retells the story of the mask's spiritual origin, which is also that of the people. The stories that are danced go backward in time from the present to the moment in the past when the people emerged from the sacred, cosmic animal spirit who is their common ancestor. The masks are gradually revealed as the dance proceeds over several hours' time. The most spectacular of these dances involve multilayered "transformation masks," which the dancer opens to reveal one face inside another until, at the climax of the ceremony, the spirit ancestor finally appears, a radiant face with both human and animal features, resurrecting and reliving the legendary moment when the two converged.

These multiple functions of the dance mask as an object that is both material and spiritual, and as the main performer in an event that is both sacred and theatrically entertaining, were already complex within the traditions of the many Native tribes that existed in the past, and remain so even in the much smaller number that survive today. This complexity has been compounded since Europeans first arrived on the Northwest Coast in the eighteenth century, in that the masks have been a highly visible flashpoint of conflict in the struggle of Indigenous people to save their historical and cultural identity from being erased by the colonizing Europeans and their hegemonic modern descendants. Edward Said's defining image of cultural hegemony applies here: the colonized land is an exotic stage set where the colonized is only a puppet and the colonizer is the real actor, the sole agent of historical action.[14]

Paths through the Forest of Symbols:
Authentic Theatricality

Inspired by Lévi-Strauss's structuralist work, anthropologist Bill Holm has, over the five decades of his career, decoded the system of forms carved and painted on the Northwest masks and other objects, forms which singly and in unison represent a cosmology.[15] In turn, Holm's fellow anthropologist George F. MacDonald, through his long study of the traditional designs of Coastal people from Alaska to Oregon, as well as the stories attached to these designs, began to unlock the long-hidden meaning of the pictorial "writing" that linked the ancient salmon-based economy and the cosmology that developed along with it: an "economy of souls" that had to be shared equally by the human and salmon peoples.[16] This eco-cosmological system connecting material and spiritual, secular and sacred, was honored by all who lived from the salmon, presaging the environmentalist movement. Indeed the concept of a shared economy of souls is still reflected in the widely observed ritual of returning the salmon's clean, intact skeleton to the river from which it was caught, thus releasing its soul to swim safely on its journey toward everlasting life.

This interlinking of secular and sacred worlds also is the main reason that, for the Northwest Coastal Natives, theatricality is at home in both realms. It is the accepted medium for both sacred and secular and sustains Native identity rather than threatening it. Even the most sacred mask dance performances are highly theatrical and contain secular elements. But Native performance does show a clear distinction between the ritual object and the object used in everyday life. By contrast, from the largest architectural structure to the smallest prop, the modern western stage makes little distinction between ordinary and extraordinary things, at least not on its visible surface. The dance masks, both sacred and secular, are often mimetic, in that the mask maker and dancer have obviously paid close attention to animals and people in the real world and have usually recreated them to be recognizable. That the masks are both mimetic and authentic, sacred and theatrical, is an unacceptable paradox in Platonic and Cartesian thinking, even though the European medieval theater accepted it.

Anthropologist Michael Taussig proposes a new definition of mimesis that respects the creation of non-European-based cultures, including those of the Indigenous people of the Americas. In Taussig's view, mimesis is not just a copying of exterior surface, which is still the predominant Western definition articulated by Plato. Instead, "the mimetic faculty carries out its honest labor suturing nature to artifice . . . by means of what was once called sympathetic magic, granting [to] the representation the power of the represented."[17] Here mimesis also involves embodiment, not just the replication of surface, and by embodying powerful spirits, one is both empowered by and protected from them.

Taussig's concept of mimesis applies to Pacific Northwest Native representation in general. From prehistoric times to the present, depictions of animals and humans on masks, house posts, totem poles, trunks, and other carved wooden objects typically show, in a stylized manner, multiple simultaneous views of the body's surface, skeleton, and internal organs as part of an overall design, a design in which outside and inside flow into and out of each other. Because this multidimensional mimesis draws no closed boundary between exterior and interior space, or between animal, human, and spirit, it is able to encompass and embody the cosmic system of life itself. An orca whale dance mask may incorporate in its design not only the spirit and physical form of the Killer Whale, but also that of Wild Forest Woman, the human children whose souls she has captured, and the double-headed Lightning Serpent, whose two heads are those of wolves. Thus, homage is paid to two great hunters, the Wolf on land and the Orca in the sea. Sometimes the Eagle, the greatest hunter of the sky, is also represented on the same mask. All these make up a cosmic system that includes the human Hunter-Warrior Spirit, who is not always shown. In some orca masks this Warrior Spirit actually appears as a tiny human figure standing in the place of the whale's dorsal fin, poised over the blowhole. The same cosmic system is shown in wooden boxes and totem poles: the carved and painted body of the whale extends over all surfaces of the box or pole, but the eye of the whale is simultaneously also the body of a salmon, and a closer look at the whale's round blowhole reveals a small human face looking outwards.

Without doubt the most awe-inspiring spectacle of the belief that humans are descendants of primeval animal spirits is performed by the transformation masks used in many tribes on the Northwest coast, for example, the Sun Transformation Mask of the Nuxalk tribe. The dancer first appears wearing the closed mask, carved and painted in the form of the Thunderbird, whose realm is the outer sky, close to the sun. At the moment of transformation, the mask is opened suddenly into a large circle with a wide-eyed human face in the center, surrounded by four beings painted on the circle. The inner circle of the face and outer circle of souls also form an image of the eternal sun. A second look reveals that the nose of the human face resembles that of the Thunderbird, a sign that the transformation is not completed and that Thunderbird and human still belong to one family and share their souls with each other.[18]

The spiritual life of the Kwakwaka'wakw (formerly called the Kwakiutl), and other Northwest Coast peoples from the Columbia River in the south to Alaska in the north, was already profoundly theatrical—and mimetic—long before the arrival of Europeans. The dance masks had two functions, for imitative secular performance and ceremonial religious performance, with the spirits of humans, animals, and plants appearing in both. Imitative dances were directly controlled by individual performers who were communicating their observation and knowledge of animal, plant, and inanimate beings in the real world. Caroline Budic retells an account recorded in 1741: a Tlingit from the Alaskan coast was dressed in a bear skin and mask and performed on the beach so realistically that "the Russian explorers were lured ashore to hunt him" and were soon killed by the dancer's fellow tribesmen waiting in ambush.[19] Such imitative masks were relatively lightweight, allowing for freer, more naturalistic movement, in contrast to the large, heavy ceremonial masks used in the slower and more restricted motion of the sacred dances. Whereas one performance embodied the real-world animal, the other embodied the spirit world through the animal's form.

Trompe l'oeil theatrical effects also abounded in the sacred spirit dances, especially for the Kwakwaka'wakw people of British Columbia. Always held during the four months of dark, rainy, mild winter, when there was much leisure time, these ceremonials utilized fire, firelight, smoke, shadow, and a curtain, as well as simulated blood, deaths, burials, and voices from the spirit world. In initiation ceremonies the spectators knew that the young initiate would only appear to die and would miraculously be brought back to life again at the end, but they didn't know *how* the illusion would be effected, because these techniques were a closely guarded secret of the performers themselves. Franz Boas, who spent years with various Kwakwaka'wakw clans, recounts the initiation ceremony of a young woman into the spirit society of the Wolf Clan, to which her family belonged. That is, the clan traced its ancestors back to the primordial Wolf Spirit by reenacting in dance and song the moment of transformation from wolf to human. For this event the longhouse was lit dimly by a central fire, with the audience seated according to their relative social standing, all facing a circular performance area. The masked Wolf Spirit dancers, wearing wolf headdresses and hides, came out from behind a large curtain and danced around the fire, casting long shadows that indeed resembled those of wolves. A pit had been dug in this area and disguised with a stand of tall grass so that, to the spectators, the woman appeared to be sinking into the earth. Then, as the grass was set afire, the longhouse filled with smoke. As the fire burned down and the air began to clear, a pile of smoking bones appeared where the woman had been, and her voice was heard coming from the bones. Actually, the initiate now lay in another disguised pit some yards away speaking through a buried length of kelp. Her relatives knew she wasn't really dead and would in the end be restored to life, but they "cried and cried anyway."[20] Indeed, she finally appeared to rise from the still-smoking bones in the place where she had originally disappeared. Tellingly, the Kwakwaka'wakw word for the winter ceremonials, *ts'ets'aeqa* (or *t'seka*), literally translates as "fake" or "everything is not real."[21]

The Hamat'sa, or Cannibal Spirit ceremonies, of the Kwakwaka'wakw would gain the most notoriety, especially those moments when the dancers seemed to be cutting pieces of flesh from the spectators, the initiate, or a human corpse. Cuts were superficial, however, and dancers concealed small bladders filled with berry juice or animal blood, breaking them when the spectacle called for a flow of blood. With the indispensable help of George Hunt, his longtime collaborator and informant who was half-Tlinget and half-Scottish, Boas records that in the climactic moment of the ceremony, if the visibly starved initiate accepted a bite of actual human flesh, it was never from the corpse of a person killed for this purpose, but of a relative who had died of natural causes long before the celebration began and whose body had been emptied out and hung up to be smoked and dried. In later times the "corpse" was usually an animal carcass carved to resemble a human body. Despite the white majority's belief that the Kwakwaka'wakw and other Northwest Coast people were cannibals, there

is no physical evidence or record from oral history or ancestral stories that
they had ever practiced cannibalism, even though they did often place
the skulls of their dead together, in the belief that communally preserved
skulls would preserve the souls of the dead. In fact, the whole purpose of
the Hamat'sa was exactly the contrary: to assure that the Native people
would never become cannibals, because if they did they would lose their
humanity. As today's Kwakwaka'wakws explain, "The most important of
our sacred dances is the *Hamat'sa* or cannibal dance. This dance is the
re-enactment of a young man's possession by a cannibal spirit living at the
North end of the world. *Dance and songs along with rituals tame the man,
bringing him back to his human self.*"[22]

Theatrical Authenticity on the World Stage:
Photographs and Film

More than fifty years before Lévi-Strauss's first encounter with them, the
dances and masks of the Pacific Northwest had already made their debut on
the world stage, first through the photographs and prolific writings of Franz
Boas and the exhibits in museums and fairs, and then through the work
of his contemporary Edward C. Curtis, who produced twenty volumes of
photographs and descriptions of the American Indian. Curtis aimed in his
photographs and later in his 1914 film, *In the Land of the Headhunters*,[23] to
eliminate the evidence of white culture's influence, which had begun in the
mid-1700s. To this end, Curtis lived three years with the Kwakwaka'wakw
in British Columbia, using their advice and help to reconstruct an "ethnic
present" from precontact times. He aimed to resurrect what he considered
their "lost spiritual values," despite Canada's ongoing governmental ban
of ritual objects and dancing (from 1884 to 1951). George Hunt, Boas's
translator, informant, and collaborator, also assisted Curtis as "dramaturg,
designer, and stage manager" for *In the Land of the Headhunters* and other
projects.[24] Hunt himself had known initiates in the *Hamat'sa* and had
witnessed firsthand the theatrical devices that were an inseparable part of
both sacred and secular performances. However, despite this knowledge,
Hunt helped Curtis create the spectacle of an "ethnic present" that would
meet the expectations of white spectators.

Curtis's method of constructing scenes from the past and filming this allegedly lost spirituality drew directly on the popular theater of melodrama, from the love-story plot of a young man and woman from feuding clans, to the painted scenic backdrops, in front of which the Kwakwaka'wakw, in purportedly "traditional" costumes, were crowded among totem poles, masks, caches of skulls, war canoes, and longhouses, most of which were removed from their original settings in villages along the Pacific coast. Although the Northwest Native dress had never included feather headdresses, they were given to the Kwakwaka'wakw actors for the sake of "Indianness."[25] Without this iconic sign, Curtis believed, the majority of white spectators would not accept these Indians as authentic. And yet the Indian actors themselves, like the artisans who built the war canoes and totems, were enthusiastic and enterprising partners, who eagerly learned from tribal elders the long-forbidden arts of the dance, whale hunting, and canoe handling. This same enthusiasm for theatrical self-representation was shown generations later in the Kwakwaka'wakws' collaboration with Bill Holm on the 1972 restoration of Curtis's film, for which the young actors learned, again from their elders, the old language and songs and recorded them for the new soundtrack. However, this time the Kwakwaka'wakw, deeply offended by the misleading original title, *In the Land of the Headhunters*, demanded that it be rereleased under the new title *In the Land of the War Canoes*.[26]

The World's Fair

The fame of the Kwakwaka'wakws was enhanced at the St. Louis World's Fair in 1904 when two tribesmen advertised as "cannibals" carved lamb meat into a human form that resembled an African pygmy whom they had bribed into playing the initiate. Breaking a bladder of blood they had hidden under the pygmy's shirt, and making the sound of a spirit whistle, they performed his "murder" by whisking him behind a curtain, replacing him quickly with the carved lamb carcass, and proceeding to eat from the carcass as the curtain reopened. At this point the pygmy "victim's" fellow tribesmen, on a nearby stage of their own, believing that they had witnessed actual murder, rushed forward toward the "cannibal" stage with spears in hand and were pushed back by the guards at the last minute. All of this unfolded before thousands of white spectators. By their own account, the Kwakwaka'wakw performers were proud of the flashing Kodak cameras and credulous amazement of their audience, and proud of their ability to use the mimetic theatrical apparatus to take control of this particular Indian show.[27]

The question of authenticity was to these performers a pragmatic matter of theatrics. Even Boas himself had a double standard of authenticity, especially when it came to his own films: for the films he made as a record for himself, he did not construct a false "present from the past" but filmed his subjects in their usual modern clothing. However, for films intended for the white public he had them dress in traditional costumes, and even constructed sets, creating, as Curtis did, an aesthetic frame drawn from mainstream Western theater and white expectations of "Indianness." Yet Boas never questioned the reality of the spirit world for Native Americans or their right to express it in seemingly contradictory ways. Confronted on one hand by the wide variations from tribe to tribe, and even family to family, of how each spirit, mask, and dance originated, and on the other by the unmistakable similarities in the dances and masks themselves, Boas concluded that the masks and dances had outlived the memory span of the performers, a memory that he and Hunt were recording as quickly as possible before time ran out.[28]

The Natural History Museum

From the latter part of the nineteenth century on, museum exhibits have also been important venues for the Pacific Northwest dance masks. Life-size dioramas were created from collections of artifacts, a painted backdrop of forest and ocean, and mannequins or live persons arranged in tableaux of ceremonial or everyday life. In a 1962 interview, Samuel A. Barrett, retired director of the Milwaukee Public Museum, recounted his experience of 1915 on Vancouver Island, where he collected artifacts and gathered data on precontact life from Kwakwaka'wakw elders and reassembled them for a diorama. In his own words, Barrett made "a real killing in the collecting of masks and other ceremonial material."[29] Using artifacts and drawing on the memories of elders, he constructed a life-size diorama that represented Indian life before the whites arrived. The diorama was shipped to the Milwaukee Public Museum. Such reconstructions that ignore contemporary Indian life have dominated both museums and fairs, from the 1893 World's Columbian Exposition in Chicago, for which Boas was the chief assistant in anthropology,[30] to the 1909 Alaska-Yukon-Pacific Exhibition in Seattle, to the highly regarded Burke Museum today. These reconstructions also still dominate film representation, even though real forests, water, and skies have replaced the painted backdrops.

Tillicum Village: An Authentic Tourist Trip

> Your experience includes a delicious buffet featuring traditional
> Indian style baked salmon; a build your own salad bar; delectable
> Tillicum whole grain bread; new red potatoes and a unique
> "Boehm's" chocolate salmon.
> —Brochure, *Seattle's Tillicum Village*, 2005–2006[31]

In the 1995 seminar where the present study originated, we saw the trip to Tillicum Village as a chance to explore how cultural identity is negotiated, both that of the Native Americans and our own as non-Native tourists with varying awareness of the social and economic stakes involved. What happens, we asked, in a context where cultural identity seems to be packaged, bought, and sold? We wanted in particular to learn how the Native American employees viewed their own performance. Tillicum Village, located on Blake Island eight miles from Seattle, was conceived in the 1960s era of the pan-Indian cultural revival as an ethnic theme restaurant that offered a literal taste of Northwest Coast Native tradition, condensed into what today's promotional brochure, distributed throughout the Northwest, describes as "A Four-Hour Adventure: A World Famous Salmon Bake, Cruise and Show." Here the dances and masks are staged to satisfy a secular white clientele with a commercial packaging of ethnic cultural identity. Tillicum Village was founded forty-five years ago by the late Bill Hewitt, a white man and caterer by trade. He originally aimed to open the restaurant in time for the 1962 World's Fair but missed it by a few months. The double purpose of the restaurant was to become a showcase for Northwest Coast Native culture as well as a financially lucrative business. Fittingly, the word *Tillicum* means "friendly people" in Chinook, which was the common language of trade in Puget Sound. At Tillicum Village, men and women from several clans and tribes, not all from the Pacific Northwest, are hired as dancers, artists, cooks, and greeters, as well as artisans who weave the funnel-shaped grass hats, decorate the red Chilkat blankets, sew beads, or carve sculptures from red cedar in the Northwest Coastal style.

Leaving the Mainland

The memory of our direct encounter with the masks, actors, and artisans remains most vivid. Other memories contextualize and frame the trip as a whole. On the Seattle waterfront where the Tillicum ferry was docked, there were many other attractions: Ye Olde Curiosity Shoppe, where cheap plastic totem poles, expensive carved canoes, seashells, Chinese statues, and other curios from many cultures were offered for sale; a streetcar from the waterfront to the famed Space Needle, also built for the 1962 World's Fair; and a seafood restaurant with a Scandinavian name. As Tamara Underiner and Katie Johnson, who were present on this trip, recall:

> The stage is thus set before the ferry leaves the dock: There are sights to be seen, "cultures" to be sampled here. Indeed, the utterly eclectic mixing of cultures in this tourist economy has the troubling effect of suggesting that all cultures, from Norwegian to Native American, are equally consumable, providing one has the economic wherewithal to take advantage of these offerings.[32]

Crossing the Water and Landing on the Island

After the ferry left the dock, we had a guided tour around Seattle's waterfront on Elliot Bay, then sailed across Puget Sound to Blake Island, where Native women in traditional dress waited on the beach to greet us as we got off the ferry, offered hot clams in plastic cups, and showed us how to crush the white shells under our feet. This embarrassing little ceremony, which seemed to demean the smiling Natives who welcomed us, was the first point at which we became acutely conscious of how uncomfortable we were in our role as tourist-researchers. It became obvious later that at every phase of this tour we were keeping a kind of mental score sheet between what Tillicum Village claimed it was representing as authentic Northwest Native culture, and what we suspected or knew was not. We did not realize at the time that our search for authenticity was, on a deeper level, not so much a scientific attitude as what Sartre called a "vertiginous" sense that our own identity was drifting away from its usual safe place tied to the solid ground of routine.[33]

Into the Longhouse

Viewed from the Seattle ferry, the main building of Tillicum Village resembles a traditional longhouse, which was constructed of cedar poles and boards up to sixty feet long, with enough room for several families. But here the longhouse shape was retained only in the frontal view. Several rooms had been added over the years, forming a large, irregular space covered with one roof. First, we entered a large, two-level anteroom with Native artifacts on the walls, quite unlike the Burke Museum's cozy longhouse interior. On the upper level, one Native woman sewed beads, while another worked on a blanket. To reach the dining hall, we passed by a pit of smoldering alderwood, where young Native men in black aprons tended to the salmon, which was split in butterfly style and mounted on sharp cedar sticks set vertically into the pit. This method of cooking is a long tradition of the coastal Indians, as described in 1824 by the Englishman John Jewitt, a shipwreck survivor who spent three years as a slave for the Nootka tribe. "This kind of food, with a little salt," he writes, "would be found no contemptible eating even to a European."[34] Already a discerning tourist, he notes his disappointment on realizing that this method of cooking was rarely used; typically, the fish, blubber, or clams were steamed or, more often, boiled in a tub of water, into which hot stones were dropped periodically "until the whole [was] reduced to one mass."[35]

A Potlatch Performance

The largest room was the dining hall, where long tables were arranged perpendicular to a small proscenium stage upon which *Dance on the Wind* was performed, accompanied by a tape of Native music and a narrator's voice. The thirty-minute performance began at the dessert stage, just as we were finishing our small but "unique Boehm's chocolate salmon."[36] The house lights dimmed, followed by the sound of drums and a spirit whistle, then the slow illumination of silhouetted rocks, evergreen trees, and finally a circular clearing center stage. A reassuring baritone voice narrated the story. First came the Paddle Dance: three young Indian women disembarked from their canoe to join the potlatch, to which the audience was also invited; then came the Ancestral Mask Dance, where several spiritual traditions were performed, including the thanking of a tree after taking its bark; and third, the Lummi Blanket Dance, which acted out the story of the blankets, moss yellow and cobalt blue, owned by the wealthy and worn on special occasions. In the next event, The Terrible Beast Dance, a Timber Giantess roamed the forest looking for children, and then disappeared in a puff of smoke. Next followed the story of Raven, the trickster who stole the light of the world from an old chief who was hoarding it. Then, in an unhappy variation of the story, Raven becomes the prey of the Eagle instead of spreading the light to the dark world, as in most versions. The last dance was the Parade of Masks, where the masked ancestral spirits reappear and dance in a circle to the sound of drums as the moonlight fades on Raven, Eagle, Thunderbird, Owl, and Bear, all of whom disappeared as the dawn broke.

The salmon meal and performance are promoted in Tillicum's publicity as the heart of the journey, and likened to the traditional Northwest potlatch. But we paid with dollars for these gifts, not, as in the Native tradition, with a declaration of goodwill toward our hosts, and an invitation to a future potlatch. As individuals we were not hierarchized according to social status, but as white tourists we became a de facto upper class because we had a privileged view of our Indian hosts and entertainers, while we could remain anonymous in the dark, watching a production that was intercultural in a hegemonic way. In half an hour, we were shown a selection of the most beloved and enduring Northwest Native traditions. Yet the small proscenium stage in the large dining room and the condensation of all the performance elements into the framework of a potlatch were clearly in the European theatrical tradition. Indeed, the publicity of Tillicum Village states that the Native dances and myths "are combined with the theatrics of the stage to enhance the ethnic and cultural heritage of an exceptional people."[37] In other words, the Native heritage alone is not enough; it needs to be "framed by and for European conventions and taste."[38] The elements of the performance, each one uniquely important to Native culture, were crowded into a space and time too small for them, a spectacle that echoed the "Indian Holocaust," the forced roundups and marches across the continent and away from their homelands.

Historicizing the Present

> In [Ned Blackhawk's] bathroom: a poster of Sartre.
> —Sherman Alexie[39]

This tragic parallel from the past is important, but the Natives' story does not end here. The fact that *Dance on the Wind* was produced by Greg Thompson, who also produces Las Vegas spectacles, does not negate the declaration of the Native performers at Tillicum Village that they take pride in their performance. As Bill Hewitt proudly explained in an interview, the method of preparing the salmon, as well as the dances and masks used in the production, was created and legally owned by Native Americans and approved by tribal elders, and the Native artists take all the profits from the sale of their works exhibited in the art gallery, in addition to being paid for serving as live exhibits of authentic Native artists at work.[40] In the same interview, Hewitt also remarked that over the years he had hired not only Native Americans, but the occasional Vietnamese, Latino, and African American as dancers, salmon tenders, or greeters. These employees are, as Hewitt explained, "trained to be polite" as they interact with the tourists in what McCannell, borrowing the terms of Erving Goffman, calls the "front space." The "back space," on the other hand, is where the "service people" work. In the Tillicum longhouse this includes the kitchen, storage closets, tourists' and employees' restrooms, and rooms where both "front space" and "back space" employees take their breaks and socialize with each other.[41] Here, it is not so important to "look Indian."

The memory of this compromised but powerful performance of potlatch and masked dance is made indelible by knowing the history of their suppression. In 1921 Charles H. Burke, Commissioner of the U.S. Department of the Interior, issued a directive to the Bureau of Indian Affairs entitled "Indian Dancing," which plainly exposed the white colonizers' attitude toward the culture of the colonized:

> The latest reports [on the Indian dances are encouraging], [they] are growing less frequent, are of shorter duration, interfere less with . . . farming, and have fewer barbaric features. They are . . . more orderly because better supervised than formerly. On a number of reservations, however, the native dance still has enough evil tendencies to furnish a retarding influence.[42]

Burke lists the forbidden dances and describes the potlatch as "the destruction of clothing or useful articles, [and] the reckless giving away of property." Reflecting the general consensus of the white, middle-class, Christian majority, Burke viewed the dances and potlatch as a "perversion of those industrial and economic essentials which underlie all civilization."[43]

At base it was the Indians' communal culture itself that had to be controlled, even though this amounted to an annihilation of their historical identity. Burke asserts that it could be accomplished without "offending [their] communal longings or robbing [their] nature of its rhythm." They could then be, Burke says, "fit to survive in the midst of all races." In fact, "communal longings" are antithetical to the desires that drive competitive capitalism and private property, desires idealized as the natural survival of the fittest.[44] While many religious, artistic, and economic practices of Native peoples were banned in Canada and suppressed in the United States for nearly seventy years, both governments gave Christian churches free rein to gather converts among the Indians.[45]

Marketing the Past

> I have a serious lack of rhythm and pitch. I always figured I would be
> insulting thousands of years of tribal traditions if I sang or danced.
> My entire family agreed with me.
> —Sherman Alexie[46]

After the performance of *Dance on the Wind* we were led to the gallery and invited to watch the artists and ask them questions as they worked. Two of the dancers from the performance also joined us, demonstrated how to articulate the huge, heavy masks, and encouraged us to try them out ourselves. The conversation starkly juxtaposed the social roles that were being played out as identity positions in this situation: one white visitor (we were all white, but from different cities, states, and countries) addressed her question to a young Lummi artist who was carving a mask: "It must be wonderful to live here. Do you like it?" At this the artist gave a short laugh, glanced briefly at the Raven dancer, and explained that they just came to work every day on the ferry but lived in apartments in Seattle like everyone else, and that he himself had another job in the off-season. Another tourist asked the Native dancers and artists as a whole, "How can you hang on to your old religions after all this time? I would have thought you'd be over them by now," to which the Raven dancer politely replied, "I don't know. How can you hang on to yours?" This remains a central question in the negotiation of cultural identity.

Reconstituting Agency and Identity: The Masks Today

> The American Indian Movement . . . found its genesis in the late 1960s and early '70s when young, educated, urban Indians . . . were searching for tribal connections. Rather than returning to their specific tribes . . . urban Indians often find solace in a kind of pan-Indianism, a contemporary reinvention and meshing of many different tribal influences.
> —Sherman Alexie[47]

Performance scholar Dwight Conquergood approves of the "brilliance and deconstructive force" of Lévi-Strauss's analysis of a shaman's performance that is both "real" and "made up," but finds that the analyst is missing "a performative appreciation for *historical process*, how practices cumulatively interact and develop through time, reconstituting agent and agency and reconfiguring context." Identity is thus "conjunctural, not essential," a meaning emerging "through dialogue and encounters, along borders and intersections."[48] As Alexandra Harmon notes at the beginning of this essay, Native Americans do not base their identity on "an unshakable core of tradition, a self-definition that resists change." All "emerged from the same historical maelstrom with self-definitions their ancestors would not recognize. Yet all define themselves as Indians . . . largely on the basis of history."

In the Pacific Northwest today, the masks still perform their traditional functions at tribal ceremonies that have been revived since the Canadian government ended its anti-potlatch law and the United States gradually replaced its fear of and disdain for Native people as violent heathens with the sentimental image of a noble, wise, but doomed "vanishing race"; an image fed by countless photos, paintings, plays, and films, all with the same "end of the trail" theme. Only with the Indian liberation movement and pan-Indian cultural renaissance of the 1960s were these entrenched stereotypes publicly challenged. With the cultural renaissance, many traditional arts were revived, not only for tribal functions but for the larger marketplace. The ritual value of Native artifacts meant nothing to the dominant white culture, but when these same artifacts rose in exchange value as reified products, the Natives wanted some control over the process. At present many masks made by Native artists are either commissioned for public sites or sold privately, mostly to white collectors through galleries that are increasingly owned and run by Natives themselves as tribal or intertribal businesses. The masks, totems, and other objects made by today's artists often use principles of contemporary design, but always in combination with traditional Native forms and principles. For most artists mask making is paid labor, but this labor is more than an individual capitalist exchange; it is also a communal exchange, voluntary but widely practiced, in that tribal elders or chiefs decide which masks may be sold and displayed publicly and which may not, according to the masks' traditional tribal roles. Likewise, before culturally important (and usually expensive) masks are sold, they must first be honored, purified, and reborn in a sacred spirit dance for the people who are part of the spirit's human family. Sometimes the artist himself has the privilege of wearing the mask and performing the dance, which is also an honor for the guests in attendance. Every week or two a "repatriation" ceremony of a mask or other revered object is held somewhere in Canada and the United States. Seattle's Burke Museum has often hosted these ceremonies. Typically, an area of the museum is closed off to the general public, and hundreds of Native Americans, often from more than one First Nation, come to attend the all-day ceremony.

In fact, as Lloyd Averill and Daphne Morris document in their indispensable book, *Northwest Coast Native and Native-Style Art: A Guidebook for Western Washington*,[49] every Native artifact with spiritual significance that is sold for public display, including dance masks, must have its own ceremony before it is established outside of its Native home. These artifacts are located at hundreds of sites in the cities and rural areas of Puget Sound, some highly visible while others are passed by regularly without being noticed: elevator panels, airport murals, paper napkins, welcoming figures at college gateways and on beaches, canoes hanging over diners in seafood restaurants, and manhole covers in downtown Seattle, a host of authentic spirits continually adapting to a new world.

CHAPTER 3

Owners of the Past

Readbacks or Tradition in Mi'kmaq Narratives[1]

ANNE-CHRISTINE HORNBORG

IN THE 1960S, many Canadians could watch a television series produced in Halifax, Nova Scotia: *The Adventures of Glooscap.* The main character, Kluskap,[2] was a mighty culture hero,[3] depicted in old myths among the Mi'kmaq and their neighbor tribes on the east coast of Canada. In the old stories he transformed the landscape by hunting a beaver,[4] and many Mi'kmaqs knew of his mighty power. But in the 1960s the oral storytelling tradition was looked upon by the dominant white society as emanating from the past, when the Mi'kmaq were hunters and education had not distanced them from premodern beliefs and animistic notions.

Thirty years later, in 1989, Grand Chief Donald Marshall asked one of the Mi'kmaq warriors to investigate if there was any truth to the rumors about a proposed granite quarry at Kelly's Mountain on Cape Breton Island.[5] The rumors were found to be true and, in response, some Mi'kmaq traditionalists organized a peaceful chanting and drumming ceremony in Englishtown, a little village close to Kelly's Mountain.[6] To establish a quarry on the mountain would be an insult to Mother Earth, said the Mi'kmaq, also asserting that the mountain and its cave were the home of Kluskap and the place where he was expected to return to his people. Did the Mi'kmaq still really believe in fairy tales? Or was their knowledge about Kluskap acquired only through contemporary readbacks of texts by non-Native authors? "Readback" is a concept, defined here as "the phenomenon of native informants giving anthropologists information on their ancestors' way of life that they themselves acquired from reading anthropological reports and publications."[7] The dispute over the quarry awoke an enduring debate between constructivists and essentialists as to how tradition is transmitted. In this case the debate also had political implications, since a constructivist approach might have questioned the authenticity of the Kluskap stories, thereby threatening the mountain.

This chapter seeks to examine the Mi'kmaq relation to that Kluskap tradition, which has been depicted by non-Native authors in books and television series and performed in theater plays. How do the modern Mi'kmaq themselves evaluate the dominant society's texts about their culture hero? Let us go back in time and look at the stories of Kluskap.

White Society and the "Discovery" of Kluskap

The first to write down Kluskap stories and the one who is credited with "discovering" him is Silas Rand.[8] He was a missionary who came to know about the Mi'kmaq culture hero at the middle of the nineteenth century, when he was trying to convert the Catholic Mi'kmaq into Protestants. He writes that "the most remarkable personage of their traditions is Glooscap. The Indians suppose that he is still in existence, although they do not know exactly where."[9] Since Rand considered it his mission to work for a Protestant evangelization of the Mi'kmaq, he preferred to dismiss their stories as nonsense. However, he had to admit that these stories spoke of a world that was, at the time, still very important to the Mi'kmaq.[10]

Rand is the first to admit the continuous transformation of the stories. He gives many examples of European influences in the stories—money, iron, kings—and stresses that at that time the Europeans had inhabited the American continent for more than four hundred years.[11] But at the same time, in *The Prince and the Peasant-Girl*, he also gives examples of how European culture has been integrated into Mi'kmaq lifeworlds. Two neighboring kings live so close to each other that a prince could bring his princess bride home within the same day. Furthermore, it is the king's duty to look after the poor, so that they will not starve but have access to seed potatoes. In both cases, the king reminds the reader more of a Mi'kmaq chief than of a European monarch. A poor peasant girl's lack of education or status does not meet with any obstacles at the court. As long as she is kind, beautiful, and well dressed, she is completely suitable "to set before the king."[12] Note that Rand tends to conclude that these unlikely elements derive from Mi'kmaq society rather than from European folklore.

Another famous collector of Kluskap stories was the great romanticist

Charles Leland. Leland's mission was quite different from Rand's. His task was to gather and write down interesting data for the sake of posterity: "I believe that when the Indian shall have passed away there will come far better ethnologists than I am, who will be much more obliged to me for collecting raw material than for cooking it."[13] Yet he seemed tempted to speculate about the similarity that he saw between Algonkin myths and the Scandinavian Edda sagas. He pondered whether the similarities might have survived from contact with the Vikings.[14] He particularly emphasizes the character of Kluskap, "who is by far the grandest and most Aryan-like character ever evolved from a savage mind."[15] Leland sees a possible route for the transmission of the stories:

> When we, however, remember that the Eskimo once ranged as far south as Massachusetts, that they did not reach Greenland till the fourteenth century, that they had for three centuries intimate relations with Scandinavians, that they were very fond of legends, and that the Wabanaki even now mingle with them, the marvel would be that the Norsemen had not left among them traces of their tales or of their religion.[16]

Leland had spent a long time in Germany and was fascinated by the European romanticists' ideas of a "*Volk*-soul," which connected people with their land. Back in America, it was not in the works of Tennyson, Longfellow, or Thoreau that he found the depth of the American *Volk*-soul, but among the Indigenous inhabitants who, for generations, had roamed the landscape, lived close to it, and enticed it to disclose its secrets. Leland edited a variety of Algonkin stories into a grand narrative that, in accordance with the spirit of romanticism, would embody a folk soul corresponding to that of European folklore.

However, a closer look will reveal that both Rand and Leland have maneuvered their stories into a magnificent opus of fairy tales or legends. Rand wrote in his introduction to the story "The Magical Coat, Shoes, and Sword":

> As towns, intoxicating liquors, soldiers, and sentinels are referred to; the story must be of comparatively recent origin. But it is none the less interesting on that account. Its reference to transformations and magic, in general, seems clearly to point to an Indian origin, though the "invisible coat," "shoes of swiftness," and "sword of sharpness" look wonderfully like some fairy tale of European birth.[17]

Leland was more radical than Rand in editing the Mi'kmaq stories. To come as close as possible to what he saw as the "original poetry of the *Volk*," he even changed details that he interpreted to be later additions. In the legend of the *Chenoo*-girl, a despairing girl begs her parents to kill her. She had become the victim of sorcery after having rejected the courtship of a man, and she felt her inner nature slowly transformed into a violent character:

> "How can we kill you?" her mother asked.
> "You must shoot at me," she replied, "with seven arrows. And if you can kill me with seven shots all will be well."[18]

Leland commented on the story in a footnote by saying that the oral version actually spoke of guns, not arrows.[19]

Leland did not see any future for the Indians and predicted that they would soon be devoured by modern society and disappear, and that all their rich traditions thereby would be lost forever.[20] Leland was not alone in nourishing the belief that the stories carried an essence from an original, pre-European Indian culture.[21] In 1937, when Alfred Bailey examined the conflict in early European and eastern Algonkin cultures from 1504 to 1700, he discerned that Kluskap was confused with Noah in the traditional Mi'kmaq stories,[22] but he still looked for what might be the Mi'kmaq essence in these tales. He criticized Leland's theory of Viking contacts and instead distinguished the following types of stories: "The first has purely Indian elements. The second shows Indian motives together with mixed decorations. The third has purely European constituents. And the fourth gives evidence of having arisen from contact of Europeans and Indians in the Euro-American environment."[23] Bailey said that the distinctions may be arbitrary but nonetheless useful, and he pointed at the seventeenth century as the greatest period of cultural fusion, especially before the English expelled the Acadians[24] from the province. Since the first contact in the early sixteenth century, many French had married Mi'kmaq women, and their children had surely become familiar with European fairy tales, either through their father's relatives or by meeting other French people who had moved to New France.[25]

We must also take into account that when Leland and Rand collected the Kluskap stories, the Mi'kmaq were in the midst of a very turbulent time. They had been forced by the British, at last, to settle down in reserves and so give up their former lives as hunters. Life on the reserve affected the stories about Kluskap, and by and by he was transformed from a great hunter and culture hero into a messiah who had left Mi'kmaq land with a promise to return in the future to save all the oppressed Mi'kmaq.[26] Although at the end of the nineteenth century the Mi'kmaq were said to be Catholics, they still had faith in Kluskap.[27]

When the early ethnographers like Elsie Clews Parsons, Frank Speck, and Wilson Wallis collected their stories, their ambition was to reflect the storytellers and the Mi'kmaq lifeworld more closely than Leland and Rand had done.[28] Since they documented oral stories, the ethnographers also indicated how the stories were performed and tried to document the narrative context. For example, Wilson Wallis described the interplay between the storyteller and the audience as follows:

> The manner of telling the tales in 1911 was much the same as that described by Rand. A story was usually prefaced with *mado wiga djik ki ci gu,* 'there, at the home place, among the old people.' Auditors responded with *geskwa,* 'go on.' The introductory word, or phrase, was used only in this context. In relating the tales there was no apparent effort at rhetorical effect. The narrator proceeded as one giving information on some point in which all were interested. During the telling of a story, auditors did not interrupt with question or remark, except to grunt, now and then, as an expression of assent, or to interpose a note of surprise or of derision, or otherwise indicate interest or emotion.[29]

Isabelle Knockwood remembered from her childhood how the storytelling could go on for days. Jokes and laughter accompanied the memories. The children were not allowed to interrupt the elders or stand between the storyteller and the audience. According to her, the stories were an important source of tribal knowledge for the children.[30]

In Speck's collection of Mi'kmaq stories from Cape Breton, Kluskap is embedded in local places on this island.[31] He described a local variant of the widespread motif of Kluskap as a "culture hero chasing a beaver" that appears in the Algonkin mythology. In this story the home of Kluskap is Fairy Holes on Cape Breton, a place that Speck locates between St. Ann's Bay and Great Bras d'Or; undoubtedly the cave in Kelly's Mountain for which the superquarry was planned in the 1990s. The story reveals how

Kluskap altered the landscape with his escapades and includes reference to Kluskap's home at "Fairy Holes (Gluska'be wi'gwôm, 'Gluskap's wig-wam'). Just in front of the caves at this headland are three little islands in a straight line, long and narrow, known as Ciboux Islands. These are the remains of Gluskap's canoe, where he left it when it was broken. At Plaster Cove (Twô´butc, 'Looking Out') two girls saw his canoe broken into three pieces; and they laughed, making fun of Gluskap. At this he told them that they would remain forever where they are; and today there are two rocks at Plaster Cove which are the remains of these girls."[32]

In Parsons's stories, it is a local Mi'kmaq identified as Isabelle Googoo Morris's "grandfather's father" who, together with six other men, looked for Kluskap in a cave at the mountain Smoket and became a target of his tricks, and it is Joe Nuelich (little Newell) who actually found the mighty hero later on.[33] But Parsons and Wallis also discovered that the Kluskap stories, over the course of time, had turned pale. While Rand writes that the faith in Kluskap was very much alive in the 1850s, Parsons says that in her time there was no longer a large body of stories about him, and that the ones that were still being retold referred to one anecdote or another but did not add up to a longer narrative.[34] One explanation for this could be that nearly eighty years had passed between Rand's and Parsons's collections, and during this time the modernization process on the reserves had advanced.

Wallis, who visited the Mi'kmaq both in 1911–12 and 1953, wrote in his 1955 Mi'kmaq monograph that he was worried about the traditional Mi'kmaq culture. He saw a "culture loss" and said that "Gluskap legends may be unchanged but few know them and we heard them only from people over sixty who no longer dominate the social scene."[35] Beliefs in magical power and spirits were held largely by those of the older generation, who still remembered who *pugulatamutc*—the stone dwarfs—were. Some thought they lived near the reserves, while others said they had gone to more distant places. However, the younger generation conflated Mi'kmaq traditional beliefs with western fairy-tale figures. When Wilson Wallis asks twelve-year-old Leo about *pugulatamutc*, the boy's answer shows that he is acquainted with his grandfather's oral tradition, but also that he is familiar with the Disney animated movie *Snow White* (1937), resembling the earlier pattern in the nineteenth century of European influences on Mi'kmaq culture.[36]

Wallis expresses his disappointment over how much the old tradition and stories had faded away and says that the art of storytelling went into the grave with an earlier generation. Many of the long, richly embroidered stories had been transformed into synoptic variants. By the 1950s, contemporary versions of the Kluskap legends were only short accounts of how he chased a huge beaver and destroyed the beaver dam and told of the implications of this beaver hunt in terms of transforming the landscape.

When Philip Bock did fieldwork on the Restigouche reserve in the 1960s, he was even more pessimistic than Wallis about the future of Kluskap stories. He spoke to many Mi'kmaq in their thirties who admitted that they had never heard about their traditional culture hero. It seemed like settled life, the modernization of the reserves, and compulsory attendance at English-language schools had transformed the former Mi'kmaq hunters into modern, Canadian citizens.

But new forums had developed where the Mi'kmaq could learn about Kluskap. One story was kept alive because it could be found both in schoolbooks and in tourist literature.[37] In school, the Mi'kmaq children read about "Kluskap hunting a beaver," but in the classroom reader, the story was in the context of a fairy tale. Instead, the "true story" about how Nova Scotia came into being was not performed by the elders but found in books of natural science. Thus, the school established a discourse in relation to Kluskap's influence on the landscape. By placing such stories alongside other fairy tales, society had told the Mi'kmaq in what context such a text belonged.

Watching a television series about Kluskap also would affect how the Mi'kmaq kept the Kluskap tradition alive. Many young Mi'kmaq admitted to Bock in the 1960s that they had never heard about Kluskap before they saw the program (or read the monograph by Wallis and Wallis). Bock saw in this phenomenon a huge problem for further research in Mi'kmaq traditional stories.[38] How might future scholars distinguish modern influences from traditional beliefs? Would this be something to strive for, or even something possible to achieve?

Cultures are always subject to change. To look for an "ancient belief" is to depict culture in an essentialist fashion, whereby the mission of the scholar is to hunt for original elements and thus the most authentic story. All cultures are open to the integration of new ideas and practices. To close this door for the Mi'kmaq is to consign their way of being to a pre-Columbian lifestyle. A more interesting task for the scholar would be to compare the experiences that the dominant society has forced on the Mi'kmaq—experiences that are still creating a cultural trauma for their people—with those features that have been integrated into their traditions through their interaction with contemporary culture.

The Return of Kluskap

Bock's fieldwork was carried out in the middle of the Mi'kmaq modernization process. Since both he and Wallis had an essentialist view of culture, they saw every disappearing cultural feature as a "culture loss." There are ambiguities in Bock's pessimistic predictions for the Mi'kmaq future, which with hindsight modern scholars with a constructivist view of culture might interpret somewhat differently.

Many events in Western society in the 1960s and 1970s affected the reserve inhabitants and were handled with new strategies by them.[39] Protest movements were growing during this time—U.S. civil rights, Black Power, and the peace movement, to mention a few. The green movement and various radical organizations looked for alternatives to western society's way of thinking. For some of them, the lifestyle of the Native people became the prototype for a more humble, respectful, and sustainable way of treating the world. Resistance against the dominant society grew stronger within Native society. An important organization for North American Natives was formally constituted in 1968: the American Indian Movement (AIM), whose members wanted to construct a positive self-image, especially amongst the younger generation. The members often participated in sit-ins to spread their message through the media to the general public.

This movement to "revive the Indian" in society during this period, both in the dominant society and within the reserves, also spread to Nova Scotia. Non-Native authors began to rewrite older texts or produce new ones about the Mi'kmaq culture hero. The new literature about Kluskap referred to earlier spread very quickly to the reserves. An early and very popular television series about Kluskap was produced in the 1960s by the Halifax Canadian Corporation. An author, Kay Hill, was asked to rewrite some Kluskap stories so that children could enjoy them. The series became so popular that Hill wrote three books based on these adaptations: *Glooscap and His Magic, Badger the Mischief Maker,* and *More Glooscap*

Stories.[40] Movies in this genre include *Glooscap Country* (1961), directed by Margaret Perry for the Nova Scotia Information Service, and *Glooscap*, directed by Harry Pierpoint in 1971 as part of the American Folklore Series.[41] Another Kluskap program aimed at a more adult audience was created by Daniel and Diane Bertolino in 1982 as part of their series *Indian Legends of Canada*.[42] The popular programs were surely watched with great interest in those Mi'kmaq homes where there was a television. They presented a positive image of the culture hero and, evidently, made the Mi'kmaq proud of their traditions.

A theatrical production based on Kluskap legends, staged for children, received a great deal of attention at the beginning of the 1970s. The play was written and directed by Evelyn Garbary at the Mermaid Theatre in Wolfville, Nova Scotia. Garbary had emigrated from Wales and was a close friend of William Butler Yeats.[43] Inspired by this poet and his romantic and Celtic motifs, she set about to showcase what she saw as being the ancient history of Nova Scotia, the Mi'kmaq legends. She was astonished to see how unfamiliar the Mi'kmaq children were with their own cultural heritage, and she decided to take the play and the actors on a tour to the reserves. In a 1998 interview, Sten Eirik, one of the actors, recalled how the ensemble came to the Eskasoni reserve on Cape Breton on a summer's evening in 1975.

An older Mi'kmaq met them at the reserve. He told them that there were several young Mi'kmaq who wanted to "research" their own ancient culture. The play lasted about an hour and was a success with the younger Mi'kmaq. It mingled more serious adaptations of Kluskap legends with burlesque and included funny stories about the animals in the forest, such as that of the loon. Sten Eirik and the other actors were not prepared for such enthusiasm and thirst for the stories. For hours after the performance, they sat in discussions with the young audience. Two attitudes dominated among the older Mi'kmaq. Some disapproved that the actors had come: what were white men doing on a reserve—portraying Mi'kmaq stories to the Mi'kmaq? Others thought that the Kluskap stories were like fairy tales: children's stories, not to be taken seriously. But the young audience saw fantastic visions in the stories. They wanted to raise money for a theater group of their own.[44] Sten Eirik says that the Mi'kmaq ethnicity had been growing stronger at the end of the 1960s and early 1970s and that the play emerged at the right moment in this Mi'kmaq revitalization. He ended our conversation with an apology: "It was really not us who should bring this tradition further."

Fairy Tales and Prophecies

As well as the new interest in the dominant society for the Native traditions, the revival of traditions among different Native groups during the 1970s also affected the Mi'kmaq. Anthropologists noted that *sweat lodges* were being built on the reserves, and powwows and sweetgrass ceremonies were being held. When the Mi'kmaq heard of the superquarry plans at Kelly's Mountain in 1989, they were in the middle of this revitalization. Some traditionalists organized a peaceful ceremony close to Kelly's Mountain.[45] One of them, who said he represented the Grand Chief, explained that the quarry plans were an insult both to the Mi'kmaq and to Mother Earth. Their main arguments against the quarry concerned both the environment and their traditions.

The authorities tried to parry these arguments by ensuring all parties that they would use safe methods to avoid any potential environmental impact. More difficult for them to discuss was the Mi'kmaq argument that the mountain and its cave were sacred and belonged to their god Kluskap. One Mi'kmaq traditionalist compared Kluskap's Mountain with other sacred sites: "[L]ike any other spiritual beliefs we have certain sites that are more important than life itself . . . the degree of offense would be equal to that felt by Christians if a super quarry were placed at the Holy Sepulchre, or by the Hebrews if the Wailing Wall were removed for a motel, or by Muslims if a casino were placed in Mecca."[46] The cave was also likened to a church: "How would you feel if someone was going to destroy your church and all your sacred gods in it?"[47] Another traditionalist took the opportunity to explain that the fact that many Mi'kmaq are Catholics also had a negative influence on the Kluskap tradition: "We are mostly Catholic and because we worship the prophet Jesus we don't pay too much attention to our prophet, Kluscap. And it suffers. And that is why there hasn't been a great outcry from the Native population about what is about to happen, the destruction of the most Sacred site in the world."[48] However, some critical voices said that challenges to the quarry were only staged by the militant Mi'kmaq traditionalists to gain attention and to challenge Canadian society. The following polemic statement

from Mi'kmaq traditionalist Sulian Stone Eagle Herney, also one of the
spokesmen for Mi'kmaq Warrior Society, expressed the distrust that he
met as a traditionalist and defender of his heritage. He strongly attacked
those who questioned his commitment by asking them:

> . . . where were you in the nineteen fifties when the road
> was being built?
> I'll tell you where we were:
> We were in residential schools
> we were hungry
> we were uneducated
> we were beaten
> we were a controlled and oppressed nation
> our hair was short and we tried to
> walk in the footsteps of the White man
> (pause)
> Our hair is long
> and we walk tall
> we don't want nobody's footsteps
> we blaze our own trail
> and the good thing about it is
> we have people of the rainbow following behind us.[49]

The Mi'kmaq first tried to use peaceful methods to protect the mountain.
A spokesman for the Sacred Mountain Society thus turned to the Human
Rights Commission in December 1992 to help with the Kelly's Mountain
issue. David Beaton of the Human Rights Commission let his secretary
answer on December 29 that he was not responsible in this matter and
referred them to the Department of Culture (Nova Scotia Museum). They
answered to the Mi'kmaq spokesman on January 7, 1993: "Since the cave
is not an archaeological site, it does not fit within the usual interpretation
of the Special Places Protection Act."[50]

A curatorial report by the Nova Scotia Museum also found a lack of
"evidence for significant cultural resources."[51]

Their failure to persuade the authorities to protect the mountain forced
the Mi'kmaq to mark very clearly how important the mountain was to
them. For a growing number of Mi'kmaq, Kelly's Mountain became
Kluskap's Mountain and, as such, a symbol for spiritual values and hope

and an anchor in a world rife with unemployment, high rates of suicide among the young, poverty, and drug abuse that led to disease, depression, divorce and family abuse.[52] If this place was threatened, so were the Mi'kmaq. The traditionalist Sulian Stone Eagle Herney warned of the consequences if the plans for a quarry were realized:

> . . . People of the faith that I follow have pledged themselves at the cave to die before they will see a quarry there. And if a person is willing to die, let me tell you a person is willing to kill. . . . We are just recently now starting to wear our hair in braids again, taking up the drum again, given back the identity to our people, the pride of our people. . . . I am one who pledges to die at the mountain, and believe me I will, and I can kill, and it's as simple as that.[53]

The Mi'kmaq had their own ways of evaluating the dominant society's interpretation of their traditions, and of looking for evidence concerning their traditional beliefs. When the Mi'kmaq spoke about their tradition, they sometimes used scholars' texts ("readback"), but it was equally common and important to refer to the memories of the elders. To strengthen the credibility of these memories, the Mi'kmaq stressed that they had been related by reliable witnesses. Herney thus said:

> I have spoken with some of the elders, and one of the elders, who unfortunately has passed away, was Annie Mae Bernard. *She was the daughter of the late Grand Chief Gabriel Sylliboy.* She gave living testimony at the base of the Sacred Mountain at a demonstration there in the fall of '88. . . . She told us about when she was a child, her father, who was Grand Chief at the time, took trips to the cave twice a year and these pilgrimages consisted of all the family. . . . When they arrived there, at the mouth of the cave . . . There are three flat rocks . . . where they would leave offers on this table.[54]

When the same speaker stressed elsewhere that it was neither a new invention nor mere politics of the Mi'kmaq to speak of the mountain as sacred, he once again referred to his mother: "My mother is eighty-two years old; she is a living witness that it was sacred when she was a child."[55]

To depict Kluskap merely as a figure in a fairy tale is, according to one Mi'kmaq traditionalist, simply a way to continue colonial, ethnocentric oppression: "For you see Glooscap was not a bedtime story to tell our children but he [*sic*] some of the creator. Glooscap was and still is a prophecy of our people."[56] The Mi'kmaq showed that they knew the scholars' work, as well as the books and the television series by Kay Hill. Older texts (i.e., by Rand, Leland, and Parsons) were used in the Kelly's Mountain issue, but the concepts or texts were a bit modified and expressed in a counter-discourse. The Mi'kmaq said that it was one thing for anthropologists to look for facts about their tradition, but it was quite another thing for scholars to interpret facts based on a biased perspective: "According to legend, Kelly's Mountain is the final resting place for Glooscap—who anthropologists call a *mythological Micmac hero*."[57] It is noteworthy that the above Mi'kmaq spokesman said it was an anthropologist who interpreted Kluskap as a "mythological Mi'kmaq hero." The implication is that the Mi'kmaq have other ways to talk about Kluskap. Bock saw a growing problem in the 1960s in the fact that the Mi'kmaq, by reading books and watching television, would be influenced by the dominant society's Kluskap stories. But maybe this was more of a problem for the scholar than for the Mi'kmaq. Thirty years later, we can thus read that the Mi'kmaq had their own opinion about how stories by non-Native authors should be read. Since Hill's stories originally were produced for children, she had radically changed Rand's and Leland's original versions, because some parts might otherwise have been frightening. The final structure was arranged like a fairy tale. Hill's books were often invoked in the debate about Kelly's Mountain, often with political intentions. The Mi'kmaq knew the stories but stressed that they were a product of a white author's fantasy and thus should not be equated with Mi'kmaq traditions. One Mi'kmaq traditionalist thus said: "There are several people who have done books, Kay Hill, an author from Halifax, *Legends of Kluscap*. In the Native community we weren't over excited about her interpretations of our stories. They do not run parallel to what I was taught. I get my teachings from my elders."[58] The same Mi'kmaq traditionalist referred to Hill's stories during a very heated meeting between the Mi'kmaq, the authorities, and environmental activists on the Eskasoni reserve in March 1992:

> You are talking about a prophet
> and a prophecy
> and there is [*sic*] two things you do not (begrudge?) a man:
> You do not get in the middle of a husband and his wife fighting
> and you do not get in between a man and his god
> you will die, or you will kill . . . "[59]

But the Mi'kmaq could also allude to or draw on older written and scholarly texts, weaving them into their own stories. For example, the Mi'kmaq poet Rita Joe must have known Parsons's text about Kluskap's Cave when she wrote her poem "The Legend of Glooscap's Door."[60]

Rita Joe's text (1988)	*Parsons's text (1925)*
There is a doorway to Glooscap's domain Where you throw dry punk and fish For his fire and food. But you must not enter Though you may leave a gift on stone Waiting to feel goodness. This is the way the legend goes So the Micmac elders say.	Gluskap's door is at St. Ann's. There you would throw in some dry punk and a little fish for his fire and food. You say, "I wish you give me good luck." So the Micmac elders say.
At Cape North on a mountain you whisper, "My grandfather I have just come to your door I need your help." Then you leave something you treasure Taking three stones. This is your luck. This is the way the legend goes. So the Micmac elders say.	"When you go to see Gluskap, at Smoket, Cape North," you say, "My dear Grandfather, I just come on your door. I want you to help me." You leave money inside door, pieces of silver. You take two or three stones away with you, that's your luck.
At Cape Dolphin near Big Bras d'Or There is a hole through a cliff It is Glooscap's door. And on the outside a flat stone It is his table. The Indians on a hunt leave on table Tobacco and eels. This brings them luck, so the story goes The legend lives on.[61]	At Cape Dolphin [Dauphin], Big Bras d'Or, there is a door through the cliff, Gluskap's door. Outside, there is a stone like a table. Indians going hunting will leave on it tobacco and eels, to give them good luck. They do this today.[62]

Rita Joe wrote her poem just before the quarry plan was announced.[63] Over the years, she had made friends with the ethnographer Ruth Whitehead. For an essentialist scholar, this way of writing poems would be seen as plagiarism, but for constructivist scholars it could be a way of creating tradition by engaging in the dialectic of history and the present. It is a way of retelling the stories.

Whitehead was one of the key scholars in the quarry debate. It was she who examined the historical-ethnographic details concerning Kelly's Mountain.[64] The scholars were asked by the Grand Chief Donald Marshall to look for Mi'kmaq petroglyphs inside the cave, but they found that the ceiling had collapsed twelve years earlier. All they found was graffiti left by a Canadian military group on an exercise in 1921.[65]

In an article, Whitehead commented on the examination and mentioned that Cape Breton had played an important role in the Kluskap tradition. From this island, one of three "doors" went to Kluskap's new home. The first "door" was at Smokey, Cape North, and the other at St. Ann's. The third door was very important and could be found at Cape Dolphin. Here, two important rocks stood right outside the entrance to a cave. One rock was Kluskap's Table; the other, the Mother-in-Law (or the Grandmother). The cave was called Kluskap's Cave, Kluskap's Door, or Kluskap's Wigwam. Whitehead says that for generations offerings were made there and that this continues today. It was common for the Mi'kmaq to put fish bones on the rock in front of the cave (Kluskap's Table). When Nova Scotia Museum staff visited the place, they found tobacco and sweet-fern offerings, both on the "table" and inside the cave.[66] The delicate question of whether there were traditions connected to these offerings at Kluskap's Cave could become a political matter. Essentialism thus turns into politics: were these offerings evidence of an ongoing tradition or a newly invented rite? What constitutes a traditional rite, and when does a tradition start? Could there be interruptions in tradition? And when it revives again, is it still the same tradition? Who has the mandate to start a tradition? If we try to look for an ongoing essence in the transmission of traditions, we will always be hunting for the most authentic story, as the above-mentioned Charles Leland did. Remember, it was Leland, not the Mi'kmaq, who commented on the guns and arrows in the story of the *Chenoo-girl*. The question of guns or arrows in the original story didn't bother the Mi'kmaq storyteller when he or she was telling the traditional story.

Respectful cooperation between scholars and Mi'kmaq could be illustrated by Ruth Holmes Whitehead's documentation of Mi'kmaq culture. Her work on Mi'kmaq traditions had been read and appreciated by many Mi'kmaq,[67] and Rita Joe had dedicated a poem to her:

A Special Friend

Somewhere there I have a friend
In this place without end . . .
Somewhere there I have a friend
The archives are her trade,
A chronicler bringing nobility
Together we relate the wonders of my nation,
Our song a landing place.[68]

The poem shows how closely today's Mi'kmaq could work with scholars. The reconstruction of old traditions for the Mi'kmaq has typically
involved balancing information drawn from scholars' texts and a reluc-
tance to become too reliant on them. In the case of Kluskap's Cave, the
colonized people have also been put in the awkward position of having
to prove their traditions. Since the stories were traditionally transmitted
orally, they have to refer to early scholars' work in political disputes in
order to strengthen their cause. However, the scholars' texts do not carry
the whole truth, and the Mi'kmaq commonly take a critical attitude to
them. The critique, aimed at non-Native scholars, mostly concerns what
the Mi'kmaq regard as their shortcomings in analyzing the Mi'kmaq
material. Non-Natives are thought to grasp only the surface of the data,
or to reshape it so it fits European models. The Mi'kmaq student Eleanor
Johnson takes as an example a female scholar, Jeanne Guillemin, who has
studied Mi'kmaq tribal consciousness. According to Johnson, Guillemin
is a "cognitive tourist" and a good example of how western scholars lack
a deeper understanding of the Mi'kmaq spirit: "These 'cognitive tourists,'
such as Guillemin, come into the communities doing their fieldwork with
preconceived notions or professional methodologies about the so-called
Indians."[69] Johnson expresses her concern about the approaches of non-
Native scholars: "They're legitimate, maybe, in some studies but they
ignore the heart of the people and this is what needs to be developed.
This is what I was trying to do when I was writing 'Tribal Consciousness.'
You know, look at us deeper than our statistics."[70] It is from this difference
and creativity that Mi'kmaq identity is formed and their traditions are
revived today.

Epilogue

Today it does not seem that the plans for a quarry will be realized. The plan to destroy Kluskap's dwelling in Kelly's Mountain was seen by the Mi'kmaq as an act of disrespect for their traditions. It was more important for them to discuss Kluskap with respect for their traditions than to answer questions from non-Natives as to whether they still really *believed* in him. Whatever the main reason for not building the superquarry, Herney later summarized what he saw as a significant learning process in the battle of Kelly's Mountain:

> The mountain has to support the unity, of not only the Mi'kmaq population but also the world community, and . . . an awful lot of good has come out of the mountain. More human relations, healing, solidarity, union, unity has come out of that mountain than any of the gravel and granite that could have been possibly shipped anywhere, more than any jobs that could have been created as a result of that superquarry. I think what the mountain has produced is something that can't be bought. . . . It produced a lot of pain, but it produced a lot of education, healing, tolerance, pride, spirituality and identity back to the people.[71]

CHAPTER 4

The Pocahontas Myth and Its Deconstruction in Monique Mojica's Play

Princess Pocahontas and the Blue Spots

MARIA LYYTINEN

> It is through our collective memories, found in our stories, through our self-description, that we can come "home" to ourselves and the wisdom holding the vibrations of eternity.
> —Neal McLeod, "Coming Home through Stories"[1]

FEW NATIVE WOMEN have gained as much attention in colonized North America as the Powhatan girl Pocahontas, who lived in the area of modern-day Virginia during the setting up of the Jamestown colony in 1607. Her figure has inspired numerous stories, poems, plays, and films in the past centuries, and she continues to spark the imagination of Americans. Her historical background and her significance in both Native and non-Native America have been much contested over the years. Pocahontas's figure has come to represent both a savior to the colonizing Europeans and a traitor to her own people. The colonizers' versions of Pocahontas's legend have dominated the scene until recent years, but her story has also been taken up by Native American artists and writers. In this chapter I shall trace the journey of parts of the Pocahontas story through North American literature, from the nineteenth century to the present day, and particularly to Native American playwright Monique Mojica's interpretation of her in her play *Princess Pocahontas and the Blue Spots* (1990).[2] Along with Pocahontas, Mojica brings Native American women onstage from almost the entire history of the colonial period and shows new and revealing aspects of the colonizer's stereotypical images of Native women. I look at the way Monique Mojica deconstructs the figure of Pocahontas and other stereotyped representations of Native women and how Mojica taps into the collective memories of Native women to "come 'home'" to who she is: a contemporary Native woman in North America.

In his work *Generall Historie* (1624), Captain John Smith tells his famous story of being rescued from death at the hands of "cruel savages" by *Pocahuntas*, the daughter of a Powhatan chief.[3] This rescue, according to Smith, took place in Chief Powhatan's quarters in 1607 after Smith was captured by the chief's brother, Opechancanough. Smith describes the "savage" Powhatan ordering his men to have the captive's brains beaten out, when suddenly the chief's favorite daughter, Pocahontas, interrupts and pleads with her father to save the captain's life. Consequently, Smith is released. This is the scene perhaps most familiar to us from Pocahontas's life, reproduced in numerous children's books, dime novels, cartoons, and films. In his earlier work *True Relation*, published in 1608, which also tells of his experiences in the Jamestown colony, John Smith gives no account of such a rescue, although he does describe being captured by Chief Powhatan's brother and released by the chief, but with no threat made on his life. In fact, in this earlier account he describes being treated as a foreign dignitary by Powhatan and his people.

There is indeed serious doubt as to the authenticity of Smith's rescue story. Whether it was for political motives or other personal reasons that he rewrote the history of his captivity,[4] his story became popular among nineteenth-century Virginians, many of them claiming to be descendants of Pocahontas. Furthermore, Smith's account gave birth to the world-famous legend of Pocahontas, elevating this young Powhatan woman to the position of a savior of the early Jamestown colony, and has since inspired hundreds of writers, artists, and filmmakers to retell this legend.[5]

Most of all, the story of the young Powhatan princess who rescued Captain Smith from death has had a tremendous influence in reinforcing one of the most persistent and powerful colonial stereotypes of Native American women: that of the "Indian Princess,"[6] the female version of the "noble savage," who risks her own life for the advancement of the colonists. In colonial discourse, two stereotypes of Indian women have persisted throughout the centuries; the "Princess" and the "Squaw," a parallel to the virgin/whore dichotomy of the dominant culture. Pocahontas is undoubtedly the most famous representative figure of the Princess stereotype.

Initially, Smith's story of the rescue was not widely circulated except in a few books on Virginia, but at the start of the nineteenth century, when Americans really began to search for a national mythology, the story became very popular. For Virginians, John Smith's *Generall Historie* became a relied-upon source for the history of the early days of the colony and provided a useful account of elevating their ancestor, Pocahontas, to the position of a saint.[7] Smith's account of the Powhatan Princess was resurrected, and she "began to loom large as the guardian angel of our oldest colony," in the words of Philip Young.[8] First her story was mainly taken up by historians who would praise her courage and retell the rescue episode, most of them relying on Smith's *Generall Historie* as their source. Among nineteenth-century historians, hardly anyone seemed to question the authenticity of Smith's 1624 account, and the Pocahontas "myth" was accepted as a part of the historical canon in the founding of the New World.

According to Philip Young, the first writer to make literary use of Pocahontas was Ben Jonson in his *Staple News*, which in 1625 already made a brief reference to the "Princess."[9] Then, after a gap of almost two hundred years, the nineteenth century saw a flood of plays based on the Pocahontas story, all greatly romanticized in the style of the time. Pocahontas was portrayed as the female equivalent of the "good Indian," helping the more "civilized" colonizer in the struggle against the "savages" in the woods of Virginia.

One of the earliest plays depicting the story of Captain Smith and Pocahontas (of those texts that have survived) is James Nelson Barker's "Operatic Melo-Drame" *The Indian Princess, or La Belle Sauvage* (1808). In this play we are presented with a chaste and virtuous princess whose "civilized" and "un-Indian" features are emphasized in contrast to the savage, bloodthirsty Indians. She rushes to the rescue of Captain Smith, helps save the English from an evil plot of the Indians, and falls ardently in love with a white man, John Rolfe, whom she praises as "godlike,"[10] and who has educated her away "from the path of savage error."[11]

Pocahontas, or The Settlers of Virginia (1830), by George Washington Parke Curtis, step-grandson of the first American president, is another classic example of a romanticized version. Like Barker's play, it uses Captain Smith's story as its "historical" basis and presents the Indian Princess's "enlightenment" at meeting the white settlers and her conversion to Christianity. One could hardly find a more willing convert than the Princess, who so readily condemns her own people as savages and praises the English for saving her from the "heathens." In Parke Curtis's play, on seeing the English arrive on the shores of her home country, Pocahontas exclaims, "Oh, 't was a rare sight to behold the chiefs as they leap'd on shore . . . like beings from a higher world, sent here to amaze us with their glory,"[12] incidentally elevating the English themselves to gods. Having now realized the great mercy of the Christian God for sending the English to her homeland, she cries out, "Come good, come ill, Pocahontas will be the friend of the English. . . . Since the light of the Christian doctrine has shone on my before benighted soul."[13] At the climax of the play, when Pocahontas saves Captain Smith from death, thus showing her loyalty to the English, she also denies her father and her own people: "Cruel King, the ties of blood which bound me to thee are dissever'd, as have been long those of thy sanguinary religion; for know that I have abjur'd thy senseless gods, and now worship the Supreme Being, the true Manitou, and the Father of the Universe."[14]

The storylines and the messages of other early Pocahontas plays are similar to those in Barker's and Parke Curtis's, each telling their white audiences the legend of Pocahontas the way they liked to hear it, a tale about an Indian Princess who abandons her own people and their ways for those of the "more civilized" invaders. Among many other examples of such plays are Robert Dale Owen's *Pocahontas* (1837), Charlotte Barnes Conner's *The Forest Princess* (1844), and John Brougham's *Pocahontas, or The Gentle Savage* (1855). In most of the plays the story is exactly the same; the young Powhatan girl realizes the savagery of her own people, gives up her "Indianness" (i.e., her savagery), saves Smith from death, converts to Christianity, and in some plays ultimately marries a tobacco planter, John Rolfe (as, in fact, she did in real life). In many plays Pocahontas helps the whites in other ways as well, bringing them food and giving them secret information about Powhatan's military plans against the English, and causing the Indians' attacks on the invaders to fail miserably. Most of the plays base their plots, at least loosely, on John Smith's accounts, and claim to be historical dramas, thus further spreading the dubious version of early American history.

As the character of Pocahontas was exhausted onstage, the figure of the Indian Princess was moved west to the nineteenth-century frontier. As well as Pocahontas, there were numerous other Indian Princess figures appearing in white fiction, art, and the traveling Wild West shows. These figures, which clearly represented a sexualized, exotic "Other" from the wilderness of the New World, were constructed to please the male colonizer's gaze. This romanticized image of the Princess was more acceptable as an object of the white man's desire than was the whorish stereotype of the Squaw. Pocahontas and other princesses of the white male sexual fantasy performed dance numbers in small buckskin dresses and sold snake oil and other "Indian" products in the Wild West shows. Then, with the development of the film industry in Hollywood, "celluloid princesses" became numerous just before the First World War in films such as *Pocahontas* (1908), *An Indian Maiden's Choice* (1910), *The Indian Maiden's Sacrifice* (1910), *Broncho Billy and the Indian Maid* (1912), and *The Indian Maid's Warning* (1913). The Indian maids and maidens in these films were again portrayed as rescuers of white men. The more daring "sisters" of Pocahontas also appeared as half-naked Indian damsels dancing in early Hollywood musical choruses.

In the 1940s and 1950s, yet more celluloid princesses bathed half-naked in waterfalls or streams, in such films as *The Deerslayer* (1943) and *Indian Fighter* (1955). Indian maidens, desperate in their love for white men, appeared in films like *Buffalo Bill* (1943) and *Drum Beat* (1954), or, if they managed to seduce the white man, they ended up dying tragically in films like *Broken Arrow* (1950) and *Across the Wide Missouri* (1951).[15] In every case, the "Indian Princesses" represented the colonizer's object of lustful desire; the exotic, sexual Other, or what Homi K. Bhabha calls a subject "in a narrative economy of voyeurism and fetishism."[16]

In view of how numerous the portrayals of the Indian Princess are in these early plays, films, and fiction, it is not surprising that her image has had such a tremendous influence on generations of both Native and non-Native Americans. Looking at the early representations of the Pocahontas figure, it is obvious that she represents both an assimilating "good Indian," presenting an example of how to solve the "Indian problem," as well as an exotic, sexualized Other for the male colonizer's gaze. In these early representations, there seemed to be a need to juxtapose Pocahontas, a chaste and innocent Indian, with the bloodthirsty, crude savages, as depicted in James Nelson Barker's play, and to distinguish her from the other Indians as an "almost" white person. Yet she is also portrayed in passionate love scenes with either Smith or John Rolfe, her husband in real life, and her character is obviously associated with a much stronger sexuality than are the white female figures in the plays. The figure of the Indian Princess embodies this duality of being an example of perfect assimilation into white Christian ways, having departed from any savagery, yet presenting an exciting and unknown sexual Other.

Interestingly, her figure has also been raised to the status of the "Mother of Us All,"[17] especially by the Virginians who occupy her native land. White Americans who like to claim some native connection to the North American soil have found a suitable ancestor in Pocahontas, a connection that is not linked to images of "savage Indians," but to a good Christian princess who was wise enough to switch sides from the "savages" to the "civilized." She can be seen to represent a friendly welcome on the part of the Indians toward the colonizers, and as a great ancestral mother she connects them to the early history of the New World. Through her position as "Mother of Us All," Pocahontas lessens the guilt of white Americans. Most of the numerous representations of Pocahontas work to appease white nostalgia concerning the early days of the Jamestown settlement and the early stages of white American society. Leslie A. Fiedler, in his book *The Return of the Vanishing American*, claims that the story of Pocahontas works to lessen the whites' guilt after beginning their life in the New World by killing off the original Americans, because it is a kind of "no—we didn't—*she wanted* to marry a white man" story.[18] This legacy of painless "history" in the early stages of European settlement in North America is even today resurrected in films, books, and cartoons, and the Pocahontas story remains one of the favorite colonial myths in North America.

The Walt Disney animated production of *Pocahontas* (1995), despite arising almost two hundred years after the early plays, does not differ much from nineteenth-century Pocahontas fictions in terms of storyline and approach. Again, Pocahontas is portrayed as the good Indian who is fascinated by the whites and charmed by John Smith, to the point of giving up her own heritage and causing her Indian fiancé to be killed. John Smith, who, according to Jacquelyn Kilpatrick, in real life "more resembled a brick than a blonde Adonis,"[19] and who was at least fifteen years older than Pocahontas, is in the Disney film tall, blond, handsome, and young and speaks in the voice of Mel Gibson. Neither is the Disney image of Pocahontas very likely to resemble the historical princess, since in the film she looks more like a modern-day disco queen than the timid image of her found in the only surviving portrait painted on her fatal visit to England.[20] Although the Disney feature does not claim to be historically accurate, it has unfortunately already gone down as "fact" to many children (and adults), both American and international, who have watched the film. Because of the huge popularity and wide distribution of Disney films, *Pocahontas* has the power to shape a significant part of American romantic folklore. By reusing the same romanticized version of the Pocahontas story, the Disney film reminds people of the colonizer's account of her as the white man's ideal, assimilating Indian Princess.

The sequel to Disney's *Pocahontas, Pocahontas II: Journey to a New World*, goes even further in presenting the Indian Princess's yielding to the handsome colonizers. In this film, Pocahontas is portrayed as a completely assimilated Indian Princess visiting the English court, dressed in a Jacobean-style gown, with her hair done up in the European style and her face powdered heavily to lighten the hue of her skin. Although Disney shows the Princess running to the woods, stripping off her fancy dress and washing her face, as though wishing to portray her fight against efforts to colonize her identity, she eventually yields to the advances of Englishman John Rolfe, who is the main agent of assimilation and of whitewashing the Princess in this version.[21] As Kilpatrick argues in her essay "Disney's 'Politically Correct' Pocahontas,"[22] children "will believe in the Romeo and Juliet in the wilds of North America that Disney has presented," which, as Robert Eaglestaff, principal of the American Indian Heritage School in Seattle, suggests, is "like trying to teach about the Holocaust and putting in a nice story about Anne Frank falling in love with a German officer."[23] On its official Web site,[24] the Powhatan Nation strongly criticizes the Disney film for its inaccuracies: "the film distorts history beyond recognition. Our offers to assist Disney with cultural and historical accuracy were rejected," writes Chief Roy Crazy Horse. He adds, "it is unfortunate that this sad story, which Euro-Americans should find embarrassing, Disney makes 'entertainment' and perpetuates a dishonest and self-serving myth at the expense of the Powhatan Nation."[25]

The most recent film adaptation of the Pocahontas story, Terrence Malick's *The New World*, appeared in 2005. Malick reuses the story of Pocahontas falling in love with John Smith, a nice and handsome Englishman, who in this film respects and wants to learn from the Powhatans.

Q'Orianka Kilcher's Pocahontas portrays well the young Powhatan girl's tormented feelings at which side to choose, but yet again the mythical love affair between Smith and Pocahontas is at the forefront, and the film brings little new to this stereotypical saga.

The Pocahontas story and her image have been molded in the hands of numerous white writers and artists for the past two centuries, but prior to the 1960s there were scarcely any depictions of her by Native Americans. The colonial imagery tells us little of Native American women, or Pocahontas's people, of whom we have unfortunately scant historical knowledge.[26] Theater and film have been effective media in spreading the colonial imagery of Indians, but in the more recent past, theater has also been employed as a medium for self-definition and counteracting colonization by Native American artists. Parodying the colonizer's stereo-types in Native American and First Nations literature has been common since at least the 1960s, and the stage offers a possibility for "reinscription and self-representation of colonised bodies," as Helen Gilbert and Joanne Tompkins point out in their book *Post-colonial Drama*.[27] Partly influenced, perhaps, by the 1960s Open Theatre and by El Teatro Campesino's[28] ironic juxtapositioning of imagery, experience, and embodied stereotypes to present social criticism,[29] Native American playwrights transferred their criticism of colonial stereotypes to the stage.

The late 1960s and early 1970s also saw an increase in Native American political activism following the general movement for civil rights in the United States.[30] There were significant developments in Native American civil rights in the 1970s and 1980s in the form of legal victories in land claims and increased tribal rights. This political and cultural process has also inspired writers and artists to critically evaluate the past and present of their people after five hundred years of colonial occupation. Hanay Geiogamah, a Kiowa playwright, was one of the first Native American writers to bring colonial stereotypes to the stage. In his satirical play *Foghorn* (1973), almost all of the characters resemble stereotyped colonial images, among them Princess Pocahontas, who is presented in a hilarious scene singing "The Indian Love Call" and telling her "hand-maidens" of Captain Smith's impotence.[31]

Female playwrights and theater groups have also deconstructed colonial imagery. The New York–based Spiderwoman Theater Company, which was founded by Lisa Mayo and Gloria Miguel, and which has been actively performing since the 1980s, presented in their play *Winnetou's Snake Oil Show from Wigwam City*[32] a character called Minnie Hall Runner who is "a copy of an Indian Princess who does nice sweet things but she's all show business" and Princess Pissy Willow, "a sharpshooter in the Wild West Show."[33] Margo Kane, a Salteaux/Cree actor and writer, also dealt with colonial stereotypes of Native American and First Nations women in her play *Moonlodge* (1990).[34] The 1980s and early 1990s represented a time in Canada of heightened political and cultural activity amongst the First Nations, with Native land claims and an increase in the number of emerging artists and performance groups.[35] From the same cultural scene as Kane's *Moonlodge* stems the work of Monique Mojica, such as *Princess Pocahontas and the Blue Spots* (1990).

As Homi K. Bhabha asserts in his essay "The Other Question: Stereotype, Discrimination and the Discourse of Colonialism," the stereotype is a "major discursive strategy"[36] in colonial discourse. It is "knowledge that is arrested and fetishistic and circulates through colonial discourse as [a] limited form of otherness, [a] form of difference."[37] The images of a young Indian girl both as subservient assimilationist and as the "darker," more lascivious, and available Squaw form the stereotypes of colonial discourse that Mojica has chosen to challenge, undo, and render ridiculous in the play.

Mojica is a Kuna/Rappahannock[38] writer and actor, born and raised in New York City, and both her mother and aunt are members of the famous Spiderwoman Theater Company. Mojica migrated to Toronto in 1983 and was a founding member of Native Earth Performing Arts, currently one of the leading Canadian Aboriginal theater companies. She has worked in theater and film as an actor, a director, and a writer with Native Earth, the Centre for Indigenous Theatre, and Nightwood Theatre, amongst others.[39] Mojica has said that it is as an actor that she found her way into writing. She says that her play *Princess Pocahontas and the Blue Spots* "resulted from a recognition that stories important enough to tell as performance also need to be written down, documented, [and] saved."[40] *Princess Pocahontas and the Blue Spots* was originally workshopped by Mojica and Alejandra Nuñez, with direction and dramaturgy by Djanet Sears, in 1988.[41] It was then workshopped by Nightwood Theatre in May 1989 in a coproduction with Native Earth Performing Arts, directed by Muriel Miguel. Subsequently, it was read at the Weesageechak Festival of New Work by Women, which was produced by Nightwood Theatre in November of that year. The play was finally fully produced at the Theatre Passe Muraille Backspace in coproduction with Nightwood Theatre in February 1990.

In her play, Mojica quotes a traditional Cheyenne saying: "A nation is not conquered until the hearts of its women are on the ground."[42] As a result of stereotyping and cultural colonization and the actual physical colonization of their land and homes, the hearts of Native American women have "been forced to the ground because the power of imagination, of image . . . is the power to determine a people's fate." So says Paula Gunn Allen in her influential book *The Sacred Hoop*,[43] which Mojica draws on in her play. In *Princess Pocahontas and the Blue Spots*, Monique Mojica has set about to displace the colonizer's stereotypes and reclaim the images of Native American women for the women themselves, to rebuild identity, and to restore wholeness among the Native people. Setting the task for her play, Mojica's character Contemporary Woman #1 says: "It's time for the women to pick up their medicine in order for the people to continue." She goes on to say, quoting the words of Art Solomon, an Ojibway elder, "The women are the medicine, so we must heal the women."[44] Contemporary Woman #1 then proceeds to give birth onstage, as if giving birth to the healing process; the beginning of a new era of recovery and self-definition for Native American women. This character is described by Mojica as a "modern, Native woman on a journey to recover the history of her grandmothers as a tool towards her own healing,"[45] and could be seen to represent Mojica's own voice in the play.

The process of reclaiming the imagery and image casting for Native American women is presented in a powerful series of thirteen "Transformations" (corresponding to thirteen scenes) on stage. In the original production, two actors, Mojica and Alejandra Nuñez, took on twenty-three different characters, voicing experiences from Native American women's lives, both past and present, and expressing the suffering, endurance, and pain of five hundred years under colonial rule. In this process the colonizer's stereotypical images of Indian Princess, the Cigar Store Squaw, and the Storybook Pocahontas are mimicked and mocked by a Trickster figure, Princess Buttered-on-Both-Sides. She is described by Mojica as "one of the many faces of the Trickster, Coyote."[46] The carnivalesque parodies of the Trickster intertwine with the voices of two contemporary Native women who represent North and South American female experiences, as well as with voices from history: those of the Métis wives, Native deities and gods, Malinche, and the historical Pocahontas. What emerges from the shifting, transforming, and undoing throughout the thirteen transformations are two contemporary women, reclaiming their own right to determine who they are. These two women emerge from the other figures portrayed by the same actors, as if to show that all of the experiences of the mothers, sisters, and grandmothers voiced in the play are still present in their lives. It is as if, through the transformations onstage, Mojica's Native women are able to fill the gap in their peoples' history, produced by the colonizer's distorted images of their ancestors. The women now reclaim these images by entering the "skin" (and the costumes onstage) of Malinche, Pocahontas, and the Métis women.

Princess Buttered-on-Both-Sides takes on the colonizer's popular images of Native women, and, by inhabiting these stereotypes onstage, she deconstructs and displaces them with Trickster hermeneutics. She thus liberates the two contemporary women of these stereotypes and provides another important part of the healing process. As Homi K. Bhabha suggests, for the colonized to liberate themselves from colonial discourse, it is essential to recognize the *"processes of subjectification* made possible (and plausible) through stereotypical discourse" and "to construct its regime of truth," through which process it is possible to reveal "the boundaries of colonial discourse," and to transgress "these limits from the space of that otherness."[47] In Mojica's play it is the Trickster who occupies that space of "otherness," subverting, through Trickster magic and humor, the colonial stereotypes of Pocahontas and the Cigar Store Squaw.

The very first example of the Trickster's "deconstruction" of colonial stereotypes comes in the opening scene of the play. Princess Buttered-on-Both-Sides is presented at the 498th annual Miss North American Indian Beauty Pageant, hosted by "George Pepe Flaco Columbus Cartier da Gama Smith," "coming to you live from the Indian Princess Hall of Fame."[48] Dressed in a "white 'buckskin' dress . . . carrying an oversized ear of corn," and offering the audience cornnuts, she comes in accompanied by "Hollywood 'tom toms,' the 'Indian Love Call,' 'The Good, the Bad and the Ugly' and the 'Mazola' commercial tune." Mojica's Trickster Coyote mocks the numerous Hollywood and commercial images of Indian Princesses, who are so ready to sacrifice themselves for the white man. She pronounces: "For the talent segment of the Miss North American Indian Beauty Pageant, I shall dance for you, in savage splendour, the 'Dance of the Sacrificial Corn Maiden,' and proceed to hurl myself over the precipice, all for the loss of my one true love, CAPTAIN JOHN WHITEMAN."[49]

In fact, the stage directions in this scene make specific reference to the film *Rose Marie*, a Hollywood feature with an elaborately choreographed woodland "Indian" dance number, "Totem-Tom-Tom," which Princess Buttered-on-Both-Sides performs as a "corn celebration played on pan pipes with vocalized cartoon sound effects [while doing a] Hollywood 'Injun Dance.'"[50] According to the stereotypes presented in many films, books, and cartoons of Indian maidens, Princess Buttered-on-Both-Sides proceeds to try to kill herself, stripping off her buckskin dress and throwing herself into "Niagara Falls," shouting "Geronimooooooooo!!!!!"[51] Only, as a Trickster, she survives this leap.

As some of the worst stereotypes are already mocked at the beginning of the play and are literally thrown into Niagara Falls along with Princess Buttered-on-Both-Sides, there is now space for the Native women's own voices to be heard. The two women onstage go through a historical journey of their ancestors' experiences. They adopt the voice of Malinche, the interpreter and mistress of Hernán Cortés. Like Pocahontas, who is seen by some Native Americans as a traitor who handed her territory and herself to the white invaders[52] (though she is also seen by many Native Americans as one of the only positive images of Indian women in colonial imagery),[53] Malinche has sparked fierce criticism from Native Americans and inspired several degrading idioms and songs in the Spanish language, calling her a whore and a traitor.[54] However, in Mojica's play Malinche is given a chance to voice her own version of how the conquistadors treated her.

Three different Métis women also appear onstage expressing their suffering as the wives of the first voyagers and fur traders, helping their husbands survive in the Canadian wilderness, but receiving only abandonment and abuse in return. The actors also adopt the voices of female Native deities and gods who tell how they were appropriated and exploited by the colonizers' church and religion. Amid these expressions of suppression, suffering, and survival, Princess Buttered-on-Both-Sides appears regularly, offering moments of humor and relief through her mock performances of cartoon Indians, buttering up whichever side is most advantageous each time. The Coyote figure traditionally symbolizes continuance and survival, and, as Paula Gunn Allen asserts, "it is this spirit of the trickster-creator that keeps Indians alive and vital in the face of horror."[55] Neal McLeod, a Cree writer and critic, furthers this argument, contending that "by engaging in Trickster hermeneutics . . . we move towards an ideal of Native Studies—namely self-description on our own terms."[56]

The "Blue Spots" in the play are the "doo-wop girls who back up Princess Pocahontas and her band" when Princess-Buttered-on-Both-Sides, disguised as the Storybook Pocahontas, performs a vaudeville-style song "*à la Marilyn Monroe*,"[57] which ridicules Hollywood musicals' use of half-naked "Indian" maidens in their choruses. The Blue Spots scream "¡Capitán! ¡No te vayas!"[58] to support the Trickster's attempts at seducing "Captain Whiteman." At the same time the Blue Spots point to the "true sign" of Indian blood, as Contemporary Woman #1 says, which "even among the half-breeds, [is] one of the last things to go."[59] Representing the "Indianness" that will not be "whitewashed" by any efforts of cultural colonization, the Blue Spots are a sign of resistance and survival. Thus, the Blue Spots also represent a type of Trickster figure, mocking the false "Indian" imagery and appropriation of Indian Princess figures, and reminding the audience of the true sign of "Indianness."[60]

The Trickster Coyote disguised as the Storybook Pocahontas also gives a parodical performance of the John Smith rescue story as told in stereotypical colonial fiction. Accompanied by a Troubadour from an "Elizabethan court," she ridicules the multitude of romanticized dime novels, epic poems, and other literary versions of the myth. In this scene Mojica could be seen to be mimicking, for instance, such epic poems as *My Lady Pocahontas* by John Esten Cooke from 1885, Mary Virginia Wall's *The Daughter of Virginia Dare* from 1908, or indeed the very origin of the myth, John Smith's *Generall Historie*.[61] Again, Princess Buttered-on-Both-Sides embodies the white man's fictional Indian Princess, as she performs a vaudeville and Wild West show number with all the ludicrous stereotypes of the sacrificial virgin, desperate in her love for Captain Whiteman. The Troubadour and Storybook Pocahontas sing together:

Her father was a stern, old chief,
Powhatan was his name-O
Sweet and pretty was Pocahontas
As he was ugly and cruel-O.
Then into her village strode a man
With steps so brave and sure—
Said he in a deep voice like a God's
"My name is Captain John Smith-O."[62]

In response the chorus sings, "Heigh-ho wiggle-waggle / wigwam wampum, / roly-poly papoose tom-tom, / tomahawk squaw,"[63] lampooning the colonizer's way of constructing an "Indian" image by merely lumping together any words depicting "Indianness." Mojica thereby illustrates the way in which "Indians" have come to be recognized by the symbols that the colonial entertainment industry has attached to them (the compulsory feather headdress, tomahawks, wigwams, totem poles and canoes, buckskin dresses and braids), many of which tend to appear in the same "Indian" story, irrespective of tribe or region.

Mojica then juxtaposes her picturebook Pocahontas, who happily rejects her own people "for the sake of her one true love, Captain Whiteman,"[64] with a more tragic aspect of the story. She has the same actor transform into Lady Rebecca, the Christianized Pocahontas who cries out: "My heart is on the ground!"[65] This Pocahontas has been stripped of her true self, her people, and her identity, and forcibly molded into the figure of a Christian, Europeanized woman who is literally stuck in an Elizabethan lace collar and cuffs onstage. She is also "stuck" in a picture frame that she is holding—perhaps a reference to the only portrait of the real Pocahontas—in which she has been turned into the colonizer's image of civilization. The actor in the picture frame onstage offers an effective "counter gaze"[66] to the gaze of the colonizer. The same Native American actor who embodies Contemporary Woman #1, Malinche, the Trickster Coyote, and Pocahontas stares back at the audience from the colonial picture frame as the portrait of an "assimilated Indian."

In addition, a character called Matoaka, which was Pocahontas's private and personal name among her own people, appears onstage as a joyful and innocent Powhatan girl, with none of the airs of the cartoon seductress performed by the Trickster in an earlier scene. By presenting these different faces of Pocahontas, the white mythical rescue story is constantly questioned and undermined as it is played out simultaneously onstage. At the point where Mojica, impersonating Pocahontas in the original performance, swoons for the love of "Captain Whiteman," she suddenly transforms into the character of Contemporary Woman #1, who asks, "Where was her mother?"[67] Coming out of the theatrical costume and stance, she poses the question directly to the audience.

Mojica constantly plays with the ideas of defining and subjectifying in this play. The multiple layers of time, the transformation of the two actors from historical figures into stereotypes and back into themselves, the juxtaposition of the colonizer's images with those of the Native women themselves, all disrupt the discourse of "Indianness." By using the Trickster figure, Mojica avoids merely reversing the colonizer/colonized dichotomy. As Gloria Anzaldúa observes in *Borderlands/La Frontera*, which deals with the experiences of Chicana women in the United States, the juxtaposing model of "oppressor/oppressed is too simplistic." It is of little benefit to have the oppressed colonial subject (or former colonial subject) merely "stand on the opposite river bank, shouting questions, challenging patriarchal, white conventions."[68] According to Anzaldúa, this sort of a counterstance "locks one into a duel of oppressor and oppressed."[69] With the use of the Trickster figure, however, Mojica makes it impossible to "lock" the oppressed into any fixed position, since the Trickster is a shape-shifter who, in this play, embodies the colonial stereotypes and, through excessive parody, strips them of their power and authority. The colonized is thus empowered toward self-determination.[70]

The climax of the reappropriation of colonial signifiers by the Trickster, and their transformation into objects of laughter and ridicule, comes toward the end of the play when Princess Buttered-on-Both-Sides reappears, this time disguised as a Cigar Store Squaw. Now she represents the image from cigarette and match boxes and tobacco ads: the appealing, lustful Indian maiden inviting you for a smoke, the Squaw of the virgin/whore dichotomy. She carries an oversized bunch of cigars (obviously phallic), offers them to the audience, and says: "I wanna be free to express myself! . . . I wanna be the girl next door! . . . I wanna have lots and lots of blonde hair. . . . I wanna be Doris Day, Farrah Fawcett, Daryl Hannah!"[71] Instead of settling for her stoically silent stereotype, Mojica's

Cigar Store Trickster wishes to take on the stereotypes of white American women as pretty, blonde neighborhood girls or glamorous Hollywood stars to represent an ideal American beauty queen. "I wanna be a cover girl, a beauty queen, Miss America, Miss North American Indian!"[72] At the same time that she mocks the white man's Squaw image, she plays with the "Pretty Woman"/prostitute image of Hollywood. She then proceeds to stuff herself into a shimmering evening gown "of the tackiest sort" and says, "So, here I am, a finalist in the Miss North American Indian Beauty Pageant! Think of it! Little me from in front of the tobacco store, fighting for DEMOCRACY!"[73]

Mimi Gisolfi D'Aponte argues that, as opposed to using the Greek concept of catharsis "and the purging of pity and fear through witnessing tragedy in the theater, and [considering] such purging [as] a form of healing," in Native plays the idea of "comic rhythm" as the "rhythm of survival" is central.[74] For Monique Mojica, as for many Native American playwrights and writers, the process of healing partly takes place through laughter and humor. A "comic rhythm" works through all the thirteen "Transformations" of Mojica's play, though she often weaves tragic elements into the parodies of the stereotypical images of Native women, as in the case of the Storybook Pocahontas. Mojica portrays her both as entirely ridiculous and as a sensitive young girl whose family has abandoned her, thereby contrasting the colonizer's image and that of a Native woman speaking for herself.

In the final part of the play, called "Una Nación" (one nation), the two Contemporary Women reappear from all the costumes and props. Throughout the play the two actors have been peeling off layers of stereotypes, and as the characters onstage change their clothes and strip off colonial symbols, eventually Contemporary Women #1 and #2 end up ritually and literally washing each other. This time they represent no one but themselves: two modern Native women who are expressing their right to define who they are. Contemporary Woman #1 discards white feminism and states the need for standing on her own feet, in her own shoes: "I don't want to be mistaken for a crowd of Native women. I am one. And I do not represent all Native women."[75] She also calls out for "friends, sisters, guerrillas—the women—'Word Warriors,'[76] to help" in the process of healing.

Mojica is certainly a "Word Warrior," composing an outspoken and powerful text of resistance to cultural colonization. *Princess Pocahontas and the Blue Spots* has recently been included in the syllabi of many American and Canadian universities' and schools' drama programs, which is a clear sign that the canon of representations of Native American women is gradually changing. Mojica continues to write and perform, and her recent play *The Scrubbing Project* deals with contemporary Native women's lives. *Princess Pocahontas and the Blue Spots* constitutes a significant postcolonial and feminist text. It has taken up the task of voicing the unsung heroines of Native women's past and delivers a liberating, self-affirming message to contemporary Native women who still have to struggle with the colonial images of Squaws and Princesses. In contemporary Native American drama, as Ann Haugo says, the "Indian Princess and the Noble Savage 'talk back,' and through the voice of the Native actors inhabiting their bodies and with the words of the Native writers, they change the terms of colonial discourse."[77] Monique Mojica leaves her audience with hope for continuance and healing. The women in her play are survivors, even Princess Pocahontas: "A nation is not conquered until the hearts of its women are on the ground."[78]

Part II

The Native Body in Performance

CHAPTER 5

Stories from the Body
Blood Memory and Organic Texts

Monique Mojica

I AM GOING TO ATTEMPT to describe a very important aspect of where my work comes from. Within Turtle Gals Performance Ensemble, Jani Lauzon, Michelle St. John, and I are keenly aware that it is the part of our process we have inherited from Spiderwoman Theater. And it is the most difficult to talk about because of its intangibility and because of its relationship to the spirit world, its connection to the land, its emotional bond to place, and its link to the healing arts. I am talking about the stories I carry because they have been passed on through my blood, encoded in my DNA.

My fellow Turtle Jani Lauzon uses the phrase, "Our bodies are our books." I would build on that thought to say that our bodies are our libraries—fully referenced in memory, an endless resource, a giant database of stories. Some we lived, some were passed on, some dreamt, some forgotten, some we are unaware of, dormant, awaiting the key that will release them.

Of course I can't and won't attempt to offer any "scientific" proof of this. However, along with my work as a performer, I am a certified Pilates instructor and I work with bodies other than my own. During the course of my training, I was struck by the way every person's body tells a story. Each injury, physical or emotional trauma, muscle imbalance, torsion of the spine or overstretched ligament tells a story. Our very breath, how it is held or released, our ability or lack thereof to connect within and be *in* our bodies, all tell a story. Our bodies house a collection of experiences as clear as tattoos on our skins.

Mining my body for these organic texts has become the primary source material for my work and I continue to be fascinated and surprised by it. When we work we use a process of deep improvisation. We stand in an empty room, witnessed by a director or by fellow ensemble members. We establish a world or a situation and we enter it with a specific question or task in mind to source information about it: what it looks like, smells like, who was there and what was said. The role of the witness is not only to watch and listen, but to tether the improvisers to the physical world. These improvisations result in raw texts that, because they are organic, often have no linear logic. It is not unusual for us not to know *why* an image or a character or place appears in our initial improvisations. Given enough time and trust, the reason an image persistently presents itself will eventually be revealed. Here are some examples.

Turtle Gals has developed a new play called *The Only Good Indian . . .* , which charts the history of Native performers in Buffalo Bill's Wild West shows in the 1880s, through P. T. Barnum's side shows, the 1904 St. Louis World's Fair (and other expositions), the silent film era, vaudeville, burlesque, and Hollywood. Now, although we were aware that Teddy Roosevelt had used General Philip Sheridan's proverbial quote "The only good Indian is a dead Indian" (the original quote being "The only good Indians I ever saw were dead") and that he had been instrumental in convincing J. P. Morgan to finance Edward S. Curtis's photographic expeditions documenting the "vanishing race," we were astonished when he relentlessly showed up in our deep investigations. What was Teddy Roosevelt doing in our play?!—a play created by Native women featuring our unsung predecessors from over a century ago? We then made some discoveries through more conventional research: the Internet, the library, and research shared with scholars such as Christine Bold of the University of Guelph. We uncovered that it was Teddy Roosevelt who flicked the telegraph key that turned on the lights at the 1904 St. Louis World's Fair where Geronimo, among others, was on display. ("Don't tell me that the lights are shining anywhere but there.") Roosevelt had to grant special permission for Geronimo to be present because he was a prisoner of war at the time and arrived at the fair in shackles. Roosevelt's wife, Edith, received one of our central characters, Zitkala Sa (Gertrude Bonin)—a prominent Dakota writer, orator, and concert violinist—in the White House. He was president when another of our central characters, Winnebago actress Red Wing, became North America's first female silent movie star. And it was Teddy again who, along with members of the elite Boone and Crockett Club (which he founded), was instrumental in bringing Buffalo Bill's Wild West Show to New York for the first time, where they paraded down Fifth Avenue before they set sail for Europe.

Which brings me to my second example: As we explored the world and time period of some of these early performers, another image recurred. It was the carousel: the old-fashioned kind with big painted horses and barrel organ music. We didn't know why it was there but we followed it down and incorporated carousel music into our piece. I had spent a lot of time on the carousel in New York's Central Park as a very small child and it had been an important special excursion for me. We then found documentation that Buffalo Bill, while waiting to sail out of New York Harbor, had taken his troupe of Wild West Show performers on an outing to Central Park—and those Indians spent hours riding the carousel! At that time it was powered by a horse and an old blind mule walking around in a pit. What an image! All the more poignant when you realize that among the Wild West Show performers were some very famous people: Sitting Bull, Black Elk, Red Shirt, Gall, Gabriel Dumont, all riding wooden horses on the carousel in Central Park.

The Central Park of my childhood was an important place not only because of the carousel, but also because of its large rock formations. They had a magnetic draw for me. Every time we passed them I had to run up and sit on those rocks, and a very specific feeling came from them, one I couldn't articulate at two-and-a-half or three years old. This is the raw text from an improvisation I did earlier this spring in which I explored that feeling.

Rocks of Central Park

I'm here! I'm here!

My rocks—I'm here—smooth with ruts in them, small holes filled with rainwater, moss—one humps up out of the other, out of the other. Somebody's feet walked over these rocks. Somebody else sat where I am. Somebody else looked at the sky upside-down like a big blue bowl— somebody else said, "I'm here."

The faces looking up out of the rocks look like me. I'm here! Where did you go? Were you lonely? Were you lonely sitting on this rock? I see him: skin dark brown and polished with long hair, black and grey to his shoulders. Here he sat dressed in deerskin, cloth, shell and antler. Not much food in the deerskin bag slung across his shoulder—just some dried meat and a horn filled with buckshot.

He is turning and looking toward the West where the tall old New York apartment buildings are now—rising like the battlements of a castle—The Dakota, and to the south, Essex House.

Somebody was lonely here. Someone was sad. Someone knew they were almost the last. Someone couldn't fight anymore. Someone couldn't walk any farther.

Could he hear the music from the carousel? I can almost hear it! Oohm-pah-pah, Boom pah-pah / Oohm-pah-pah, Boom pah-pah. The gold paint on the horses—seals, lions, monkeys. Oohm-pah-pah, Boom pah-pah / Oohm-pah-pah, Boom pah-pah Up and down, up and down, around and around. My horse is white, its nostrils flared, hooves up in the air. I can see the paddle striking the bass drum inside the organ. Around and around so fast that my hair streams out behind me—and I can't see the rocks anymore.

Another grouping of persistent imagery that may recur, in part because New York City was my first view of the world, is massive Greco-Roman statuary—not the least of which is the Statue of Liberty herself. Now *that* lady has some big feet! Interestingly, according to Cherokee scholar Dr. Rayna Green, the Statue of Liberty evolved from earlier depictions of the Americas as a Native woman—an Amazon Queen riding the back of an armadillo. Her features gradually became more and more European until we have the toga-clad figure we're all familiar with. She made a brief appearance in *Princess Pocahontas and the Blue Spots* when the clown character, Princess Buttered-on-Both-Sides, is finally crowned Miss North American Indian.

These colossal statues have always both scared and mesmerized me. So much so that when Turtle Gals was developing *The Scrubbing Project*, and looking at angels and embodiments of winged warrior women, who should show up but Winged Victory! "What's she doing here?" I asked. "She's not an Indian." However, I accepted her along with Groucho Marx and others who presented themselves in my Starworld because one of the vital questions we asked ourselves in this play about genocide is, "How do we get from victim to victory?" Whether we are looking up at L'Arc du

Triomphe in Paris, the War Memorial in Ottawa, or the Princess Gates at the CNE (complete with majestic Winged Victory atop), these monuments are all about the victors and the vanquished, the triumphant and the conquered. That has a peculiar resonance if you are an Aboriginal person on this land—a people without even one memorial to our war dead.

It was no casual coincidence that many of the residential schools in Canada and the United States had an archway at their entrances, as did the Nazi concentration camps. The immense whiter-than-white statuary at the 1904 World's Fair was constructed to celebrate the Greco-Roman roots of civilization, read "progress." In my correspondence with the director of a centennial celebration film documentary about the 1904 World's Fair, Bob Miano had this to say about his upcoming documentary project, which focuses on the Gateway Arch at the entrance to the fair: "It will be more than just a story about the building of the Gateway Arch—the 'how' of it. We'll really examine the 'why' of the monument—what it symbolizes and what it means to this country and the rest of the world. I believe it will be another important history lesson for many people." I have a feeling there may be a few more statues in Turtle Gals' next show.

I'd like to share an excerpt from that next show, *The Only Good Indian . . .* :

> First, what you need to know is that I come from a family of show Indians. My Grandpa and Red Wing's son-in-law mixed up snake oil in the bathtub and sold it. They scripted invented ceremonial skits and dances. My mom and her sisters (the future Spiderwoman Theater) rode on floats and ballyhooed to drum customers into the movie houses to see the latest John Wayne western. They posed for tourists in their buckskins and feathers and danced for the Boy Scouts. I did too, once because my Grandpa took me with him without my mother's knowledge. And boy, was she mad! She and her sisters had refused to do this once they could voice an opinion, but we were show biz Indians! Many of these show Indian families from all over converged in New York. They danced at the World's Fair and performed with the rodeo at Madison Square Garden. And when they had no place to go, my family took them in. Some stayed and raised their families and created a community in New York City.

> This is the story of a sad and magical place of memory—my grandparents' house, 50 First Place, Brooklyn.

House of Mirrors

I can see right through myself! Transparent like "The Invisible Woman"—
a cord of veins getting smaller and smaller like the branches of a tree,
the tributaries of a river. A net of life—a blue/green map of veins charts
a flow of stories that my eyes have never seen but that I know. From
behind my eyelids—images projected on the retina from the mirror in
Grandma's hand.

My Grandma's house had mirrors, mirrors on the walls! A house of
mirrors; big mirrors suspended from the ceiling that hung tilted down into
the room and reflected the aqua walls. When I looked up into it, I floated
under water in a swimming pool. And on the walls, Jesus walks on water.

There were gilded framed mirrors with a golden eagle on top, round
like a porthole of a ship. Concave, convex, it distorted my face, made my
nose long like a dog or a moose.

There was a slanted mirror under the coffee table. I would duck under
the table top to see myself reflected in the blue-tinted glass. I slip through
the beveled edge of blue mirror and I am inside Aunt Lizzie's china
cabinet looking out at my four-year-old self looking in. We touch fingers
against the glass.

I'm on the shelf among the salt and pepper shakers shaped like toma-
toes, Indian heads and animals; souvenirs from Niagara Falls and Florida,
beaded Mohawk pincushions and picture frames. On the bottom shelf
is an Indian blanket, a straw man doll from Mexico, and a rag doll Aunt
Lizzie made. She's an Indian doll with an embroidered face, moccasins,
a fringed leather vest and a beaded daisy chain bracelet.

In the mirror at the back of the china cabinet I can see the room reflected behind me over and over again, reaching back to those who came
before me and stretching on to those who'll come after. I see myself fractured on and on like on the old box of Uncle Ben's Rice.

On the orange box is a picture of Uncle Ben holding a box of Uncle
Ben's Rice, on that box is a picture of Uncle Ben holding a box of Uncle
Ben's Rice, and on that box is a picture of Uncle Ben holding a box of
Uncle Ben's Rice. On and on, smaller and smaller as far as I can see, until
it doesn't look like Uncle Ben anymore.

In the house of mirrors there was a really big table. Around it could fit
all our blood relatives and all our extended family, sometimes the neighbors upstairs or whatever Indian family was passing through the house
of mirrors, waiting to get back home after being stranded in New York
by the outfits they performed with: rodeos, circuses, exhibitions. They

brought with them the sounds of Winnebago, Kanawake, Rosebud, Hopi land and they would all tell stories about "Mrs. Mofsie, Mrs. Martin, Mrs. Deer, Douglas Grant, Blow Snake, Big Mountain, Red Wing." Stories that my eyes never saw but that I know.

Whatever celebration it was—birthdays, Christmas, Thanksgiving—Grandpa would preside over the platter—usually a turkey—and there would be big bowls with mounds of mashed potatoes and yams, corn, cornbread, pies. Or fish fried to golden perfection eaten with rice cooked in a diamond-shaped aluminum pot that Grandpa and Uncle Joe would turn red with the amount of chili pepper they shook onto it. Chili so hot it had a devil on the bottle.

And I would be under this big table sipping a 7-Up float from a tall glass that I'd stir with a long-handled spoon. It was a good hiding place. I'd sit balanced on the cross beam in the world under the table in the house of mirrors and listen to the stories. Stories that my eyes never saw but that I know: "Mrs. Mofsie, Mrs. Martin, Mrs. Deer, Douglas Grant, Blow Snake, Big Mountain, Red Wing." Images projected on the retina from the mirror in my mother's hand.

Up north—years far away from the house of mirrors—I meet two brothers from the Deer family. "I know who you are!" one brother says. "When my grandparents died, there were photographs of your grandparents in their things." "I know who you are!" I say. "Your uncle is my godfather!" "My children know who you are!" says the other brother; "I tell them, 'That's your cousin on TV.'"

Backstage, I meet a ventriloquist named Big Mountain, "I know who you are! I remember your sister, your uncle ran the elevator; I remember when he fell off the iron." Once, in a massive demonstration of one hundred thousand people—I met a Mofsie!

"I know—." We knew. We are connected over three, four generations of Indian performers—from way back.

There have been times when mining my body for organic texts and confronting blood memory has been a matter of life and death. Lest that sound too melodramatic, let me tell you this story: Two days before Christmas 1997, forty-five unarmed Indigenous women, children, and men were slaughtered while they fasted and prayed for peace in Acteal in the municipality of Chenalho, the traditional Mayan village in the highlands of Chiapas, where my husband comes from. In the early weeks of 1998, I had to watch days and days of raw footage from the aftermath of the massacre and the funeral in order to translate it from Spanish to English. I was drowning in sorrow; it was stuck in my body. I felt closer to the world of the dead than to the world of the living. I asked my close friend and colleague director/ dramaturge Kate Lushington to meet me in the Nightwood Theatre studio because if I didn't get this story out of my body I was afraid that the dead might take me with them. By plunging into that outrage and grief, I saved my own life. This is the result:

I Am Sad Still

I wake up—
　　　　　suffocating　　my mouth and nose filled with dirt.
　　　　　Was I dreaming again of drowning?
　　　　　of being crushed against the ceiling of
　　a room suddenly　shrinking?
　　　　　It's hard to breathe so I breathe as little as possible.
　　　　　My legs are cramped and I have to pee.
I wake up—
　　I am in Canada　　chunks of earth in my nostrils
　　　　　　　　　roots poking into my side
　　I taste dirt　　　　　　　and something else . . .
I wake up—
　　I see the man's face—impassive calm
　　He looks into the camera
　　　　　releases a breath
I wake up—
　　I am in Canada　　gasping to breathe against
　　　　　the dust　　　　and smell of blood
　　　　　"Bueno," he tells the cameraman,
　　　　　"I will show you where I hid."
　　An arroyo　　flies still buzzing around the sticky drying blood
　　　　　　　buzzing　　thick
　　where the bullets swarmed thick around the people of the bees
　　　　　　Las Abejas.
　　The camera moves to . . . women's shoes　　two pairs
　　　　　　　carefully set side by side.

There is a small cave in the bank of the arroyo
                           crumbling earth   dark
                  "Aquí, señores," he says, "here, I hid as if I were dead
                                 saved
                two   of my children.
             I am sad still
         My wife was killed with another child. My sister, two
brothers in-law,
        three nephews."
I wake up—
     I am in Canada   we lie very still   chunks of earth in our
          nostrils   and mouths
             not breathing—not moving
                  I have to pee.
                  Ten hours
In this hole   three of us lie.
Outside   screams
     outside hack hack CHUN of the machetes
     bullets buzzing   swarms of bullets
             swarms of flies
     Bullets made in Canada
     M-16's assembled in Canada
             bullets swarm like flies
I wake up—
     I am suffocating   my mouth and nose filled with dirt.
     My legs are cramped and I have to pee.
I wake up—
     I am in Canada
I wake up—
     on a pile of dead
I wake up—
     in the snow at Wounded Knee/ hiding along the riverbank at
Batoche/ being crushed in a boxcar to Treblinka
I wake up—
     I am in Acteal
     December 22, 1997
             and I am sad still.

Creating an organic text from blood memory sometimes occurs when there is something my body is experiencing that I can't quite put my finger on—there's maybe a certain quality of light and I think, "I've been here before" when I know I haven't. As a contemporary Native theater artist I feel it is crucial that we acknowledge our experience as a valid worldview—something that has been consistently denied us. We must honor the way in which we navigate what the late Chicana writer Gloria Anzaldúa called "the borderlands." This is our reality. And that reality is inclusive of worlds that are both seen and unseen.

This is an excerpt from *Princess Pocahontas and the Blue Spots*. It was written in 1989 during my first trip to Mexico with the man who was to become my husband. Several voices from parallel times co-exist in this piece. It explores those moments when the world tilts and you can suddenly see those other realities. It is also part love story, and I've used a song as a heightened form of storytelling to tell that part.

Stand Me in the Rain Forest

Stand me in the rain forest—
my soul whispers, "home . . .
home . . . "
Rise me above the rain forest—
I know every ray of filtered light that ripples
the living green

>   (*singing*) Cuando canto
>   en Tulum, en Tulum canta la
>   luna—
>   cuando canto en Tulum,
>   en Tulum canta la luna.

slant-eyed and head swinging low to the ground,
my muscles ripple from shoulder to haunch,
now running—now stopping to sniff the air.

>   (*singing*) When you
>   tasted of salt and oranges,
>   and the moon sang her
>   happiest songs to us,
>   —heart offerings

        when we remembered her—
        When you tasted of salt
and oranges,
      and the falling stars
took our breath away—the
waves of the sea
      mixed with my own salt
tears

barefoot and possessionless I
walk resigned, but not broken,
chest thrust forward I memorize
every leaf, every hill, every bird, every plot of mountain corn—
knowing these are the last things I will see.
The bus winds the mountain turns.
It begins to rain, cold drops pelting the window in streaks.
        I promise to return.
        The light in the doorways,
          the hammocks hung in
        the homes of the brown
        mountain-weathered people
        looking up from the side of
        the road.
I promise to return to carry on the light.
Swell my heart in my chest
full and warm. I turn and say,
"If I survive this journey, it is only because my
heart has decided not to burst."
        . . . and she sounds like this:
        (singing)
    ah ah ah   ah ah ah
       ah ah ah
    ah   ah   ah!
I give myself to this land.
My heart pierced my back split open. Impaled.
My blood stains this piece of earth—a landmark for my soul.
I promise to return to love you always.
        Call to me in a language I

                                       don't understand,
Curled beside me, you sleep.
Wake up! There's work to be done!
We're here.
                              slant-eyed and head swinging
                              low to the ground,
                              my spine arches from neck to tail.
                      (*singing*)
                              When you tasted of salt and oranges
                              I howled at the pulling in my womb,
                              —your own trembling
                              not quieted by whispers (of no, no,
                              no)
I crouch at the side of the mountain
the guardian—watching

                              When you tasted of salt and
                      oranges,
I put down my sorrow in
an ancient place,
ahh ahh ahh ahh

                              wordless, I walk into the sea
                              and the moon she will sing.
I wait.
                      ah ah ah ah ah ah
                         ah ah ah
                      Ah   Ah   Ah!

Sometimes the images I work with come from old photographs. Earlier this spring, while researching *The Only Good Indian* . . . , I was show-ing an old family photograph to the other two Turtle Gals. It was of a gathering of a large group of Indians at American Indian Day in the mid-thirties. Jani pointed to one striking old woman and asked who she was. I didn't know, but her face is so intense that it's impossible not to pick her out of the crowd.

    I've just returned from New York City. I went there to attend the opening of an exhibit called "New Tribe New York" at the Smithsonian–National Museum of the American Indian. It's a retrospective of Spiderwoman Theater's work and of their origins—my origins, the legacy that I am proud to have inherited.

It opened with a tribute to Spiderwoman—my mother and her two sisters. My brother-in-law's drum group drummed, my cousins and my brother and I sang. I read them the "House of Mirrors." On stage my contemporaries and I represented the third and fourth generations of interconnected Indian performing families. And there is a fifth generation of performers coming! Red Wing's family and mine have intermarried and my eleven-year-old niece, Josephine, a descendant of both these families, was on stage too. It was an intensely emotional evening.

As I walked into the exhibit itself I saw a photograph of my Grandpa projected onto the wall nine feet high! Sitting next to him in traditional dress was a gaunt elderly woman whom I recognized from old photographs in my possession—but I didn't know who she was. I grabbed my Aunt Elizabeth, the matriarch of our family, and asked her. "That's your Aunt Muriel's godmother," she told me. "She was called Princess Naomi and she was almost one hundred years old back then in 1937. She was the last surviving Manhattan Indian." As she spoke I realized that the faces in the rocks of Central Park were her people—that is her land.

Four days later, I took Turtle Gals' video camera and my videographer's skills—which leave much to be desired—and I went to Central Park with my cousin to shoot some footage of the carousel. I chose a white horse with its hooves in the air and I rode. I wanted to do it in full traditional dress, but I lost my nerve; maybe next time. I also shot footage of those magnificent rock formations, and as I walked over them I remembered Princess Naomi.

As I've told you these stories from my body, Princess Naomi and the Manhattan Indians are remembered again. You've witnessed me naming the names of my predecessors. Now their names and our stories are part of your memory, and as long as they are remembered they live on. This is blood memory. This is where my work comes from.

CHAPTER 6

Acts of Transfer

The 1975 and 1976 Productions of Raven *and* Body Indian *by Red Earth Performing Arts Company*

Julie Pearson-Little Thunder

NATIVE TRADITIONAL STORIES and cultural explanations are frequently prefaced by the phrase, "The way I heard it was . . . "[1] This qualifier points to a Native ethos, or value system, that readily acknowledges the possibility of alternative viewpoints or explanations.[2] However, this phrase has another function as well. It invokes live presence as *authorizing* the information about to be related. It draws attention to the fact that the person telling this story was once a listener, physically absorbing and storing the information he or she is about to share.

Authorization of knowledge by means of live presence is a feature of "the repertoire"—Diana Taylor's term for embodied practices.[3] These practices, which include spoken language, ceremony, sports, ritual, and games, amongst others, have long been ignored by the West as a source of potential historical knowledge.[4] According to Taylor, this neglect arises, in part, from western scholars' fondness for the archive, the "supposedly enduring materials" of manuscripts, buildings, artwork, archeological remains, and the like.[5] Yet the repertoire can also make historical claims, since it acts as a fluid and mobile means of storing and transmitting collective knowledges and histories, values and memories (between past and present).[6]

Because the repertoire occupies a central place in U.S. tribal cultures, it played a pivotal role in the development of twentieth-century Native theater. From the sixties through the mid-eighties, Indian theater companies, wishing to commit to a season of productions, faced a task akin to following the Trickster Rabbit to his home. No e-mails requesting scripts by Indian playwrights could be exchanged with playwrights or play development organizations. No anthologies of Indian-authored plays could be pulled from the bookshelf. This shortage of written scripts obliged Native theater companies to create their own scripts or to convert materials written by non-Indians into theater pieces. In both instances, Native theater workers turned to the repertoire—song, dance, gesture, and Native habitus—as well as to enactment, to transform textual representations into Indian theatrical space.[7]

Of course, theatrical performance is also part of the repertoire, a means of presenting certain kinds of content while displaying the performers' skills for a live audience. But as Taylor emphasizes, performance may also function as an "act of transfer" conveying "social knowledge, memory and a sense of identity" from one group of individuals to another and from one generation to the next.[8] In the context of theater historiography, understanding performance as an act of transfer may yield new and deeper understandings of Indigenous and other alternative theater practices.

The term "act of transfer" is particularly intriguing with regard to Native theater, where it invites application as a theoretical lens in its own right. As Taylor observes, the archive and the repertoire often "work in tandem," to transmit history in different but usually complementary ways."[9] In this chapter, I read the archive of two early Native theater productions, through the repertoire and acts of transfer, to analyze the Indian theatrical space of *Raven* and *Body Indian*. These plays, presented in 1975 and 1976 respectively by Red Earth Performing Arts Company, differed radically in style, content, and authorship. But both drew extensively upon the repertoire and acts of transfer in all aspects of their production—from rehearsal and staging to performance and audience reception.

In 1974, the newness of Native theater as genre created such excitement that the appearance of a Native play in one part of the country tended to inspire the development of other companies or productions in a ripple effect. Thus, Red Earth, known as REPAC, might be considered an act of transfer of Native theater to the Seattle Indian community by the Native American Theater Ensemble, or NATE. NATE arrived at the University of Washington campus in 1974, armed with *Foghorn*, a politically charged agitprop by the group's director, Hanay Geiogamah.[10] John Kauffman (Nez Perce), Phyllis Brisson (Assiniboine), and Terry Tafoya (Isleta/Warm Springs)—attended the production. All three had been performing Indian poems and stories in local venues, but *Foghorn* was their first encounter with an Indian-authored play.[11] After the show, the Seattle actors and the touring company struck up a friendship that would eventually become a sustained artistic exchange of personnel, texts, and tribal repertoires.[12] Donald Matt, an Indian counselor at the school who helped book the performance, was also in the audience. Matt, who had no previous theater experience, was so excited by *Foghorn* that he quit his job to tour with NATE for the next three months.[13] When he returned to Seattle, he joined Kauffman, Brisson, and Tafoya in founding Red Earth Performing Arts Company.

Aided by a grant from the National Endowment for the Arts, REPAC became a company in residence at Seattle University in the fall of '75. Their first show was *Raven*, described in the company's program as "an original play from the Indian legends of the Pacific Northwest Coast."[14] Written by Nick DiMartino, a non-Indian friend of John Kauffman, its regional subject matter and strong production values made *Raven* an immediate success. However, its viability as Indian theatrical space was due more to its use of the repertoire, and multiple acts of transfer, than to the play text itself.

Frieda Kirk describes the play as a "conglomerate of stories from the Northwest Coast and Canadian tribes."[15] The plot follows Raven's search for his brother, Nighthawk, murdered by their Uncle Bear, "through four dangerous worlds, beyond death itself."[16] Donald Matt relates that at least part of the play's action involved Raven's pursuit of Bear to avenge his brother's death.[17] However, as Kirk implies in her use of the word *conglomerate*, this mixture of stories from differing tribes and diverse social contexts had at best a tenuous connection to tribal oral traditions.

Within Native circles, storytelling is a daily act of transfer of values, social identity, and ways of being. Traditional storytelling is a highly physical act, drawing upon gesture, song, dance, and the use of props, and alternating between third-person narration and enactment. In traditional or ceremonial venues, as Diné poet Luci Tapahonso explains, storytelling becomes a "multi-media" production in its own right.[18] Listeners mentally process the images and sounds of the story in combination with the sensory effects of the story's delivery in an indoor dwelling or outdoor environment.[19] Cultural restrictions such as age, clan membership, gender, and season are often associated with the act of transfer of traditional or mythic stories, thus increasing audience investment in the story. The oral tradition is a "collective creation," not simply by virtue of its genesis, but also because the storyteller is not alone in learning and storing his/her material. Through repeated hearings, audiences also learn and store a repertoire of stories. While their rights to tell these stories may be circumscribed, this act of embodiment by audience members contributes to perceptions of the oral tradition as communal product.[20]

Red Earth members were keenly aware of the communal status of Raven stories, and anxious about how their Indian audience members might react to DiMartino's script. The author's use of American Indian oral literature, translated into English and collected in various anthologies, was not a problem per se, since REPAC actors often worked from these same kinds of archival sources. More problematic was the mixing of the tribal, social, and cultural contexts mentioned above, and DiMartino's goal in adapting this material for the stage. DiMartino admired Northwest Coast cultures, but he likely did not presume to transfer collective tribal knowledge, histories, or memories to Seattle University audiences. His purpose in writing Raven was to deliver a theatrically exciting, regionally relevant, Indian-themed play.

REPAC's use of the repertoire, Native habitus, and tribal spatial practice helped turn the play's symbolic representations into Indian theatrical space. Much of the credit for this conversion goes to Gerald Bruce Miller, the first NATE actor to join Red Earth, when he moved back to Washington. Miller, who was Skokomish and Yakima, had grown up with his tribal practices.[21] His first act of transfer was to teach his fellow actors the iconic Yakima dances and the singing style so often associated with all Northwest Coast cultures. Kauffman, who was directing the show, built much of his staging around this tribal repertoire and arranged for Miller's input into other production aspects as well.

It is important to note that practices like western dance, choreography, song, and stage blocking are also part of the repertoire. As such, they clearly contain their own "trajectories, influences, and histories."[22] Nonetheless, I would argue that Miller's acts of transfer, in this case, differed to such a degree as to be almost distinct. The primary aim of western stage blocking is to transfer technical skills and technical knowledge confined to theatrical production. In Miller's acts of transfer, technical skills could not be separated from other kinds of cultural content.

In the Native approach to teaching, cultural content and technique are imbricated. The function of performance as an episteme, or way of knowing, is obvious.[23] While instructing the group in a series of dance steps, Yakima-language words, or vocables, Miller would have emphasized the importance of the social relations embodied in the dances and songs. Working by accretion over a series of rehearsals, he would have used Native-language words, when possible, to explain the history and function of the dances, and the dancers' clothing and masks. Similarly, a western theater practitioner might also offer a contextualization of a court dance like the gavotte.[24] But the practitioner would verbally establish only as much context as she or he deemed necessary to the effective execution of the dance: the focus would be on facilitating the theater work. Miller knew that he was sharing a living practice that would be scrutinized as such by Native audience members; thus, rehearsals served as a strategic introduction to some aspects of Northwest Coast cultural etiquette. After the play closed, whether the intertribal cast traveled to Indian homes in the area, longhouse ceremonies, or Northwest Coast exhibition dances, the information they had absorbed from Miller, and now carried in their persons, would be recontextualized, added to, expanded upon. It would have a life outside of and beyond the theater.

This does not mean that Miller, or Kauffman, as the director of the play, neglected theatrical considerations when rehearsing and staging these acts of transfer. Selecting which repertoire elements are to be emphasized, mediated, and/or eliminated is a crucial step in adapting traditional singing and dancing for western performance formats. Again, the distinction to be made is between performance as an act of transfer and the use of repertoire in performance to connect past and present. Making decisions that honor the extra-theatrical aspects of the repertoire without dishonoring these same live practices in other tribal socio-ceremonial contexts is the key to creating Indian space on stage. Moreover, Miller's acts of transfer from the repertoire did not end with physical or vocal work.[25] He also guided Bill Wilkins, the show's non-Indian set designer, in creating a multipurpose longhouse with Northwest Coast Indian motifs, and the show's costumes were based upon Miller's knowledge of Northwest Coast tribal clothing and masks.

The actors' embodiment also helped connect *Raven* more strongly to tribal spatial practice. Because performance is "constitutive," in Edward

Bruner's words, the potential of embodiment for subverting, inverting, and deconstructing dialogue is well known.[26] Indeed, in the case of *Raven*, embodiment may have provided an opportunity for ironic commentary on a text that many of the Indian actors perceived as somewhat naïve, when compared to such Native adaptations or stagings of the oral tradition as *Coon Cons Coyote* and *Changer*.[27]

While Red Earth's signature style had yet to be developed, the influence of Miller in the show suggests that some stylistic elements of the troupe's work might have been present in an early form in *Raven*.[28] These elements, described in later productions, included a broad physical approach to comedy, described by Kirk as "over the top," and a large degree of freedom to improvise lines and blocking.[29] In addition to directing the show, Kauffman played multiple roles, including the lead, Raven. Most of the other actors played multiple characters as well. These included personifications of the elements or seasons, like Fog Man and Winter Girl, or animal roles—Loon Woman, Goggle Fish, Otter Boy, and Grandmother Robin, to name just a few.

Along with a farcical playing style, REPAC actors brought with them a physical habitus that reflected their tribal identities and their intertribal experiences through friendships. As John and Jean Comaroff point out, the definition of habitus as a culturally determined field of behavior must be expanded to include physical ways of gesturing, speaking, and moving, along with mental habits of thought and perception.[30] Although this behavior must be largely unconscious to qualify as habitus, the frame of theatricality foregrounds these subconscious, mechanical, and/or barely conscious physical behaviors. Along with the tribal repertoire of Yakima singing and dancing, this habitus helped win over Native spectators, wary of the playwright's status as cultural outsider, and of the script's symbolic representations.[31] The play's title virtually ensured a strong Indian turnout by signaling its cultural content.[32] Spectators of Alaskan and Northwest Coast heritage felt particularly proprietary about the material, but even the intertribal Seattle Indian community sought to assess *how* Raven stories were being represented.[33] As Peggy Phelan explains, the public circulation of images of a particular group, created by members of that group, is charged with a dual function: "to increase the pride of those within the community, and . . . to inform those outside of the strength of the community."[34] REPAC actors sought to meet these dual responsibilities in rehearsal and performance, by adding to the play's Indian spaces through the repertoire and Native habitus.

The number and quality of the acts of transfer in *Raven* affected its reception by Native spectators. While it did not transmit collective knowledges or histories except in a relatively superficial way, it did convey a palpable sense of excitement about the storytelling possibilities of Native theater. For a number of Native audience members, *Raven* inaugurated a habit of theatergoing and a growing acquaintance with theater practice that enriched Seattle's urban Indian spaces. Thanks to REPAC, Native theater became a place for Indians to come together in the city, just as they did at other kinds of Indian events.

For non-Indians, the presence of the repertoire worked in different ways and generated different acts of transfer. Like Native spectators, non-Indians welcomed the play's singing and dancing as evidence of Indian space. But many of them could not distinguish between the symbolic representations of the text and tribally generated material, nor could they appreciate the careful valencing of cultural and theatrical elements in the play. Assuming that reviewers do indeed represent a perceptive viewer, attuned to the socio-cultural currents of the day, it is interesting to read the newspaper reviews that accompanied *Raven*.[35] Both Donald Grat, writing for *Northwest Arts*, and Pamela Jennings, writing for the *Seattle Times*, praised the show's production values, but only Jennings seemed to suggest the problematic nature of the script from a tribal cultural viewpoint. She referred to *Raven*'s "assortment of characters" and "myriad of phantasmagoric places" in phrases that seem to tacitly acknowledge the script's hodgepodge of sources. But aside from noting that "dances, created by the company, graphically relate great portions of the story," Jennings failed to identify elements of tribal repertoires as the key to *Raven*'s production values.[36]

As Henry Bial observes, the language of critics is performative: it produces and reinforces constructions of difference through the act of describing them.[37] Both Grat and Jennings were impressed by the actors' animal characterizations, but Grat prefaces his discussion of these characterizations by drawing attention to the actors' theater training. Noting the return of Donald Matt from a "summer of intensive training" at the American Conservatory Theater, he praises Matt's "great dexterity in handling a number of roles." Grat then goes on to explain that "actors rarely have such a direct application of training building blocks such as animal characterization, and it is intriguing to watch the diversity and range of abilities in this style."[38] While Grat's idiosyncratic phrasing makes it difficult to interpret his meaning, this entire paragraph tends to minimize tribal cultural contributions to REPAC's performance. The skills of the actors in depicting animal characters are conflated with western acting training.

I believe tribal repertoires and Native habitus deserve much of the credit for the actors' bird, fish, and other biotic characterizations. The political, ethnic, and experimental theaters of this decade, described as "theaters of 'transformation'" did indeed turn to animal movement and vocalization in their desire to challenge realism.[39] However, the development of human characters was usually the end product of these explorations. By contrast, there is a rich stylistic and mimetic basis for animal characterization in tribal repertoires. Ceremonial and powwow dances often pay tribute to animals in stylized ways, and REPAC actors incorporated some of these stylized elements in their movement and costumes. Additionally, Indian actors in the seventies tended to maintain contact with rural homeland or reservation environments, even if they did not live in these environments year-round. This background probably facilitated additional observation-based approaches to characterizations in *Raven*.

Reviewers of the play do foreground the way in which the actors' embodiment illuminates its message of respect for different life forms and their fundamental interdependence. The notion of the basic equality of humans, plants, animals, and natural forces on a spiritual and cosmic plane informs much of Native spatial practice.[40] It is expressed in ceremony, in oral traditions concerning the intermarriage or exchange of knowledge between people, elements, and animals, in clan taboos, and in myriad other ways. The actors' ability to communicate these social relations, not simply through action and dialogue but in spite of them, comes through clearly in Grat's review. "One must divorce himself from traditional theater elements to appreciate the show. Raven is surrounded by, and on a parity with, Otter Boy, Fog Man, Eagle Boy, and other animals of the action. This natural logic is so clearly understood by Raven that the fascination of [*Raven*] lies in our deciphering the various elements of [its] world, so foreign to our perceptions."[41] Jennings also explains how the play transfers a sense of Native social relations in the words she chooses to end her review. Despite noting some glitches in the production, she praises

Kauffman's "energy, skill in dance and faith to the character of Raven," Matt's "hilarious Fog Man and Elegant Eagle Boy," and Miller's "lapping, scratching, crapping Dog Husband" and writes that "there is human and other than human spirit in 'Raven.' Praise it."[42]

Red Earth's second production, *Body Indian*, produced the following spring, could not have been more different from *Raven* in tone and content. Written by Geiogamah (Kiowa-Delaware), and set in present-day western Oklahoma, the play combines realistic and expressionistic elements in its portrayal of a group of Kiowa characters over two days of binge drinking. It is significant that the text, published in 1980, offers not only a conventional description of the set by the playwright, but an author's note in which Geiogamah explicitly addresses habitus. Calling for an "'Indian frame of mind' [to] be established in the performances from the very start of the play," the playwright adds, "this is not something the actors will build but something they will sustain throughout."[43] Geiogamah includes in the stage directions instructions for a regional/tribal vocal habitus that addresses grammar and speech patterns and vocal delivery. He stresses the need for all the actors to deliver their lines in a clipped fashion and for female actors to "lengthen vowels inordinately, as in l—ots." At the same time, he warns against "'overplaying' this Indian speech" and offers definitions of Comanche and Kiowa words used by the characters.[44] Physical habitus is also prescribed: "Group effort will produce both the proper restraint and gusto for the requisite Indian style of drinking . . . the drinking should be a controlled part of the entire performance. . . . A certain degree of rollicking is permissible, but care should be taken not to overdo . . . the Indian speech traits and the physical actions."[45]

In 1976, Geiogamah conveyed these notes in person to Red Earth cast members, who flew him in for the entire production process. Kauffman put the play on its feet, but when he landed a part in a movie about Chief Joseph, Geiogamah took over as a combination assistant director/stage manager.[46] His coaching of the actors—none of whom hailed from Oklahoma—in the proper habitus was an important act of transfer during rehearsal. He was aided in this by Marie Antoinette Rogers and Miller, both of whom had performed in NATE's original production of *Body Indian* at Café La MaMa in New York.[47]

Described by Geiogamah as his "toughest play," *Body Indian* addresses the personal and social costs of alcohol abuse from a Native perspective.[48]

Again, Geiogamah's consciousness of the way in which repertoire and embodiment need to work in the text reaches beyond a western playwright's usual attempts to imagine, visualize, and hear the script while it is still on the page. Only the proper acting approach will ensure the successful transfer of the play's content: "It is important that the *acting* nowhere is conducive to the mistaken idea that this play is primarily *a study of the problem* of Indian alcoholism" (my italics).[49] Clearly, Geiogamah is aware of the controversial nature of his subject matter, but he is counting upon the repertoire and embodiment to challenge any anthropological/sociological stance of "objectivity" on the part of non-Indian audience members, and to transform their stereotyped expectations of contemporary Indian life into an experiential encounter through performance.

Native embodiment and habitus in *Body Indian* are charged with communicating "in the here and now" five hundred years of what Eduardo Duran labels "the colonialist discourse of alcoholism." The play is ghosted by a historical consciousness of the political causes of alcoholism, made visible alongside its socioeconomic causes and effects. Duran demonstrates how Europeans used the discourse of alcoholism to reinforce binary notions of Indian identity as either the noble or demonic savage.[50] The practice of binge drinking was deliberately encouraged by government agents on the frontier during treaty-making sessions as a means for land fraud. However, another deleterious effect of this practice has been its internalization by Indian peoples and, particularly, a tendency to use binge drinking as a way of rebelling against what are perceived as white societal norms.[51]

Body Indian opens as the protagonist, Bobby Lee, arrives at his apartment, already occupied by a number of friends and relatives, with two of his aunts. Lee wears an artificial leg from a previous alcohol-related accident, and he carries sacks of groceries and wine purchased with his lease payment.[52] Lee wants to treat his relatives and friends to a party, but he also announces his plans to keep back enough money to enter a treatment program for alcoholism. By the end of the play, his friends and family have either asked for, or stolen, all his money, and when he finally passes out, they take his artificial leg to pawn.

As this plot suggests, the play is comprised of comic and serious threads, none of which can be separated from each other. *Body Indian* presents an Indian community in which the tribal values of generosity and reciprocal caretaking have been twisted and perverted by the dynamics of addiction. The tidelike rhythms of the play's drama reinforce the experience of binge drinking, from high to low, as the characters sing, fight, joke, and make clumsy sexual advances while the spirit of alcohol slowly takes over.

Significantly, Geiogamah also relies upon the repertoire to help establish the atmosphere of the play. Whereas REPAC actors had to add dance and song to the script of *Raven*, Geiogamah uses social singing and dancing to reinforce *Body Indian*'s dramatic structure. At an early point during the binge drinking, the character Howard, who is older and out of shape, makes a humorous attempt at fancy dancing—primarily a style of powwow dancing suited to teens and young men. As the drinking progresses, Geiogamah adds stage directions for the women to sing and round dance to the 49 song "Strawberries When I'm Hungry," as an ironic comment on the play's action.[53] As a post-powwow celebration, 49s offer an occasion to socialize, sing, and dance outside the strict parameters of the powwow.[54] Full of humorous lyrics, 49 songs combine a powwow singing style and English lyrics in an ironic interplay. Because of their contemporary association with drinking, their use by Geiogamah's characters makes them a fertile source of comedy. Much of the laughter that the play arouses comes from the kinds of mechanistic behaviors that characterize addiction. Each time the characters drink, they make the same assertions, resolutions, and promises, and forswear them in exactly the same way. The end of the play, in which the host of the party finds himself broke and alone, is both a familiar story and a foregone conclusion, just like the play's beginning and middle.

For the intertribal cast of REPAC, humor provided immediate access to the script and became an important act of transfer between the actors in rehearsal. "From the inside we just enjoyed *Body Indian*," says Brisson, "because we know the Native alcoholic can really come to all that."[55] If Brisson's comment reflects her situatedness, it also points to the layered and complex attitudes toward alcoholism on the part of the Indian community. Indians are acutely conscious of the role played by colonialism in alcohol abuse. Tribal values of tolerance, an ethos of collective responsibility, and the reality of extended families make it hard for Indian individuals to simply "banish" problem drinkers from their lives. Additionally, the face-to-face nature of many Indian communities ensures that daily or weekly encounters with the effects of alcohol on tribal members are not unusual. Having to deal with such encounters requires both irony and humor to release emotion and worry and to restore perspective.

Because *Body Indian*'s dialogue and situations hit close to home, the actors were more than usually aware of the rehearsal process as sited in the personal and political, and functioning as a liberating process. They brought to the play their own memories and issues with alcoholism and channeled them into the rehearsal process. Playing characters trapped in alcohol addiction empowered the actors, allowing them to mine the script for personal and group healing even as they exploited its comedy.

In performance, *Body Indian* was a complex act of transfer, communicating differently to different segments of the Native audience. For many Native spectators, this contemporary portrait of the underbelly of Indian life created a visceral reaction. They identified with the irony of the characters' lives and the disparity between their ideals, desires, and behavior, and they reacted strongly to the play's portrayal of addiction. The response of the audience was so emotional it sometimes moved people out of their seats. "When we did *Body Indian* in New York," says Geiogamah, "it was very theatrical. But in Seattle, the play acquired . . . immediacy, a more human aspect. Sometimes Indians in the audience would stand up, and it was like they were testifying. There was no fourth wall."[56] During one performance, this surreal aspect of *Body Indian* was reinforced by the presence of a drunk who wandered in from the street and took a seat in the front row. "He was laughing and joining in and partying," says Kirk, "and when the play was over, he came backstage. He thought we were going to keep on partying."[57]

While many Native audience members received *Body Indian* as the author hoped they would, others, according to Brisson, were "unsure how they felt."[58] Part of this uncertainty may have arisen from seeing this kind of material presented in a place where the audience included non-Indians. As Roberta Unamuno explains, when spectators of color watch representations of their group, they find themselves in a scopic bind. They—in this case, Indian spectators—are all too aware of "the double gaze of the white audience members, of 'them' watching the images on stage and shifting that gaze to extrapolate meaning to [Indians] seated nearby."[59] Still others vocally denounced the play as a disservice to the Indian community. They felt *Body Indian* merely perpetuated stereotypes and added to distorted representations of Indians within the dominant society. These reactions were a sobering reminder for the actors that, despite their desire to present contemporary material, some segments of the Native audience would reject any depictions of an unpleasant side of Indian life.

Body Indian also engendered complicated and layered reactions among non-Indians. Some of the same audience members who had embraced *Raven* complained to the actors that they felt "misled" by REPAC's second play. What they really meant, says Kirk, was, "How dare you be Indians and put on a play that wasn't something you can bring the kiddies to!"[60] Still other non-Indian viewers were disturbed by the character depictions and the play's realistic treatment of the effects of binge drinking. Although *Body Indian* lacks overt physical violence, one local critic who watched the play said he felt like he had been "kicked in the stomach."[61]

But non-Indian audiences also understood the humor of the play, although their laughter contrasted with that of Native audiences, because it occurred at different moments. These cultural differences with regard to humor sometimes caught the actors off guard. The Jesuit faculty who taught at the University of Seattle had a habit of attending REPAC's plays together as a group on the same night. When that night arrived, Brisson recalls, the house was so silent that the actors began running through the play as if it were a rehearsal. "The [priests] didn't make a sound, they didn't react to anything. Then, about two-thirds of the way through the play, they laughed. It was so startling, we thought, 'We've got an audience!'"[62] For these audience members, *Body Indian*'s act of transfer was to impart a better understanding of one aspect of contemporary Indian political and socioeconomic conditions. Like the Native spectators who rose to their feet while watching the play, these non-Indians embraced Native theater's ability to deliver painful truths.

To slightly revise one of Taylor's pronouncements, the strength of performance as an act of transfer is that it functions by inculcation, not by inscription.[63] "People learn . . . through enactment, and they participate . . . in the production and reproduction of knowledge by being part of the event."[64] While the importance of the repertoire has been somewhat recalibrated in Native theater today, Native theater continues to be characterized by a privileging of the repertoire and acts of transfer that connect the past and present. The ability of Native theater to transmit alternative traditions, histories, and memories, and to share different ways of knowing by means of performance, is one of its great strengths.

CHAPTER 7

Embodiment as a Healing Process

Native American Women and Performance

SHELLEY SCOTT

THEATRICAL ROLES that may be termed autobiographical have a heightened importance in work by Aboriginal women. They can be uniquely therapeutic for both the performer and the spectator, as well as aesthetically and thematically powerful. In this chapter I focus on the examples of Shirley Cheechoo's one-woman show *A Path with No Moccasins*, and Rosalie Jones's dance-drama *No Home but the Heart*. I also discuss Monique Mojica's play *Princess Pocahontas and the Blue Spots* and allude to some further examples. The autobiographical nature of the performance is quite different in each case and takes on various shades of complexity, but I will argue that in each example, the central commonality is the importance of healing and the manifestation of that mission in the body of the performer.[1]

In reference to black women writing for the stage, African Canadian playwright Djanet Sears has explained that to write is to "define ourselves, by ourselves, and create stories to keep that definition within the limits of our own controls."[2] Sears (who was the director and dramaturge for *Princess Pocahontas and the Blue Spots*) suggests that writing for theater is a form of healing, a longing to tell one's story, a process that is also a symbolic gesture to recover the past, to gain a sense of reunion and release: "We have created our own theatre from a language that was forced upon us, and we season it with our own sense of rhythm, ritual and music. Not a song and dance, but a heightened language and ritual."[3] Métis writer Maria Campbell, among many others, has argued that the storyteller has an essential place in the healthy spiritual life of the community.[4] To illustrate, Native dramatist Jordan Wheeler explains, "The victory in the aboriginal story is when harmony can be achieved between the character and his or her environment. . . . During five hundred years of contact, the lives of aboriginal people have borne the onslaught of pain and tragedy. The result is a beleaguered, traumatized people suffering deep wounds. At present the aboriginal community is healing, and stories that reflect the struggle, and the resulting harmonious existence with a given environment, help the healing process."[5] It is not surprising that this healing through storytelling should take place in the theater. Tomson Highway suggests that the Native "oral tradition translates most easily and effectively into a three-dimensional medium. In a sense, it's like taking the 'stage' that lives inside the mind, the imagination, and transposing it— using words, actors, lights, sound—onto the stage in a theatre."[6] Theorist Barbara Godard writes that it is useful to think about oral literature *as* performance, because it:

> distributes the emphasis equally between text and context, between text and receiver. Artistic performance sets up an interpretive frame within which the messages being communicated are to be understood. Performance as frame invites special attention to and heightened awareness of the act of expression . . . [F]ormal patterns have the power to engage the audience's participation, binding its members to the performer as co-participants in an event.[7]

It is also unsurprising that a number of Native works for theater have taken the form of the autobiographical monologue, or one-person show, since this particular form is so closely associated with issues of self-identity. Highway's analogy of taking the creative story inside one's head and projecting it onto other bodies can also apply to the process of taking one's intangible sense of identity and personal experience and transposing it into a physical form. For example, I find it telling that, while Highway is best known for his large-cast plays, he chose to use the monologue form when it came to sharing the very personal story of his own brother's death.[8]

Autobiographical and one-person shows have a strong tradition in Canadian theater, and much of their power resides in the phenomenon of the actor-writer "playing" himself or herself. In performance, it is the artist's physical presence, his or her body, that becomes the signifier of authenticity and the site of lived experience. Women, especially, often associate their experience of their own bodies with a lack of control, a sense of alienation and even loathing, which is further compounded by histories of abuse. To reclaim one's own body, to physically re-inhabit it in a public ceremony of sorts, can be both personally healing and artistically profound. As Muriel Miguel, founder of Spiderwoman Theater, notes: "How do you express . . . in a gesture, in body language, with sound, not using the word? . . . Those are the really interesting things when you start looking into what the body does, where sound comes from, working hard enough to try to get rid of your clichés."[9] Although she has problems with her own one-person play, *Moonlodge*, being labeled as therapy, Margo Kane recognizes that it "may be therapy to some because it is a story that can assist in the healing process. These stories developed out of a need to say something about native experience, not to educate people about spiritual ways but to remind and state that these practices are still alive — they are necessary for the healing of our people. That we, ourselves, must reconnect. That healing can occur even against all odds."[10] Kane is correct in noting that the critical reaction to theater from an identified community, whether feminist or "ethnic," is often patronizing. However, I think it is quite common for audiences and critics alike to feel that a one-person show is a unique theatrical form; when the actor is also the author, when the work has autobiographical elements, and when it explicitly addresses a loss of identity, it would be unusual not to assume the work has therapeutic benefits. Art and therapy are not mutually exclusive. Part of the reason that a work is healing is that it is aesthetically rewarding. It uses the artificiality of performance to, paradoxically and metaphorically, speak the truth. Since Aristotle, the potential for a therapeutic catharsis has been part of the theoretical discourse about traditional tragedy. What is different in the shows under consideration here is the immediacy of the autobiographical material, and the presentational configuration of the author-performer enacting not the mimetic trajectory of a character's discoveries, but her own.

Shirley Cheechoo is a multitalented Cree artist who expresses herself not only as an actress and playwright, but also as a painter, musician, singer, director, and producer. She is also the founder of Debajehmujig Theatre Group, a unique theater company and training environment for Native artists, located on the Wikwemikong Unceded Reserve on Manitoulin Island, where her play *A Path with No Moccasins* premiered in 1991.[11] In summing up the play's impact, the *Regina Leader-Post* proclaimed it to be "introspective, haunting and appalling in its blunt blast of reality to anybody who claims to know what life was like in Indian residential schools."

NOW Magazine said: "*Path with No Moccasins* confronts painful memories in a gentle style full of good humor and sharp observation and rich in remembered detail."[12] The reviewer of one performance wrote that "it worked because this woman was so emotionally involved in her play that the audience feels immediately drawn into her life story. Cheechoo cries true tears, and the audience realized that this was not just acting. After all, the play is about her life and the pain of her past and is a play that could not be captured by any other actor."[13]

Shirley Cheechoo spent her early childhood on traplines with her parents and brother but was sent to residential school at the age of nine. There she was beaten and told that her parents would die if she ran away. As punishment, her hair was cut and the other children were encouraged to taunt her with the nickname "Woody Woodpecker." Cheechoo left the school at fifteen and went on to struggle with substance abuse. When she was twenty-three, she almost killed a friend while drunk. This incident spurred her to change her life and led, in turn, to the exploration of her artistic talent. Cheechoo explains: "When I began my work I wanted revenge on people for what they had done to me as a child. Once I had healed, I began to look for things in my culture that I could use to reflect reality."[14]

In my opinion, the most intriguing aspect of *A Path with No Moccasins* is its autobiographical structure. Over the course of four sections, Cheechoo represents herself at four different ages. The play follows Shirley from residential school at age nine, through periods of alcohol abuse and searching for identity in her twenties, to a healing closure on Manitoulin Island at age thirty-five. The play takes the form of a healing ritual in which, by embodying her own trauma and addiction, the actor emerges renewed and stronger after each performance. In the dedication at the beginning of the published text, Cheechoo writes that she has "transformed [her] life into a 90-minute play, not knowing that it would be seen by so many people."[15] The printed text is not an unbroken monologue but indicates to whom the various speeches are directed, usually "To Us" or "To Herself." But often the indication is "Reliving," and, significantly, at the end there are three speeches in a row that are labeled "She Connects":

• This is my body. No one is allowed to touch it unless I allow it. I have the choice to dance, to dance the dance of life. I hate those men for not dancing with me.

- The eyes of others are my mirrors. What I put out will come back to teach me. Is that why everybody was so angry around me because I was?
- Those sleeping children taking a path with no moccasins awake. I am one of them.[16]

In his introduction to the published text, Aboriginal actor Gary Farmer writes that "in reading it, we begin the process of healing for ourselves. . . . I offer my thanks to the writer for her humble effort that all may see."[17] I would argue that by "seeing" the work performed, the hope of healing becomes that much stronger. As powerful as it may be to read about Cheechoo's painful experiences, it is so much more effective to watch her become her earlier selves and live through her transformation once again.

In an issue of *Canadian Theatre Review* dedicated to the theme of "The Body," guest editor Catherine Graham comments that, increasingly, we are coming to understand that there is a kind of knowledge that is developed and transmitted through the body, challenging the "exclusive use of conceptual reason" as a means to make sense of our world.[18] An insistence on ignoring the body and denying its role in our cognition of reality is "not borne out by practical experience" and amounts to a kind of sickness or, as Daniel David Moses explains it, "that alienation from yourself that the mainstream mindset creates. Up in your head you're separate from your animal self."[19] Cognitive scientists have posited that cognition "is not the representation of a pregiven world by a pregiven mind but is rather the enactment of a world and a mind on the basis of a history of the variety of actions that a being in the world performs."[20] Graham points out that this is a description of social behavior, conditioned by the gender, ethnicity, and class of the body in question, and that it is also a description of how an actor creates the fictional world of performance—by imagining and "being" within that world.

In the same issue of *Canadian Theatre Review*, director Michelle Newman writes that "when one is working with the body, with presence, incarnation, one is also working with absence incarnate. With the wounds, losses, traumas, memories, dreams, imaginings, desires, even the other bodies that this body incarnates. Of course, in the theatre, one regularly works with many of these categories of absence."[21] Newman says that the impulse is usually to cover over these wounds, to create the image of a "unified body." She advocates instead allowing the actor to identify the symptoms of absence and to move from there:

> What if the body could give body to, could transform, could dance with loss? What other movements, embodiments, remembrances might be possible? . . . What if the body was at last allowed to mourn? . . . For we live in a world, a culture decimated by violence, trauma, ashes still around us everywhere, and yet we are not really permitted to mourn, neither our public nor our private disasters, without always being urged toward forgetting, containment, closure of the wound.[22]

This is a fascinating theory when applied to the examples in question here. It is possible that a performance such as Cheechoo's does just what Newman asks: it is an act of mourning, an act of remembering physically, of making those absent (like Cheechoo's deceased father, like the child that Shirley Cheechoo once was, like all those displaced and lost in the process of colonial invasion) present again, but in the contained and sacred space of the theater. Thus, the wound is not denied, but neither is it kept open in "real life." In this theatrical setting, it can be honored in a way that provokes a special kind of recognition in the audience, in what Hélène Cixous calls "a sanctuary of recollection."[23]

Barbara Godard identifies another way in which Native performance works: "it posits the word as a process of knowing, provisional and partial, rather than as revealed knowledge itself, and aims to produce texts in performance that would create truth as interpretation rather than those in the Western mimetic tradition that reveal truth as pre-established knowledge."[24] I find this especially relevant to the three examples under consideration here. In these plays, there is a strong sense that truth is being created in the moment, and I think that this distinction comes from the presence of the performer. It is not a question of a lecture, revealing pre-known facts, or of an actor playing a rehearsed part. Rather, what the audience witnesses and participates in is the performer discovering and creating a truth for herself, making contact with it physically, a kind of epistemology (and epiphany) of the body. Inhabiting this self, breathing as she did, I come to understand her.

Native performance culture has a particularly complex and rewarding set of circumstances to work with. Writers such as Agnes Grant have noted the importance of dreams and the belief in shape-shifting in Native spirituality and have argued that this lends itself to the creative imagination: "Shape-shifting, the transformation of the body form, which is found in myths and legends, was not merely a literary device; it was an article of belief and it surfaces in contemporary writing. Visions and the importance of dreams still play an important role in some contemporary societies so they too are reflected in the literature."[25] Rosalie Jones (who goes by her performance name, Daystar) recounts that an elderly Native woman once asked her after a performance whether the subject matter had come from a vision. This realization that her work is both an artistic activity and a visionary process came as a revelation for her: art is a new way to seek visions. Daystar encourages everyone to look at storytelling, the story of her or his own life and family, and how it relates to history and to the circumstances of growing up. The "talking circle" can be a healing form of personal and group storytelling. As she explains, "I feel my family story is a very universal one because many Native Americans have a similar story: intermarriage between tribes or with non-native people; the whole process of assimilation and acculturation; adapting to the modern world and changes as they occur. . . . Being a dancer and wanting that to coincide with who I am as a person—Native American and non-Native American. This is actually what the performance is all about. Identity is at the root of it."[26] Or, as an art teacher once advised her: "You'll never do any really good work until it comes out of who you are as a person."[27]

Daystar's *No Home but the Heart* is autobiographical, subtitled "An Assembly of Memories," although here the embodiment is not only of the author's self but also of her foremothers. The structure is multilayered, drawing upon events in the lives of the choreographer's ancestors but also taking creative license to weave them into a larger context. Daystar, who is of Pembina Chippewa ancestry, was born on the Blackfeet Reservation in Montana. From an early age she was intrigued by stories her mother told about her grandmother and great-grandmother. In *No Home but the Heart*, Daystar has tied these stories and selected events from the lives of her female ancestors to historical events that affected the resettlement of Native peoples on the Northern Plains. As she explains, "History has to be brought down to a personal level. The watermark events that spark personal transformation also mark the passage of time in this production."[28]

Daystar developed her performance *No Home but the Heart* over a period of five years, beginning in 1995 when, after a career of interpreting

traditional tales, she decided it was time to tell her own story.[29] She uses
her own family as a vehicle to show how Natives have adapted and been
assimilated over a hundred years through events that had an impact upon
both Canada and the United States, such as the 1837 smallpox epidemic,
the creation of reserves, railroad expansion, selling lands, and boarding
schools. The challenge was to contextualize these events within a dramatic structure with scenes, lines, and resolution. Daystar wrote down
what she remembered in a "free flow" until she saw structures emerge
and themes reoccur. The form came naturally by asking about each generation of woman: where is she when she is young, and where in age?
If she were alive today, what would she want to say? Only the daughter,
who represents Daystar but is played by another dancer, remains young
throughout, because she suggests a resolution in the present. This structure tells the story in capsulized form, leaving the middle of each story up
to the audience's imagination while still allowing for continuity.

The particular qualities of each of her female ancestors energize Daystar, as she fleshes out the transformative quality of each character. Susan
Big Knife was Daystar's great-grandmother, who came from Canada with
the Little Shell Band of Chippewa to live on the Blackfeet reservation in
Montana and spoke a dialect of French Cree. Daystar learned that Susan
Big Knife was a medicine woman and also that she lost one eye at some
point in her life. These two facts coalesced into a defining and emblematic
image through which to connect with her ancestor. Daystar has chosen
to imagine this as the event where the spirit came and made her great-
grandmother into a medicine woman. The spiritual power of the healer
is then grounded and made manifest through her physical tools. Accumu-
lating the physical objects that her great-grandmother would have had,
such as a medicine bag, Daystar began to experiment with moving to the
drum until, in her words, the breath came. Once she was able to inhabit
her great-grandmother by embodying the way she might have moved and
even breathed, the connection was made. Daystar comments: "I'm only
now getting . . . where it feels like it's authentic, that I'm not pretending to
be old."[30] I think that this element of authenticity comes from her working method being rooted in physical movement. As Daystar herself ages,
her connection with her great-grandmother becomes experiential, and the
performance takes on a deeper level of identification.

After Susan Big Knife, we are introduced to Rose Jackson, Daystar's grandmother. This scene reminds me of playwright Beth Herst's remarks on the importance placed on the body in theater by Canadian women. Invoking Audre Lorde's concept of auto-bio-mythography, Herst emphasizes "the centrality of the body, its insistent, problematic presence as the site and source of dramatic conflict," and "the preoccupation with a wounded yet enduring body."[31] It is interesting too that the woundedness of the three bodies being considered here (Cheechoo, Jones, and Mojica) is not immediately or visually apparent—all are strikingly beautiful, strong-looking women. They display endurance, and they have to work at revealing their pain. This is particularly vivid in the case of Daystar and her depiction of her grandmother Rose Jackson, whose uterus was displaced after many childbirths. Jones, who is tall, straight, and graceful, becomes contorted with pain, wrapping black ribbons around her head and twisting her legs up into the air in a wordless evocation of the home remedy prescribed for her grandmother, whose legs were tied with a rope and hoisted in the air, suspended from an iron hook in the ceiling to give her some relief. As Herst writes, the body is ultimately inescapable, a source of suffering and of strength: "It is memory, identity and story too."[32]

Monique Mojica's play *Princess Pocahontas and the Blue Spots* is not, strictly speaking, autobiographical.[33] Nevertheless, as Ric Knowles and Jen Harvie point out, "as an antihegemonic revisioning of dominant myths of Native women, written and performed by Mojica out of a strong and resisting subject position, from which its various characters, historical and contemporary, seem to emerge—it can be seen as a kind of spiritual/historical autobiography."[34] The play aims to recover a lost sense of self by portraying a strong, stable, and empowering community of Native women, and to explicitly tie identity to the biological marker of a blue spot at the base of the spine. Mojica incorporates the story of the blue spot as a sign of authenticity, and the play is concerned with the differences between "storybook" and "real" Native women. However, the play demonstrates an awareness of how "authenticity" is complicated by factors other than biology and acknowledges that the presence of a physical characteristic does not guarantee that one is sure of her identity. In performance, Mojica was accompanied by Chilean-Canadian musician Alejandra Nunez, who contributed material about the *mestiza*, the offspring of the Spanish and Native Americans. Mojica, as the child of a Kuna/Rappahannock mother and a Jewish father, is herself concerned with issues of hybridity. As

Knowles and Harvie point out in their discussion of the play, "the myths
of Native identity that it attacks or constructs are indiscriminately drawn
from all of North, Central and South America; and the hybrid nature of
Native and other ethnicities is asserted at every turn and embodied in the
author-performer."[35] The play features a recurring theme of Indigenous
women as collaborators, acting as guides and interpreters, and bearing the
children of white men. In one sense, through this collaboration, women
ensured the survival of their race, sometimes at great personal sacrifice,
but on the other hand, they were sometimes condemned as traitors.

Princess Pocahontas and the Blue Spots has a complex structure, rooted
in a valorization of nature and a matrilineal tradition that Mojica claims
was inherent to the characters.[36] In the play, Contemporary Woman #1
states, "I do not represent all Native women. I am one." Yet she also embodies countless women across five hundred years of history and suggests a
commonality between them based on race and gender. The published
version (Toronto: Women's Press, 1991) explains the play's structure,
which consists of thirteen "transformations," but the distinctions between
each character and entity are not as evident in performance. As Mojica
moves from one transformation to the next, it is as if she is illustrating
different aspects of a single subject—evidence, I think, of her deep desire
to express solidarity with her foremothers. Ric Knowles points out that the
play works across many geographical and historical locations and transgresses the borders of performance genre, history, fiction, and myth: "In
fact, the play might seem to combine the shape-shifting qualities of the
Trickster figure ubiquitous in various Native cosmologies."[37] Indeed, the
transformational structure of the play and its fluidity in performance are
themselves a model and a call to arms for Indigenous women.

Mojica's more recent work continues to defy boundaries in this way.
As one-third of Turtle Gals Performance Ensemble, with Michelle St.
John and Jani Lauzon, Mojica has created The Scrubbing Project, which
was developed while the three women were in residence at Nightwood
Theatre for the 1999/2000 season. In 2007 they produced a show called
The Only Good Indian . . . , which explores the history of Native per-
formers "from the 1880s in Buffalo Bill's Wild West shows through P. T.
Barnum's side shows, the 1904 St. Louis World's Fair (and other exposi-
tions), the silent film era, vaudeville, burlesque, and Hollywood." Like
Princess Pocahontas and the Blue Spots, the work was not autobiographi-

cal in the traditional sense, but it sought to place the artist within her very particular lineage. In an article entitled "Stories from the Body: Blood Memory and Organic Texts," Mojica explains, "First, what you need to know is that I come from a family of show Indians" (see chap. 5, this vol.). She talks about her grandfather making up ceremonial skits and dances to accompany the sale of "snake oil"; her mother and aunts posing for tourists and riding parade floats wearing feathers and buckskins; and her family providing accommodation for other Natives who came to New York to dance at the fair or to perform in rodeos. Mojica concludes her article by recounting the opening of an exhibit at the Smithsonian National Museum of the American Indian called "New Tribe New York," a retrospective of Spiderwoman Theater. She expresses her pride by dancing onstage with her brother, her brother-in-law and cousins, and a niece who represents the fifth generation of performers in her family line.[38]

There are other examples of work by Native women that might also be discussed in terms of autobiography and embodiment. Lori Blondeau of Saskatoon, for example, creates performance art that draws on her personal encounters with the stereotypes of "Indian Princess" and "Squaw." One piece is based on an incident from her own childhood when she attempted to bleach her skin whiter. Native women's performance troupes that draw on the personal history of their members include Spiderwoman Theater, particularly in their show *Sun Moon and Feather,* from 1981, and Coatlicue/Las Colorado Theatre Company's 1992 production, *Blood Speaks and Cloud Serpents.*[39] Interestingly, both are troupes of sisters who draw on their own family histories. The title *Sun Moon and Feather* is taken from parts of the Native names of the three Spiderwoman performers: Lisa Mayo, Gloria Miguel, and Muriel Miguel (Kuna/Rappahannock). Elvira and Hortensia Colorado of Coatlicue explain: "These are the stories of our lives," and "Our theater work consists of personal stories coming from our oral traditions, which not only entertain, but educate and heal."[40] There have also been collaborations between these two troupes, such as *Power Pipes* (1992), and Hortensia Colorado appeared as one of the performers in Spiderwoman's *Winnetou's Snake Oil Show from Wigwam City* (1991). Even in plays like this one, which are somewhat less autobiographical, the performers appear as themselves at some point in the presentation. In the cast list, each actor is listed as playing a number of roles, but each is also listed as "playing" herself. For example, as well

as playing the characters Gunther, Witch #2, Princess Pissy Willow, and
Demon #3, Lisa Mayo writes, "at certain moments, during the serious
times of the play, I am Lisa Mayo, Cuna/Rappahannock."[41] Similarly,
in *Open Wounds on Tlalteuctli* (1995), "a series of vignettes of Native
women's experiences in the Americas," the Colorado sisters draw on their
Chichimec/Otomi storytelling tradition for a declamatory delivery and
the adoption of many roles.[42] As in the case of Cheechoo, Daystar, and
Mojica, the acknowledgment of the performer *as* performer is crucial to
the meaning of the performance, embodied in her physical presence as a
self-identified Aboriginal woman.

One of the reasons the autobiographical show is so popular is that
it draws attention to an essential element of theater: finding an authentic self. As Ann Wilson notes, in a world that has alienated us from an
innate sense of wholeness, "theatre promises to repair the damage and
allows for a recuperation of this lost human essence."[43] Wilson argues,
however, that the story one tells about oneself must take into account the
forces that have shaped that story—the conditions of living in contemporary society—and must not rely on some ahistorical sense of untouched
authenticity. The best autobiographical performances are the ones that
"render the self as complex," and one might argue that such complexity is unavoidable for the contemporary Native performer. As Elizabeth
Theobald, an American director of Cherokee descent, observes, "to say
the least, identity in a Native world with 500 different Nations and 500
years of oppression, acculturation, adoption, boarding schools, intermarriage, and forced migration can be very confusing. Our stories are unique,
individual, and we wear the scars of our histories on our sometimes dreary
day-to-day lives."[44]

Yet the very act of rendering this complexity visible can be seen as empowering. As in Monique Mojica's example of the presence of a blue spot, the
authenticity and meaning of the body are most effectively explored through
the physical presence of the storytelling performer. Daniel David Moses
comments:

> One of the words that always comes up in Native gatherings, and particu-
> larly among Native artists, is that it is part of our jobs as Native artists to
> help people heal. . . . I think our cultures probably allow us to be more
> autobiographical than the mainstream. . . . I think it comes from the atti-

tude that everyone is an individual spirit with something unique to say which is important in the life of the entire community. And most Native writers are . . . speaking first to their own community.[45]

In these works by Aboriginal women, the scars of history are worn on the body and made visible by a kind of storytelling that is a mixture of public testimonial and personal healing. While it is primarily the performer herself who is healed, by witnessing their performances, that embodied healing can be shared by the audience and wider community.

CHAPTER 8

The Hearts of Its Women

Rape, (Residential Schools), and Re-membering

RIC KNOWLES

THE BEST-KNOWN SCENE from First Nations drama in what is now Canada is from Cree playwright Tomson Highway's *Dry Lips Oughta Move to Kapuskasing*, and it depicts a brutal rape.[1] The quotation most frequently cited by First Nations playwrights in Canada is the traditional Cheyenne saying that a nation "is not conquered until the hearts of its women are on the ground."[2] Among the lines most frequently cited from First Nations plays produced and published in contemporary Canada are those in Kuna-Rappahannock playwright Monique Mojica's *Princess Pocahontas and the Blue Spots* concerning the difficulties experienced by Mojica's alter ego, "Contemporary Woman #1," as she attempts to make "feminist shoes . . . fit these wide, square, brown feet."[3] Finally, as Ojibway playwright and essayist Drew Hayden Taylor has noticed, while "perhaps [the] most pervasive" feature of First Nations theater is "a female character who suffer[s] some form of sexual or physical abuse," the most pervasive feature of current Native writing in all genres in Canada seems to be the impact of "Residential schools—past, present, and future" on Native children.[4] These are the Christian-run schools to which First Nations children were taken by force, removed from their communities and denied access to their languages and cultures, by government decree for over a century from the mid-1800s until the 1970s.[5] It is the intersections between these moments, subjects, and quotations, and the related and all-pervasive issue of embodied, performative First Nations cultural memory, that I wish to explore here.

My focus is on plays by First Nations women in contemporary Canada in which rape and sexual violence are represented as individual and community dismemberment that can be healed only through an embodied cultural re-membering. These plays, unlike those by non-Natives and by

Native men, represent rape and sexual violence not as emblematic, but as real, material technologies of colonization, past and present. Rape and sexual violence are shown to be mechanisms that work together myths of authenticity and of racial and cultural purity, with ideologically coded (mis)representations of First Nations women, and with the erasure of embodied cultural memory in residential schools, as agents of ethnic cleansing and cultural genocide. Finally, I want to argue that, in the face of this dismemberment, these plays represent an act of embodied cultural re-membering as the province of First Nations women. This *re*-membering works together with a strategic pan-nationalism across the Americas to resist the global scope of the colonial project, and with strategic analyses of pan-colonialist (mis)representations of Native women, to serve as agents of anticolonial and anti-imperial resistance and healing.

I will be looking briefly at four issues: (1) the cultural role played by memorials of violence against women in non-Native and Native communities; (2) representations of rape in plays by non-Natives and by Native men; (3) representations of sexual violence, dismemberment, and enforced forgetting in plays by First Nations women; and (4) the representation and embodiment of memory across time and space in autobiographical performance as an agent of individual and cultural re-membering and healing.

Memorializing Murdered Women

My thinking is informed by my involvement in a collaborative research project on cultural memory and the feminist memorializing of violence against women in Canada. During the project, it became clear early on that attempts to create memorials emblematic of violence against *all women*, particularly national monuments, were fraught with problems posed by the different cultural roles of sexual violence and collective memory in disparate cultures.[6] One site might serve as an example.

In 1990 a committed group of Vancouver feminists set out to create a "permanent, national memorial" in honor of the fourteen female engineering students killed at L'École Polytechnique, Montreal, on December 6, 1989, because, as engineering students, they were perceived to be "a bunch of feminists" because they were studying to take their place in what he felt was a male profession.[7] The organizers determined that these women would be remembered as individuals but also as being emblematic of "all the women murdered by men . . . women of all countries, all classes, all ages, all colors."[8] The monument was installed in 1997 in Thornton Park in Vancouver's downtown eastside, just a few blocks away from the beleaguered neighborhood in which dozens of women—most of them poor, many of them prostitutes, and many of them First Nations—had been murdered or had disappeared during the previous decade. When challenged about the appropriateness of erecting a monument in this neighborhood dedicated to fourteen white university staff and students from three thousand miles away, the organizers, none of whom were First Nations women or women of color, confessed their ignorance of the local situation. They made various adjustments to the Women's Monument project, such as: the inclusion of a West Coast First Nations language, Chinook, among the seven in which the monument's dedication is inscribed; an emblematic feather etching designed by a First Nations artist; and a small tile dedicated to the downtown eastside women among a large ring of donor tiles that encircles the monument.[9] However, the monument's appropriative efforts at inclusivity failed to address sufficiently the cultural differences in First Nations women's experiences of gendered or sexual violence, or to satisfy the monument's neighbors. There have since been two local parks dedicated to murdered and missing local women, and in light of the discovery of many of these women's DNA on the farm of a man currently under trial for their murder, the local Downtown Eastside Women's Centre is raising funds to install a permanent monument in their memory. In addition to these traditional monuments, an annual Valentine's Day March, now reaching its twentieth anniversary, remembers local victims performatively, as participants pay tribute at each of the sites of the previous year's murders. Unlike the permanence of the Vancouver Women's monument, carved in stone, and in resistance to official attempts to erase Native cultural memory at the residential schools, the Valentine's Day March performs embodied, dialogical memory.[10] It does so, moreover, on the contested site at which Cree/Métis playwright and performer Marie Clements locates her powerful and poetic docu-memory play *The Unnatural and Accidental Women*, which tells the story of the serial murder of Native women in the same neighborhood.

Those aspects that the organizers of the Vancouver Women's Monu ment failed at first to acknowledge are representative of the kinds of omissions that can often characterize work about First Nations experience by non-Natives, creative and scholarly, including my own. Among them is the inscription of white experience as universal and, in an attempt to be inclusive, the concomitant failure to acknowledge that women of color, First Nations women, or the poor are much more likely to be victimized by femicide than white professional women or university students. As they raised upwards of $160,000 for the installation of "public art," and while shelters and social service agencies in the downtown eastside remained chronically underfunded, the organizers of the Women's Monument also failed to acknowledge that the impulse to memorialize gendered violence emerged among white feminists only after white women from relatively privileged situations had been victimized. Finally, the organizers failed to notice that an attempt to build a "permanent *national*, memorial"[11] discursively reenacts a colonization of Nations indigenous to the land that was later carved up, parceled out, and colonized by European settlers/invaders—land that was never ceded by its original inhabitants, whose strategic self-identification *as* "First Nations" people bespeaks their ongoing resistance to any claims to legislative or judicial authority over them by the latter-day Canadian nation-state.

What I wish to focus on here, however, is my understanding that the historical and continuing causes and consequences of sexual abuse and rape (I am not, of course, attempting to speak of any individual woman's experience) are materially different within the dominant cultures of North America than they are in the cases of First Nations women. Within the former, rape and other sexual violence operate fundamentally as tools of patriarchal control and cultural reproduction. In this context, gendered violence serves to ensure the stability and sustainability of the gendered hierarchies, patrilineal successions, and homosocial exchanges (and objectifications) of women upon which western patriarchal capitalism relies. Within these dominant cultures, rape is, quite literally, a technology of cultural reproduction. However, the stakes are very different in other cultural contexts. African American women, for example, have stressed the intolerable role that "rape and forced childbearing" played in "[making] the black woman the legal instrument of her people's slavery."[12]

Rape as Emblem

Canadian drama has a history of sympathetic representation of First Nations women and their experience of sexual violence, the best-known of which occurs in Ukrainian-Canadian playwright George Ryga's 1967 play *The Ecstasy of Rita Joe*. Helen Gilbert and Joanne Tompkins point out that "both native and non-native dramatists [in Canada and elsewhere] have featured inter-racial rape as an analogue for the colonisers' violation of the land, and also for related forms of economic and political exploitation."[13] Ryga is no exception:

> This play figures Rita Joe as the site on and through which the disciplinary inscriptions of imperial patriarchy are played out as her body is progressively marked by capture, assault, and sexual penetration. Politically, she functions less as an individual than as an emblem of native cultures in Canada; hence, her death signals the grim triumph of the imperial project.[14]

Penetration and rape are well-established metaphors for imperialism. Moreover, the tendency to treat rape and sexual violence as emblematic is not limited to plays by non-Natives. Both of Tomson Highway's professionally produced "Rez" plays, for example, risk dematerializing the experience of their female subjects by metaphorically representing the effects of Christianity and colonization on Native spirituality through rape.[15] Gilbert and Tompkins note that "*The Rez Sisters* . . . stages rape as a violation not only of the land but also of the very spirit of native culture [when] the mentally disabled Zhaboonigan Peterson's revelation that a gang of white boys penetrated her vagina with a screwdriver"[16] is accompanied by the agonizing contortions of Nanabush, the central, ungendered figure in Cree cosmology, here performed by a male dancer. In *Dry Lips Oughta Move to Kapuskasing*, Dickie Bird Halked, a victim of fetal alcohol syndrome, uses a crucifix to rape the sympathetic Patsy Pegahmaghabow, an embodiment of Nanabush, who is played by a woman in this play. Gilbert and Tompkins suggest that Dickie Bird's repeated stabbing of the earth with the crucifix, while Patsy/Nanabush reveals her bloodied body, "points to the desecration of indigenous land/culture by the colonising forces,"[17] and indeed, much has been made of Highway's assertions that "on a metaphorical level, the scene symbolizes the matriarchal religion raped by the patriarchy."[18] But a First Nations woman might be forgiven for saying of either of these scenes, in the words of Scottish-Canadian playwright Ann-Marie MacDonald, speaking in another context, "Good going, boys, but get your fucking metaphors off of my body."[19] And Highway's play *has* been criticized by First Nations women on these grounds.[20]

If, as Jacques Lacan argues, "the symbol . . . is the death of the thing,"[21] or at least, as in semiotic theory, the sign marks the absence of its material referent, it would seem that the extensive use of rape in scenes that symbolize the colonial project and its impact on Native culture risks replacing and effacing both its lived, material reality for the women who are its victims, and the actuality of its gendered and raced practice, both historical and contemporary.

Sexual Violence in Plays by First Nations Women

To turn to plays by First Nations women is to turn to a broader range of representations of sexual violence. *Annie Mae's Movement*, by Métis Yvette Nolan, artistic director of Toronto's Native Earth Performing Arts, focuses on the life and death of Anna Mae Aquash, the Mi'kmaq activist from Nova Scotia who became a leader in the American Indian Movement (AIM) in the 1970s. In this play, rape, murder, and (literal) dismemberment are represented as fundamental components of the routine exertion of power by the police, who function as a repressive state apparatus. Like *The Ecstasy of Rita Joe*, *Annie Mae's Movement* reaches its climax with the rape and murder of its central character. Ryga's play, however, ends with an emblematic "no more," and the ecstatic sacrificial ascension-in-song of the heroine-as-martyr.[22] Nolan's play concludes as Anna Mae—no mere victim—recites an anachronistic list of "sisters," the recognizable names of First Nations women writers and actors and their creations (or what Paula Gunn Allen calls "Word Warriors"):[23] "Gloria and Lisa and Muriel, Monique, Joy and Tina, Margo, Maria, Beatrice, Minnie, April, Colleen." "You can kill me," she cries, dying, "but you cannot kill us all."[24] "You can kill me, but my sisters live, my daughters live."[25]

Cree/Métis playwright and actor Marie Clements's evocative and powerful *The Unnatural and Accidental Women*, which is also based on documentary sources, diverts focus from the isolated sacrificial victim to represent a series of femicides committed by the same man in Vancouver's downtown eastside between 1965 and 1987, using the same modus operandi. Nevertheless, the women's deaths were all ruled to be "*unnatural and accidental*'" by the coroner, who astonishingly found "no evidence of violence or suspicion of foul play."[26] Full of humor, poetry, and filmic theatricality, the play succeeds in representing the women themselves as vibrant, sensual, and life-affirming (even after death). It represents the tenacity of embodied memory and offers a trenchant critique of state neglect and the tacit judicial approval of gendered and racial violence. It ends with the daughter of one of the murdered women enacting an equivalent revenge: she kills the murderer by the same means and in the same place as he had killed his victims, while their ghosts act as witnesses.

Another of Clements's plays, *Now Look What You Made Me Do*, explores cycles of so-called domestic abuse and the relationship between "domestic" or intimate sexual victimization and prostitution. The latter is perhaps a social manifestation of the systemic sexual exploitation and violence masked by such ungendered neologisms as the phrase "domestic abuse." The central character, a Métis woman, herself a victim of sexual violence and, ultimately, of intimate femicide, asks of her older friend, a prostitute: "I wonder if she ever stopped dying. I wonder if every time she slept with another john she'd die just a little more. Piece by piece. Flesh ripping raw in their grabby hands leaving her gaping just a little more. Blood seeping bright and crimson on the sheet spunked out with sperm fishing to death."[27]

Rape and Re-membering
in Autobiographical Performance

Helen Thomson, in an article on Australian "Aboriginal Women's Staged Autobiography," quotes Joy Hooten's claim that "no document has a greater chance of challenging the cult of forgetfulness than a black [by which she means Aboriginal] woman's autobiography," and this is especially true of embodied autobiography performed by its author and subject.[28] Citing "forgetfulness" as "a politically charged strategy that has characterized settler history,"[29] Thomson surveys a range of autobiographical performance pieces by Aboriginal women that bring together sexual violence and the removal from their homes of the "stolen generations" of Aboriginal children and children of mixed descent, in ways that resonate with performances by First Nations women in Canada. Both *Moonlodge*, by Salteaux/ Cree/Blackfoot Margo Kane, and *Path with No Moccasins*, by Cree Shirley Cheechoo, include stories of early childhood, of the "scoops"—forced removals to residential schools and foster homes—of sexual abuse and rape, and of the active attempt to re-member: to reconstruct coherent psychological and social subjectivities through embodied cultural memory. Eschewing the sensationalism of Ryga and Highway, both plays represent rape in ways that are, perhaps, most shocking for their apparent ordinariness. They are presented as quotidian, hegemonic practices of subjugation that virtually come with the territory of being both Native and woman in Canada.

In *Moonlodge*, Margo Kane's central autobiographical subject, Agnes, sings "On the Street Where You Live" from the musical *My Fair Lady* as she is raped by a biker with whom she has hitched a ride.[30] This First Nations woman, who has been forcibly removed from her own culture, educated in a Christian school, and raised by a white stepmother, evokes disturbing associations as she cites the musical based on Shaw's *Pygmalion* (a story of class-cultural erasure performed by an English academic on a cockney flower girl) while being raped. Without dematerializing the experience of rape, its role as a material agent of colonialism is made readily apparent.

In Shirley Cheechoo's *Path with No Moccasins*, the autobiographical subject passes quickly over her rape at age twelve by a gang of boys, assuming the blame herself, and commenting only that it "seems like no matter how old I am, someone always wants to do this to me. I don't want to be beautiful like Ann-Margret any more. It's my fault for asking to be a movie star."[31] The play is full, on the one hand, of recollections of a residential school where she is "not supposed to speak Cree" (19) and not allowed to attend her grandmother's funeral (33) and, on the other, of dreams, voices, and images that invoke remembered traces and traumatic scars of sexual violence. In one dream, she sees a "pack of wolves tearing my clothes and these wolves turn into men on top of me" (40). In another, she dreams of a brutal vaginal evisceration performed by a male doctor (33), and in another she imagines herself trapped in silence "in a box of cockroaches crawling all over me, sexually abusing me against my will, telling me they loved me" (39). Sandra Richards has argued that cultural memories and traditions passed on in unspoken, embodied, and performative ways through everyday habit and ritual can work to resist attempted erasures, as was the case for diasporic Africans in the wake of the slave trade.[32] The colonialist project of cultural erasure through the removal of children from their communities directly attacks this embodied continuity of memory, and, in this play, this project is closely allied with attacks on the hearts and bodies of First Nations women. The play asserts its autobiographical content by naming its central character "Shirley Cheechoo" in the text itself (16), thus allowing its author/performer to articulate and perform an embodied struggle to remember and awake from the colonial nightmare. It concludes as the "sleeping Indian children taking a path with no moccasins awake. I am one of them" (41; see also 38, 39).

Monique Mojica

I referred earlier both to Monique Mojica's difficulties in making feminist shoes fit her "wide, square, brown feet" and to the potentially lethal embrace of inclusiveness in feminist memorializing.[33] Mojica's radio play *Birdwoman and the Suffragettes* might indeed be read as a response to such problems. It stages Mojica's liberation of the living memory of Sacagawea—guide to the American Lewis and Clark expedition (1804–6)—from the dubious "honour[s]" bestowed upon her by a cabal of 1905 suffragettes, as she is "captured again" (83), within a bronze memorial statue dedicated to her as both a "trusty little Indian guide" (67) and as the spirit of "the eternal womanly" (83). Both this play and Mojica's *Princess Pocahontas and the Blue Spots* offer alternatives to such memorializing-as-monumentalizing, which buries the past rather than keeping it alive. As James Young argues, to "the extent that we encourage monuments to do our memory-work for us, we become that much more forgetful."[34] For Mojica, as for many First Nations people, memory, unlike history in its European context, is embodied and therefore potentially active. In *Birdwoman and the Suffragettes* this embodiment takes the form of orality through scenes that depict the grandmothers and grandfathers as bearers of tradition. In *Princess Pocahontas* it takes the form of bodily enactment, as Mojica's foremothers come alive within her and speak through their descendant. In both plays, memory serves, not to keep the dead dead, but to keep the ancestors alive. In addition to a more active mode of remembering over time than is available in European cathartic memorial practices,

Mojica's work invokes a kind of resistant pan-nationalism that, while not effacing the differences between First Nations, resists the global scope of the colonial project by acknowledging coalitions of difference across the Americas and by conducting a transnational strategic analysis of colonial (mis)representations of First Nations women.

As such, in *Princess Pocahontas and the Blue Spots*, sexual violence appears as a rupture in a seemingly disconnected scene not long before the play's final "Transformation." The central focus of *Princess Pocahontas* is the intersection between the journey of "Contemporary Woman #1," Mojica's alter ego, "to recover the history of her grandmothers as a tool towards her own healing" (14), and the enacted stories of four women or groups of women from history: Mexico's La Malinche, partner of the Spanish invader Hernán Cortés; the First Nations wives, *a la façon du pays*, of the fur traders in Canada; the conflated Woman of the Puna/Deity in colonial Peru; and, of course, Pocahontas herself (in various historical and contemporary guises). But late in the play Contemporary Woman #1 and #2 tell horrifying, filmically intercut stories that appear to have little connection to the rest of the action. They tell the story of Anna Mae Aquash, "beaten, raped, shot in the back of the head" and dismembered (53–54), and of a thirteen-year-old Chilean girl who was tortured and interrogated "by inserting a live rat into her vagina" while the tail of the rat was attached to an electric shock system. "And the rats," we are told, "are really big in Chile" (54).

But the scene is by no means gratuitous. Just prior to the activist conclusion of the play, in which female word warriors are marshaled in a call to arms and a leap of faith, the brutal materiality of the sexual violence and coercion that underlie the stories of each of the characters and underwrite the colonial project is brought to the surface. Each of Mojica's principal historical characters is made the object of sexualized exchange between men, each mothers a mixed-blood race, and each one is both blamed by her own people and celebrated by the colonizer for her role as the agent (translator, traitor, mistress, and whore) of the destruction of her people.[35] Sacagawea, a "captured" "Slave girl" to another tribe (69) in *Birdwoman and the Suffragettes*, is "won gambling" (73) by a husband "well known for raping Indian girls" (72), before her child is taken from her by Clark (in a deal, between men, with her reprobate husband) to be "educate[d]" (79) in the ways of the colonizer, after the fashion of the residential schools. In *Princess Pocahontas*, the title character is "kidnapped" and removed from her people to die, left—significantly, given the Cheyenne saying with which we started—with her "heart on the ground" (29). Yet along the way she says, "I provided John Rolfe with the seeds to create his hybrid tobacco plants and I provided him with a son, and created a hybrid people" (31). Similarly, the Quechua woman of the Puna/Deity/Virgin in the Andes (Mojica's conflation of real, historical women who refused to become Christianized with various goddesses [Nusta Huillac, Tonatzin, Coyolahuaxqui] and the Roman Catholic virgins into which they were refashioned), "of [her] membranes muscle blood and bone . . . birthed a continent" of mixed-race peoples (36). As Mojica insists, whether she was "abducted or / ran of [her] own / free will / to the / Spanish miner/ Portuguese sailor-man / . . . / creation came to be" (36).

The women in Canada, who were provided as guides, workers, translators, and sexual partners for the fur traders, to "translate/navigate/build alliances with our bodies/loyalties through our blood" (*Princess Pocahontas*, 43), were also treated as objects of exchange: "When there is no more to trade, our men trade us. / Fathers, uncles, brothers, husbands, trade us for / knives, axes, muskets, liquor" (*Princess Pocahontas*, 46). These women, too, who were eventually "turned off" (46) in favor of late-coming European wives, "were the wives and daughters and granddaughters of the founders of this country" (47), and they "birthed the Métis" (22). But the archetype, perhaps, is Malinali, Doña Marina, or La Malinche, known to her own descendants in Mexico as "'La Chingada'—the fucked one" (14), the despised mistress of Cortés, who "was a gift. Passed on. . . . Stolen! Bound! Caught! Trapped" (24), but who mothered the Mexican nation. In response to the descendant who shouts abuse at her, she cries, "Traitor! Whore! You are the child planted in me by Hernán Cortez who begins the bastard race, born from La Chingada! You deny me?" (23)

If rape, then, is both a metaphor and a central technology of colonization, at least as important to the colonizing project is the mechanism of control over reproduction represented by various pan-national myths of racial and sexual purity and authenticity; control that helps in the process of cultural and racial erasure through the production of mixed-blood people who can, in turn, be portrayed by the colonizer as impure, debased, or inauthentic. Such people—"not really Indian," or "only half,"—can then be assimilated.[36] It is not accidental that Mojica's work has focused most directly on women who have been put into service by the colonizer as faithful or unfaithful translators and mediators, as well as faithful or unfaithful mistresses and mothers. Celebrated by the colonizer as "Indian princesses,"[37] these same women have frequently been condemned by their own people as unfaithful traitors and whores. To translate, according to the proverb, is to betray.

Cree/Métis scholar Kim Anderson has articulated the cultural function of the "Indian princess" myth in ways that directly resemble the role played by Mojica's satiric representation "Princess Buttered-on-Both-Sides," as Captain Whiteman's "buckskin-clad dessert" (Mojica 25, 26):

> "Indian princess" imagery constructed Indigenous women as the virgin frontier, the pure border waiting to be crossed. The enormous popularity of the princess lay within her erotic appeal to the covetous European male wishing to lay claim to the "new" territory. This equation of the Indigenous woman with virgin land, open for consumption, created a Native female archetype which, as Elizabeth Cook-Lynn has pointed out, could then be "used for the colonizer's pleasure and profit."[38]

"It is possible to interpret characters like Pocahontas, Sacagawea and la Malinche as strong Indigenous leaders," argues Anderson, "but the mainstream interpretation of these mythic characters is quite the opposite: Native women (and, by association, the land) are 'easy, available and willing' for the white man" . . . "[T]he 'good' Native woman who willingly works with white men is rewarded with folk hero or 'princess status.' Racism dictates that the women of these celebrated liaisons are elevated above the ordinary Indigenous female status."[39] But not in their own communities.

If Mojica's play deconstructs the ideological effects of non-Native historical representations of Native and mixed-blood women, it also explicitly aligns itself with, and quotes the work of, mestiza women such as Gloria Anzaldúa and Cherríe Moraga, "Word Warriors"[40] who have set out to recuperate the reputations of the mothers of the mestizas. *Princess Pocahontas* undertakes to recuperate these same historical figures across the Americas as leaders, mothers, and grandmothers, transforming the internalized racism and self-hatred of their mestiza, Métis, and mixed-blood descendants into a re-membering of those individual and communal bodies that have been dis-membered through colonization.[41] In a solo performance in which she depicts women's history as autobiography, Mojica's ancestors are re-membered and brought to life in and through her body. According to the brief biography in the published script, she performs as "a Kuna [a Central American Nation]–Rappahannock [the nation of Pocahontas] half-breed, a woman word warrior [like Anzaldúa, Moraga, and Paula Gunn Allen], a mother [like Pocahontas, La Malinche, Sacagawea, and the fur-trade women] and an actor" (86).

In fact, Mojica embodies a matrilineal performative tradition in still more direct ways. She trained as a creator/performer with New York's Spiderwoman Theater, which consists of her mother, Gloria Miguel, and two maternal aunts, Muriel Miguel and Lisa Mayo, and she works in a tradition that is continuous with theirs in both form and content. In their play *Reverb-ber-ber-rations*, Mojica's mother says, "My grandmother stepped into my head and behind my eyes. / She talked":

I've been here for a long time planted on earth.
I am a mother.
I am a grandmother.
I am a lover.
I am a sister.
I am a daughter.
I am a granddaughter . . .
My heartbeat and blood carry messages from the past
through me into the future.[42]

The Scrubbing Project

Mojica's most recent work, *The Scrubbing Project*, is also a collaborative performance with two other women—Cree/Métis actor-singer Jani Lauzon and Pequot/Carib performer Michelle St. John—who together constitute The Turtle Gals Performance Ensemble. Indeed, both the ensemble's December 2000 workshop production at Toronto's Buddies in Bad Times Theatre, and its national tour, in a revised version in 2006–7 were directed by her aunt, Muriel Miguel. *The Scrubbing Project* addresses *métissage*, both in form and content, more fully, and genocide more directly, than any of Mojica's previous work, and it enacts in the present, trans-national resistance. An outrageous, formally hybrid mélange of vaudeville, American musicals, Marx Brothers movies, winged warriors, and survivor testimony, the show is extremely difficult to characterize, shifting as it does from pure shtick to personal reportage that ranges from the hilarious through the uncomfortable to the harrowing. Its formal hybridity is matched by a focus on the mixed heritage of its creators, all of whom identify as Native, and two of whom (Mojica and St. John) also have Jewish parentage, and one of whom (Lauzon) has Finnish ancestry (she describes herself as "Finndian").

Perhaps the most characteristically daring moments in the show are the recurring "Living with Genocide Support Group" scenes—"My name is Esperanza and I am living with genocide"[43]—and the related "Dancing with Genocide" song:[44]

> reservations, relocations, missionary education,
> subjugation and starvation, "put them in their place"
> anorexic, diabetic, mutant children from the tailings
> of uranium excavation. . . .
> epidemic and systemic incest, battery and rape . . .
> [. . .]
> living with genocide
> born into genocide
> breathing this genocide
> resistin' this genocide
> we're doin' the genocide blues. (37–38)

Like *Princess Pocahontas and the Blue Spots*, the play addresses sexual violence directly only in one full scene that occurs late in the action. "Branda," a doughnut-shop worker, whose daughter has been taken from her by the government, falls from the play's STARWORLD, where she plays a Valkyrie (she also plays Chico Marx and a "Wannabe Jew"), into a prison in an unidentified country, where she is forced to perform fellatio on a prison guard. The scene is performed to the tune of "Would You Like to Swing on a Star": "Cause she had / High hopes / she had high hopes / she had high apple pie / in the sky / hopes" (44).

This scene, "Dancing with Genocide," together with another in which "Ophelia," a seven-year-old saint-in-training, is verbally abused and labeled as a "fucking squaw" by teenage boys (40), frames a monologue spoken by Mojica in the role of Esperanza ("Hope Rosenberg"), a "massacre collector and atrocity tourist" who, fifteen years earlier, witnessed a massacre in a village in Mexico, where she worked with a weaver's co-op (n.p.). Esperanza finds death camps in her "bundle"—Mojica's father was a Holocaust survivor—and she carries *among* her bundles a bag of human bones. For her, memory is testimony: "Yes, I want them to rest, I want to rest too, but I can't yet . . . They are the proof of my declaration . . . I'm not going to bury them yet, I want a paper that tells me they killed them . . . and they had committed no crime" (10, ellipses in original). She tells the (true) story of the December 1997 massacre at Acteal in Chiapas, Mexico, of forty-five Indigenous people: nine men, twenty-one women, and fifteen children, including one infant, by sixty paramilitary men sponsored by federal and state governments.[45] In spite of the gendering of the massacre, it has not been reported, even by Amnesty International,[46] as an act of violence against women. Mojica, whose partner is a Chiapan activist, recorded the monologue for a *Songs for Chiapas* CD. She performs it on that CD and in the show itself, in a way that powerfully brings together several of the central strands of my argument: resistant transnationalism, activist and performative memory-making, and genocide, together with a range of imagery and breath control that evokes the events at Acteal, such as the massacre of mainly Native women by men, *as* gendered violence.[47]

Before each "I wake up," Mojica gasps, taking in a recovery breath that suggests both suffocation and the traumatic memory of sexual abuse:

[*Sharp intake of breath*] I wake up—
  suffocating   my mouth and nose filled with dirt
  Was I dreaming again of drowning?
  of being crushed against the ceiling of
a room suddenly   shrinking?
  It's hard to breathe so I breathe as little as possible.
  My legs are cramped and I have to pee.
[*Sharp intake of breath*] I wake up—
  I am in Canada   chunks of earth in my nostrils
  roots poking into my side
  I taste dirt   and something else . . . (38)

(See the end of chapter 5 for the full text.)

Conclusion

What the plays I have been discussing cumulatively suggest is that, within First Nations cultures in the Americas, violence against women functions

not only in the service of maintaining gendered hierarchies and repro-
ducing patriarchal cultures, but more significantly to perpetuate rape
and murder as the gendered and raced technologies of colonialism and
ethnic cleansing that efface difference, not emblematically, but materially
and literally. However, as Mojica and her collaborators demonstrate in
performance, embodied memory, recovered habit, testimony, and social
ritual—including the social rituals of theater and performance themselves—are also mechanisms through which First Nations cultures can
form coalitions of difference and through which *métissage* can be recu-
perated, not as an emblem, but as a tool for resistance, for survival, and,
perhaps oxymoronically, in the words of *The Scrubbing Project*'s support
group, for "living with genocide" (24).

Part III

Native Representation in Drama

CHAPTER 9

"People with Strong Hearts"

Staging Communitism in Hanay Geiogamah's Plays Body Indian and 49

JAYE T. DARBY

We pray.
We are a tribe!
Of people with strong hearts.
Who respect fear
As we make our way.
Who will never kill
Another man's way of living.
—Hanay Geiogamah, 49, scene 12

As is often said, community is the highest value for Native peoples,
and fidelity to it is a primary responsibility.
—Jace Weaver, Other Words[1]

Our abilities as writers—as novelists and poets, playwrights and
essayists—are a gift given to us by the Creator. It is our obligation
to return that gift, to make use of it in a way that serves the people
and the generations to come.
—Joseph Bruchac, "The Gift Is Still Being Given"[2]

THE 1960S AND 1970S in the United States saw the rise of American
Indian activism, sometimes called the Red Power movement, as Native
activists pushed for increased Native rights, tribal sovereignty, and self-
determination.[3] These efforts resulted in a number of acts of resistance.
The National Indian Youth Council, a Native-rights organization founded
in 1961, supported the Northwestern tribes' "fish-ins" in Washington and

Oregon held during the sixties to reclaim tribal fishing rights established in earlier treaties. The American Indian Movement (AIM), founded in Minneapolis in 1968 to address police harassment, rapidly became a militant force for Indian rights throughout the country. On Thanksgiving Day, November 20, 1969, United Indians of All Tribes reclaimed Alcatraz Island to expose the injustices perpetrated against American Indians and to establish cultural and educational centers. In 1973, members of AIM occupied Wounded Knee on Pine Ridge in South Dakota, site of the U.S. Army's 1890 massacre of nearly 300 Minneconjou Lakota men, women, and children.[4]

During this period of political upheaval, Hanay Geiogamah, a young Kiowa-Delaware activist in Oklahoma, became interested in the possibility of theater as an agent of Indian cultural renewal. In recalling this time, he wrote, "By 1968 my political crusading and my interest in theater began to merge, initially in a conception of writing plays which would depict the *truth* about the condition of American Indians."[5] Four years later, as a member of the National Indian Youth Council, and encouraged by the possibilities offered by the free theater movement in the sixties, on March 1, 1972, in New York City, Geiogamah founded the American Indian Theater Ensemble (later renamed the Native American Theater Ensemble) at La MaMa Experimental Theatre Club with the help of Ellen Stewart.[6] With the dual goals of establishing a resident company in Indian Country and helping develop Native performing arts within interested tribal communities, Geiogamah began the theater as a collaborative endeavor by recruiting a group of Native American artists from a range of communities, who formed the creative core of the new theater company.[7] Recognizing the potential of performance as a means to revitalize cultural continuity after centuries of European American disruptions, Geiogamah described contemporary American Indian theater as "a logical development because in the tribal past, before the breakdown of the classic modes, communication had been person-to-person, group-to-group, through storytelling and dance and the symbolic communication provided by ceremony in a familial situation."[8] For Geiogamah, "The stage therefore seemed to offer Indians—provided only that they could control it—a means of self-realization and of presenting culturally authentic images of themselves."[9]

Hanay Geiogamah's early work with the Native American Theater Ensemble offered a comprehensive vision for theater that imagined community in this broad sense, a vision that continues to resonate today. During the next three years, Geiogamah wrote three major plays—*Body Indian, Foghorn,* and *49*—which were workshopped and performed by the Native American Theater Ensemble. These works displayed a distinctive American Indian aesthetic of theater that fused Native traditions and current issues, ushering in "the contemporary era of Native American playwriting," according to Mimi Gisolfi D'Aponte.[10] Intentional in his positionality, Geiogamah locates his drama within his own Kiowa-Delaware traditions and larger pan-Indian experiences while recognizing—as a secondary influence—western theatrical traditions. Centering his work in the nurturing reciprocity of stories and the "rich and complex inheritance" of tribal cultures in American Indian communities, he defines stories broadly as "dances, rituals, ceremonies, customs, and traditions . . . instructions, regulations, and laws."[11] Thus, Geiogamah's criterion for contemporary Indian theater lies in its inherent value to Native people: "In judging an Indian play, readers and viewers should keep in mind that the most important function of the Indian dramatist is to communicate with his own people. The major questions are: Does the play speak effectively to Indians? Can Indians understand what is happening on stage? If there is a message, is it communicated clearly and effectively in Indian terms?"[12] Implicit in this approach is drawing the theater audience together as a community.

In his important book *That the People Might Live: Native American Literatures and Native American Community,* Cherokee scholar Jace Weaver provides a theory of "communitism," a term combining "community" and "activism," to describe "a proactive commitment to Native community, including the wider community" as an underlying tenet of much of Native writing during the last two hundred years.[13] Geiogamah's emphasis on serving the community positions his work within the communitist tradition in Native theater. This chapter analyzes the integrated dramaturgical enactment of Native community and cultural praxis in two of Geiogamah's major plays, *Body Indian* and *49.*[14] *Body Indian* exposes the aftermath of the allotment of Native lands in Indian Territory, later the state of Oklahoma, and the breakdown of tribal values in its depiction of contemporary struggles with poverty and alcoholism and the evocation of traditional kinship obligations within the community. In response to forced cultural disruption, *49* turns on the centrality of the vision quest in Plains traditions to serve the people. This essay takes its theoretical orientation from recent Native literary and theater critical studies, what Cherokee critic Daniel Heath Justice describes as "keeping Native concerns and issues firmly at the interpretative center."[15] As dramaturgical analysis, the discussion moves between script and performance, following the arc of each play as it unfolds theatrically.

Several critics have examined the complex interplay of community and writing in Native literary and theater studies. For more than twenty years, Paula Gunn Allen, Laguna Pueblo/Sioux scholar and writer, has argued that conceptions of significance and aesthetic values are culturally specific and in the case of Native writing deeply embedded in specific spiritual, historical, gendered, and aesthetic tribal contexts, reflective of the diversity and multiplicity of more than five hundred nations. In the introduction to the Modern Language Association publication of *Studies in American Indian Literature*, Gunn Allen calls for an understanding of Native works on their own terms, recognizing "American Indians as people with histories, cultures, customs, and understandings worthy of study."[16] She more fully develops this critical approach in *The Sacred Hoop: Recovering the Feminine in American Indian Traditions* and *Off the Reservation: Reflections on Boundary-Busting, Border-Crossing Loose Canons*, which stress the holism of Native literature, oral traditions, ceremony, and Native communities.[17] Just as understanding the influences of European literary traditions—the Bible, English history, and Aristotelian conceptions of drama—is helpful in approaching Shakespeare's work, Gunn Allen suggests that study of Native works, such as N. Scott Momaday's *House Made of Dawn*, is made richer by knowledge of "Walotowa, Navajo, and Kiowa" traditions, as well as Roman Catholic influences. Similarly, Leslie Marmon Silko's *Ceremony* is enriched by the feminine principles and ritual contexts from Laguna Pueblo communities.[18]

In *That the People Might Live*, Jace Weaver builds on the work of Native intellectuals Paula Gunn Allen, Vine Deloria Jr., Gerald Vizenor, and Robert Warrior, among others, theorizing that responsibility to the community is integral to a substantial amount of written Native literatures. Defining these literatures broadly to include novels, poetry, drama, tribal histories, biographies, autobiographies, essays, and tracts, he traces the works of well-known and lesser-known writers from the 1700s, beginning with Samson Occom and other missionaries and continuing into the 1990s with contemporary writers.[19] Resisting essentialism, Weaver recognizes the "many different kinds of community—reservation, rural, urban, tribal, pan-Indian, traditional, Christian"—in North America, and the manifold responses Native writers have had.[20] Within this pluralism, he looks at interrelationships among oral traditions, land, culture, spirituality, historical forces, current conditions, Native writing, and recovery as defining elements in much of Native writing during the past two hundred years. Implicit in his view of communitism are "the valorization of Native community and values and a commitment to them."[21]

Weaver's critical perspective acknowledges the complexity of those Native literatures engaged in communitism as simultaneously rooted in ancient traditions and spiritual obligations and situated in present realities still rife with poverty and oppression. Communitism, as conceptualized by Weaver, reflects larger spiritual beliefs, ceremonial traditions, and sacred responsibilities going back to Creation that define community for each tribe as a way of being and living in the world. These beliefs, which vary in their manifestations tribe by tribe, integrate the sacred and the secular, focusing on the interconnections between all beings and the land, what Weaver calls "the entire created order, including plants, animals, Mother Earth herself," and communitarian values of responsibility, respect, balance, and kinship.[22] Communitist writing also remembers, mourns, and contests multiple historical atrocities that occurred throughout North America, as well as ongoing daily oppressions from European American colonization. According to Weaver, "to promote communitist values means to participate in the healing of the grief and sense of exile felt by Native communities and the pained individuals in them."[23]

In counteracting the continued psychological, spiritual, political, and material effects of colonialism, Weaver argues for the restorative power of Native writers to heal and offer possibilities for new conceptions of community. In describing Weaver's work, Daniel Heath Justice notes, "Native continuity through community is central to his scholarly ethic." Seeing communitism as transcending "pretty catch-phrases of pan-tribal unity," Justice explains that "it requires deep, systematic, and often painful decolonization of mind, spirit, and body."[24] Moving between literary, performative, and social worlds, many contemporary Native writers, according to Weaver, push for new visions of community to heal the past and create the future. As he explains: "By writing out of and into Native community, for and to Native peoples, these writers engage in a continuing search for community," thereby "creating in the process new, praxis-oriented views of identity and community," which extend into the lived world.[25] Thus, rather than merely resisting, the act of communitism liberates and transforms. So powerful is the work of these Native writers, Weaver asserts, that "they write that the People might live."[26]

Body Indian

By interrogating the raw realities facing many members of the intertribal community in Oklahoma in the 1970s, and the collapse of community ties after centuries of cultural dislocation, Body Indian stages a poignant appeal for the restoration of communal responsibility. The play, originally partnered with Na Haaz Zaan, a traditional piece arranged by Robert Shorty and based on the Navajo creation story, premiered in the American Indian Theater Ensemble Company's debut on October 25, 1972, at La MaMa in New York.[27] Even though the production was in New York, Geiogamah wrote it for the Indian community, articulating his purpose in a La MaMa press release: "It is a play of the past and the present, but hopefully not of the future. I am trying to depict how Indians abuse and mistreat one another in a dangerously crippling way, not with physical violence but with actions and gestures that most of them do not see as being insulting, abusive, and defeating."[28]

The play opens with a tableau of Bobby Lee, on crutches, struggling into Howard's one-room apartment, introducing the subtext of poverty and the larger American society's complicity in this, which resulted from allotment, the impoverishing loss of land, and the systematic breakdown of tribal values. Having lost his leg in a train accident in a drunken stupor on a track and now living in Oklahoma, Bobby Lee lives from check to check of lease money. In this room, strewn with liquor bottles where four people on a bed and a mattress on the floor have been sleeping off the effects of too much alcohol, the audience sees poverty with all of its attendant ills—deprivation, violence, despair, and alcoholism.

As a result of U.S. federal allotment policies, Indian lands were broken up in Indian Territory, now Oklahoma, in the late 1880s and early 1900s. Each Native head of household received 160 acres apiece, which many began to lease out under the control of the Bureau of Indian Affairs. This small allotment was in replacement of millions of acres of land taken from the tribes.[29] In 1969, Bobby would have received about $400 per month for his share of 80 acres of land. In addition to taking large tracts of land for European American settlers, allotment policies were designed to sever communal ties, foster individualism, and disrupt traditional religious practices.[30] Jace Weaver describes the spiritual, psychological, and cultural ruptures resulting from forced displacement: "When Natives are removed from their traditional lands, they are robbed of more than territory; they are deprived of numinous landscapes that are central to their faith and their identity, lands populated by their relations, ancestors, animals and beings both physical and mythological. A kind of psychic homicide is committed."[31] *Body Indian* stages this "psychic homicide," compassionately probing the subsequent collapse of the traditional tribal values of respect and responsibility, and positing alcoholism as both the common consequence of and catalyst for degeneration.

As the action unfolds, events play against the centrality of kinship in Plains communities and the responsibilities inherent in such relationships. "Kinship and clan," according to Vine Deloria Jr., "were built on the idea that individuals owed each other certain kinds of behaviors and that if each individual performed his or her task properly, society as a whole would function."[32] The opening of scene 1 clearly delineates kinship ties through dialogue and staging. Thompson, a contemporary of Bobby, and his wife, Eulahlah, invite Bobby in. Using the Kiowa term *hites* for a friend who is like a brother, Thompson warmly welcomes Bobby with, "Well. I'lll beee! B—obbye Leee! Come in, hites, come in! Long time no see" (9). Bobby, then emphasizing communal responsibilities, asks Thompson to "go down and *halp* my aunts up the stairs," which he does (9). Bobby Lee calls Howard, an elder, "Uncle" as a token of friendship and respect. Onstage, when Howard is joined by Ethel, his girlfriend, she reminds Bobby that they are related. Howard confirming that "ya'll are kin" carefully articulates the kinship ties: "Ethel is related to your mother, Bobby. Your mother was my dad's sister. Ethel's dad was kin to both of them" (12).

Yet as the drinking escalates, the play quickly exposes the fragility of these kinship ties in the face of poverty and alcoholism, revealing what Kenneth Lincoln calls "a bracketed tribalism, where 'kind' means ideally cultured communal, yet realistically born destitute."[33] Bobby, who plans to use his lease money to go to an alcohol rehabilitation center in

Norman—"a A-A deal for alcoholics"—finds himself trapped in his old destructive pattern of bringing his lease money to Howard's apartment where his friends and relatives are drinking (20). Consequently—each time with their encouragement—Bobby loses his resolve in a bottle. In a stark reversal of kinship obligations, his friends and relatives, themselves victims of larger social forces, become predators. In five meticulously constructed scenes, they "roll" Bobby for more drinking money, each theft escalating the violation done to Bobby Lee's body and to the community's values. The sound of a train punctuates each act of violation—a reminder of Bobby's accident, the complicity of his friends and relatives in perpetuating his suffering, and the subsequent loss of community ties. Annamaria Pinazzi suggests, "The title of *Body Indian* refers both to Bobby Lee and to Indians collectively."[34]

The first "rolling" depicts the erosion of the moral role of elders as exemplars of communal values, purpose, and fortitude in tribal life. So important are elders in sustaining the community that Vine Deloria Jr. describes them as "the best living examples of what the end product of education and life experiences should be."[35] Howard and Ethel, Bobby's relatives, cynically expressing concern about the pain from his prosthetic leg, use the opportunity to frisk him and to steal from his pockets. In scene 2, following the dire example set by their elders, Thompson and Marie—a cousin to whom Bobby turned to help him get into the detox program in Norman—roll him again and fight over the money. Then, Bobby's aunts Ethel, Alice, and Eulahlah, who earlier danced a round dance of friendship with him and openly acknowledged their obligation to help him as both a relative and an injured person, steal from him, enacting a perversion of responsibility and another communal collapse. The staging punctuates their guilty actions: *"The women quickly return to their dancing and singing, pretending they have not rolled Bobby"* (26).

A chance for atonement and redemption of the community exists briefly in scene 4 when Bobby wakes up and realizes that most of his money is gone. Barely able to sit up, he confronts the other characters with slurred words, reminding them of his need to go to a detox center: "I want . . . to . . . go . . . to Norman. My money . . . money . . . is . . . for Norman" (28). Rather than heed him, his friends and relatives continue to degrade him as Howard's grandson, James, and his two friends, Martha and Fina, take the money from his shoe for more beer and gas. Jeffrey Huntsman notes that "the play develops almost ritualistically, manifesting the dark forces of a troubled society, covertly at first, in empty solicitude and forced camaraderie, and later in open and unalloyed badness."[36]

The ultimate communal transgression occurs with the elder Howard's final treachery. In his desperation for money for more alcohol, Howard leads the group, including his own grandchild James and his two young friends, in justifying the theft of Bobby's prosthetic leg and, thus, in reifying this dysfunctionality for the next generation. At this point, as Huntsman points out, "Bobby's friends are wholly engulfed by their most self-deceptive rationalization."[37] As C.W.E. Bigsby writes, "The communal efforts of those individuals who come together to steal Bobby Lee's money parody the communality of the tribe. They combine only in the process of degradation."[38] On stage, their perfidy, according to Annamaria Pinazzi, is a visceral blow replete "with Artaudian cruelty" to Bobby and the "Indian body."[39]

Through its searing interrogation of the loss of community, *Body Indian* exposes suffering and longs for amelioration. By compassionately acknowledging the anguish many tribal communities have endured, such work, according to Weaver, supports "new constellations of Native community."[40] Throughout the play the characters have the potential to engage in responsible behavior; Bobby's relatives and friends could support one another as members of a community, and each person could heed the train's sound instead of ignoring it. The play's ending testifies to Geiogamah's faith in the capacity of Native people to overcome hardships. At the end, Bobby, missing a leg, learns that he has to rely on himself. In an interview with Kenneth Lincoln, Geiogamah explains that Bobby is "taking responsibility for himself" and that "he's clean now, he's been cleaned out, cleansed."[41] In a tentative moment of restoration, the women tidy the room in the background, trying to return it, and their lives, to some sort of order. Hope lies buried at the end of the play, and the final tenuous staging of community intimates redemptive possibilities for Bobby that extend into the audience. In "Indians Playing Indians," Kenneth Lincoln clarifies the healing potential of *Body Indian*, born out of anguish, as "cathartic change—an artistic as well as social commitment to acting out the truth, hoping for a better life. It's critical trickster theater, a breed of mythic humor and psychological realism to wake the people up to themselves."[42] Uncompromising in its gaze, *Body Indian* is a play of both immense pain and fragile possibility.

49

The Native American Theater Ensemble's first production in Indian Country was an early version of 49, which opened on January 10, 1975, at Oklahoma City University. First workshopped in New York with Tom O'Horgan, who directed *Hair* and *Jesus Christ Superstar*, 49 was later reworked by Geiogamah in collaboration with members of NATE in Oklahoma.[43] The final version of 49 is a musical, with songs by Jim Pepper and Hanay Geiogamah, that integrates both contemporary issues and traditional performance elements.

Like *Body Indian*, 49 addresses a pressing community concern—the alienation and cultural dispossession of Native youth in Oklahoma in the 1970s. However, unlike the realistic staging of *Body Indian*, 49 counters one hundred years of disruptive federal colonial policies through a ceremonial form that reasserts American Indian cultural sovereignty theatrically.[44] Set on an Oklahoma dance ground, 49 transcends time and space, taking the audience through contrasting scenes with Night Walker—a Plains holy man and spiritual leader—and parallel groups of Young People in the late nineteenth and twentieth centuries. The Young People of the Past have strong traditional ties and opportunities for cultural knowledge. Those of the present, denied their rich legacies by repressive federal policies designed to strip Plains communities of their spiritual, cultural, linguistic, and governance practices, are culturally dispossessed and unaware of tribal responsibilities.[45] They turn to the 49, a free-for-all post-powwow event and party for Native young people in Oklahoma, as one of the few cultural remnants left in their lives, which are increasingly marred by danger and encroached on by police.

Pivotal to the narrative structure of 49 are the Plains tradition of the vision quest and the power of the visionary world to enlighten and serve the community through the restoration of appropriate relationships.[46] Elaborating this tradition, Howard L. Harrod explains, "Vision, the gift of power, and the normative importance of kinship—these were elements that constituted central features of Plains social worlds, formed the horizons of their moral and religious experience, and deeply motivated their actions."[47] Drawing on the vision quest, 49 stages a fusion of the sacred and the aesthetic. The arc of the play follows a ceremonial circle, pushing the white world to the margins, which is represented only by patrol voices.

Thus, in a communitist moment on the American stage, Geiogamah constructs a work in which the theatrical vocabulary creates a visionary Plains
world and reasserts Plains beliefs, values, and practices once suppressed
by the federal government. Through these elements, enhanced by music,
dance, chants, and lighting, 49 evokes a mythic reality, central to Plains
traditions, in which, according to Harrod, "the 'accent of reality' was
granted so powerfully to transcendent orders of meaning that the everyday
world was often subordinated to and shaped by the vision experience."[48]

Establishing the sacred connection to the land, the first scene of 49
opens in a ceremonial area. Night Walker calls everyone to the "ceremonial circle" and "our people's arbor" (91), the sacred center of Plains
spirituality. Immediately, the staging establishes an integrated holism of
sacred time and space.[49] As a holy man, the character of Night Walker
possesses spiritual and communal responsibilities. His role draws on the
Plains spiritual tradition of a leader who "is distinguished as someone
of power and vision, chosen by the spirits to heal," and who "works as a
medium from a deeper order of spiritual Reality to the corporeal reality people ordinarily live."[50] So important is the spiritual integrity of the
performer entrusted with the role of Night Walker that, during the first
performance, the role was played by a Skokomish spiritual leader, Gerald
Bruce Miller.[51]

In stark contrast to the mythic timelessness of scene 1, radio Patrol
Voices blast scene 2 onto the stage, exposing the physical and cultural dis-
placement of the Young People of Today, who are being harassed by the
police on their way to a 49. Far more than local police, the Patrol Voices
signify centuries of colonial control and cultural suppression, denying
the youth even this small opportunity to come together as Indians. "Colonialism succeeds," Jace Weaver writes, "by subverting traditional notions
of culture and identity and by imposing social structures and constructs
incompatible with traditional society."[52] Thus, rather than being able to
fulfill their spiritual right to come to the ceremonial circle as in the past,
in a community-affirming act, the 49 group, on the run from the police
and burdened by centuries of oppression, must hide in the bushes to
evade detection. Yet, by virtue of their resistance and the fusion of the 49
dance ground with the site of Night Walker's ceremonial circle, mythic
forces begin to act on the stage as the 49ers draw closer to their ancestral
past and their spiritual powers. By contrasting the real time in which the

Patrol Voices and actions are portrayed with the ceremonial time of Night Walker and the two generations of Young People, the dramaturgy of 49 undermines the power of colonial chronological time—what Gunn Allen identifies as "western industrial consciousness" and linear history—replacing it with mythic time, which establishes continuity and wholeness.[53]

In scene 3, the pivotal scene of the play, originally called "A Prayer for Guidance from the Power Spirits," the performer playing Night Walker is required to engage theatrically in a vision quest.[54] The staging of this scene draws on the belief that the vision quest opens a liminal space where "the spirit world and the natural world interconnect."[55] Lee Irwin describes the spiritual implications for the whole tribe: "The transformative quality of the vision experience is a consequence of actually interacting with the powers that sustain the world."[56]

In this scene, the dialogue and staging highlight the communal purpose of the vision quest and its inherent power to transform the community. Night Walker, describing himself as "a friend who has honor and respect deep in his heart for you" (96), thanks the spirits and focuses on the needs of the tribe. Asserting the spiritual interconnection of all beings, including the earth, Night Walker calls on the "holy place around" and refers to the spirits as "our friends, our brothers and sisters" (96). As he tries to make sense of his concerns as a holy man, responsible for the needs of his people, Night Walker respectfully thanks the images of the spirits that increasingly inhabit the stage world and honors them by sharing a song, story, food, and tobacco, and then, smudging the space with sage, prays for the needs of the tribe.

In his prayers, Night Walker puts the needs of the tribe first as he shares his concerns about their safety, a young man and woman's future, the growing tide of funerals, and the subsequent need for him to "talk more and more to Brother Death" (98). Night Walker's plea has intertextual resonances with the haunting call of Hehaka Sapa, or Black Elk, the Oglala Lakota visionary, for his people to receive the blessings of his great vision: "Hear me, that my people will live, and find a way that my people will prosper."[57] Instantiating communitism, Night Walker's subsequent questions to the spirits focus on future generations of youth onstage, in the audience, and in the larger Native community, and on their abilities to fulfill sacred responsibilities to the tribe and the earth, and to live.

In describing his vision onstage, Night Walker first mentions a "darkness" that is "gathering ahead on our road" (98), the darkness of a century of despair and oppression resulting from brutal federal educational and religious assimilationist policies.[58] More importantly, beyond the darkness as the vision concludes, Night Walker receives an answer that reassures him of intergenerational tribal continuity and a promise of life that he affirms in a ceremonial coda: "We will live and walk together for a long time. All of us will live and walk together for a long time" (100). The dramaturgical question raised by scene 3 remains: How? How will the people "walk through the dark that *has* passed us" and "live" (99)?

The remaining scenes of 49 answer this question by portraying the living power of a vision for the community, and the communal obligation that the visionary has to share the vision, what David Martínez refers to as "using it responsibly."[59] This communal responsibility drives the dramaturgy for the rest of 49 as the remaining scenes fulfill the other two requirements of a vision—enactment and realization, thereby staging the Plains tradition in which receiving a vision involved "an act of power by which the vision can be socially validated."[60]

In a spirit of communitism, Night Walker's enactment of the vision is intended to motivate this generation and their descendants to continue their rich tribal legacy in the face of enormous adversity through a series of performed cultural lessons that address the Young People of the Past. His lessons in scenes 6, 8, and 10 provide a similar impetus for the Young People of Today onstage and in the audience. Night Walker's educational process emulates what Vine Deloria Jr. describes as "the old ways of educating," which "affirmed the basic principle that human personality was derived from accepting responsibility to be a contributing member of a society."[61] In scene 6, Night Walker compassionately enacts his vision for the Young People of the Past, showing them both the coming darkness and the journey into the future, through song, dance, ceremonies, and "the stories of our way," all of which are pivotal to surviving and overcoming the oppression (106). Further cultural lessons unfold theatrically in scene 8, as Singing Man teaches the young people about the integration of spirituality and music, and the obligation of music in fulfilling community responsibilities, affirming kinship ties, honoring all beings, and moving into the future. Weaving Woman then teaches weaving as a means of honoring the ancestors and supporting the tribe. Each one of these lessons exemplifies what Lincoln identifies as "older, idealized tribal values," which "include sharing material and spiritual wealth, remaining loyal to the people at all costs, caring about one's place in relation to the encompassing world, maintaining an extended family as support for each individual, and being kind in the original sense of the word, that is, 'of the same kind' and 'kind' or generous within that bond."[62]

The communal stakes of the performance build as the contemporary youths' actions in scenes 4, 5, 7, and 9 increase the urgency of realizing Night Walker's vision of life to ensure the future of the tribe. Each of these scenes, in contrast to the lessons of the past, locates the 49ers within the darkness of personal alienation, cultural dislocation, selfishness, and hedonism foreseen by Night Walker. Enmity, alcohol, car crashes, and indiscriminate sex are agents of Brother Death waiting to destroy this generation.

To counter the dangers facing contemporary youth, scene 10, the arbor scene, performs a communal rededication to Plains spirituality through story and ceremony. Actors, using story theater techniques, portray Night Walker's parable of the tipi—the recovery of the lost children—thus enacting a central metaphor of the play and offering healing through story. As Jace Weaver explains, "traditional Native American tribal myths are communal in character, forming identity, explaining one's place in the cosmos, creating a sense of belonging."[63] Emphasizing the sacred tie between spirituality and community, Night Walker instructs the community: "This arbor cannot be killed. It is strong and powerful. . . . It can be burned and torn apart, but its life cannot be taken from it. It draws its life from the hearts and souls of the tribe, our people" (122). In preparing the arbor on stage with Night Walker, the Young People of the Past learn that spiritual obligations and correct practices are ongoing sources of tribal renewal and key to maintaining the community. Having the knowledge and ability to conduct appropriate ceremonies is crucial for maintaining an ordered life. Emphasizing this sacred duty, Vine Deloria Jr. writes, "Presented with the natural ordering of cosmic energies, when the people saw an imbalance they knew that their responsibility was to initiate ceremonies that would help bring about balance once again."[64]

In violent juxtaposition to the harmonious arbor ceremony, a brutal fight erupts at the 49 in scene 11, as the 49ers endure life out of balance. At this point in the play, degeneration seems to triumph: the young contemporary Indians shout for the fighters to kill one another. While on one level appearing social and personal in nature, this struggle, as in *Body Indian*, indicates a spiritual imbalance within the community—the Young People of Today's disconnection from the sacred responsibilities and kinship ties observed by their ancestors.

Elements of communitism coalesce, animating Night Walker's vision of life, when out of the fight, in a catalyzing moment as the police lights close in, the 49ers band together and form a line in the shape of a Beautiful Bird, undermining the police intrusion and defying their authority when they refuse to be removed from the 49 grounds. C.W.E. Bigsby describes the performers in this scene as "articulating their convictions about the physical nature of theatre and the redemptive power of the body."[65] While certainly a powerful physical articulation, the youths' shared purpose and unity also signals a cultural and spiritual metamorphosis, as they turn away from their earlier self-destructive behavior and selfish individualism toward the restoration of kinship ties and the sacred power of communitarianism. Jeffrey Huntsman explains that "the form of a great bird, an elaborate and living barricade against the outside intrusion," performatively marks "a realization of their faith in themselves and in their values, and that process of building is in itself where the value lies."[66] The Young People's act of community makes manifest Night Walker's vision and the innate power of the visionary experience to transform everyday lives. This staged realization of communal order also confirms the spiritual leader's power, whose "healing," according to Kenneth Lincoln, "aligns the people with the natural health and energy of the universe, the balance of all things."[67] Inconsequential in the full force of mythic power, the patrol lights and voices retreat as the Young People claim the dance ground which belonged to their ancestors.

The performance ends as Night Walker blesses and sends both the performers on the stage and the audience into the future, bringing the play full circle. The staging of the arbor lit within the ceremonial circle remains semiotically the source of renewal and continuity, mythically connecting the young people to their past, present, and future, and to all other beings. Thus, the ending signals a powerful form of Native community—one that symbolically returns Native peoples to their lands, their powerful cultures, traditions, and spirituality. By drawing on Plains traditions and by substantiating the ceremonial requirements of a vision quest—vision, enactment, and realization—49 theatrically re-envisions the future for Plains peoples.

Concluding Reflections

In his early plays with the Native American Theater Ensemble, Hanay Geiogamah, described by Jack Marken as "an authentic voice of Indian affirmation and hope," pushes for the vitality of Native community as a living force.[68] Integral to community continuance, which underlies the dramaturgy in *Body Indian* and *49*, is fulfilling communal responsibilities to one another and the cosmos. *Body Indian* evokes responsibilities of kinship that offer deliverance from the damaging effects of alcohol and poverty; *49* ceremonially leads the Young People away from Brother Death back to the tribal circle and into the future. We would all do well to heed Night Walker's call to live respectfully as relatives, and to "never kill / Another man's way of living" (132). Evoking communitism, both plays still resonate and inspire. *A-ho*.[69]

CHAPTER 10

Coming-of-Age on the Rez

William S. Yellow Robe's The Independence of Eddie Rose *as Native American Bildungsdrama*

David Krasner

[*Bildungsromane*] are the most pedagogically efficient of novels, since they thematize and enact the very notion of aesthetic education.[1]

The Independence of Eddie Rose shows a very hard slice of life, but it also provides hope.[2] The sixteen-year-old protagonist in William S. Yellow Robe's play *The Independence of Eddie Rose* must choose whether to remain at home on the Indian reservation (referred to in the play as the "Rez") or to leave for Seattle with his friend Mike.[3] In this drama, neither choice offers much reward for Eddie Rose. The reservation provides scant opportunities; little in Eddie's world is removed from the reality of poverty and ennui. However, his leaving without money or prospects seems a naïve and far-fetched possibility. From the opening of the play, Eddie is shown to be living in a dysfunctional home with his alcoholic mother, Katherine Rose, her abusive boyfriend, Lenny Sharb, and Eddie's ten-year-old sister, Theia, who is victimized by Lenny's vitriolic temper. Eddie is helped by his aunt Thelma, Katherine's sister. Still, Thelma can provide little more than emotional support. She attempts to countermand the evidence that Eddie's life is unlikely to improve if he remains on the reservation; yet the situation is hardly conducive to self-development and growth. Eddie, a high-school dropout, imagines his future will be characterized by dead-end jobs and boredom. His friend Mike, who is in trouble with the law for the crimes of loitering and smoking marijuana, tries to persuade Eddie to leave. Mike cajoles him into thinking that the big city—in this instance, Seattle—might provide adventure and at least the possibility of a better life. Mike has motivations: though his crimes are not serious, he is being hassled by the reservation's truant officer, Sam Jacobs, whose sexual appetite is directed toward him. Sam has Mike incarcerated in order to "make deals." Mike wants to escape and urges Eddie to assist him. But neither has money (they are hoping to borrow a car), nor any real experience outside the reservation.

The play is deceptively simple. The dramatic conflict is unambiguous — Eddie either stays or leaves. The playwright portrays the scenes realistically, conveying life on an Indian reservation somewhere in Montana or Idaho in detail. There is no mention of a specific national identity or "tribal affiliation"; instead, the play seeks to create a universal picture of contemporary Native life. Despite the uncertainty of the nation and locale in which the play takes place, Yellow Robe's talent for illustrating the details of a reservation is evident in the dialogue, characterization, interactions, and descriptions of everyday existence. But there is more to the play than a mere depiction of troubled life on a reservation. The play is rooted in a tradition of moral decision making that is frequently found in western dramas. Yellow Robe situates the play in a Native milieu, while building its framework on western melodramatic forms. The German term *Bildungsroman* loosely describes a "coming-of-age" story, one that is appropriately descriptive of *Eddie Rose*. In what follows I will attempt to demonstrate that *The Independence of Eddie Rose* is a "Native American Bildungsdrama" in the tradition of western literature. As a "rite-of-passage" play, *The Independence of Eddie Rose* traces the protagonist's initiation into adulthood, demonstrates his conflicts, and portrays a drama of moral choice. It chronicles Eddie Rose's passage from naïveté to awareness and builds on the framework of the bildungsroman in Native American life. I will first broadly describe the development of this genre in western literature and then examine the ways in which Yellow Robe's play deploys this form.

Bildungsroman

According to *The Oxford Companion to German Literature*, *Bildungsroman* is "a novel in which the chief character, after a number of false starts or wrong choices, is led to follow the right path and to develop into a mature and well-balanced man."[4] It calls for the subject's transition from puerility and naïveté to a broader understanding of social responsibility. As the bildungsroman, which emerged in Germany during the late eighteenth century, continues into the twentieth, it also develops additional objectives: it describes an individual's confrontation with society; it is predicated on a protagonist who profits from life's lessons; and in the course of maturing, the protagonist usually becomes reconciled to some condition of the world that he or she had previously rejected.[5]

James Hardin observes that "there is no consensus on the meaning of the term Bildungsroman." Thus, like many words that do not directly translate, it is open to various interpretations. His reasoning is based on the consideration of at least two historical definitions: "first, *Bildung* as a developmental process, and, second, as a collective name for the cultural and spiritual value of a specific people or social stratum in a given historical epoch."[6] The idea of *Bildung* as an aesthetic, moral, and rational concept was commonplace in European Enlightenment thinking, but the idea of the bildungsroman did not take hold until the late eighteenth century. In his book *The German Bildungsroman: History of a National Genre*, Todd Kontje asserts that the term *Bildung* originated in the Middle Ages as a pietistic reference to "God's active transformation of the passive Christian." As its meaning took literary form, influenced by Goethe in the late eighteenth century, *Bildung* went from signifying a passive individual, devoted to whatever mandates may have been interpreted from the Bible or from the clergy, to signifying an active citizen, asserting his or her free will while coming to terms with society. "Instead of being passive recipients of a preexisting form," Kontje contends, the characters in a bildungsroman "gradually develop their own innate potential through interaction with their environment."[7]

Credit for coining the term *Bildungsroman* goes to Karl von Morgenstern (1770–1852). In the second of his two lectures on the subject (the first in 1816 and the second, quoted here, in 1820), he maintained that the genre "portrays the *Bildung* of the protagonist . . . but also, secondly, because it especially encourages the reader's *Bildung* through this portrayal."[8] This description implies that both protagonist and reader mature as a result of the narrative. This process requires the reader to learn by casting aside his or her childlike attributes and adolescent beliefs, and by identifying vicariously with the protagonist's false starts, misjudgments, and ultimate discovery of coping mechanisms. As such, the narrative develops concomitantly between reader and subject: in the process of shedding certain adolescent behaviors, both discover more meaningful ways of living. The novel is intended to emphasize the notion that the more one disengages from certain beliefs and attitudes about oneself, the more one matures.

Throughout the nineteenth and twentieth centuries, alienation becomes a feature of the genre. The new modern protagonist generally finds society disingenuous and develops an iconoclastic antipathy toward social hypocrisies and injustices. At the end of the typical contemporary bildungsroman, the protagonist learns to compromise and sheds past rebellious values. Identity arises from flexibility; he or she incorporates an internal adherence to personal (and sometimes nonconforming) ideals, whilst adjusting these ideals to meet social requirements. Thus, the bildungsroman comes to express the inner conflict between conformity and iconoclasm. J. D. Salinger's 1952 novel, *The Catcher in the Rye*, exemplifies this pattern of rebellion, compromise, and reconciliation. The protagonist, Holden Caulfield, drops out of his elite boarding school. Rather than going home, or even telling his family what he intends to do, he wanders on his own through New York City in search of "the real world" and a better understanding of himself. Turning away from materialism and those he terms "phonies," Caulfield's wanderlust epitomizes the bildungsroman as a path toward self-realization. Caulfield deliberately wears his hunter's hat backward, which, in the 1950s, would have been a symbol of his rebelliousness. At the end of the novel, he recognizes that his responsibility to his sister, Phoebe, must override his nonconformist impulses. He adjusts his hat so that the rim points frontward, signaling his changing attitude.

There are considerable parallels between *The Catcher in the Rye* and *The Independence of Eddie Rose*; both Caulfield and Rose are adolescent rebels who learn to come to terms with their ethical responsibilities to their younger sisters. In *The Catcher in the Rye*, Caulfield finds that his sister emulates him. Despite his attempts to dissuade her, she insists on following him wherever he goes. Eventually both end up in New York's Central Park, where they stop at the merry-go-round. Caulfield pays for her ride. As he watches her, he starts to cry. He realizes that his rejection of society's pretensions must, ultimately, be tempered by a sense of responsibility to others. Caulfield, in short, cannot leave his family whenever he chooses. Phoebe's sincerity and devotion require his acknowledgment. If he tries to run away, she will tag along. He must take her into account.

Eddie's responsibilities to his sister are portrayed more starkly. Lenny's rape of Theia forces Eddie not only to protect his sister but also to obtain a court order removing Theia from their mother's home. The final scene of the play depicts a painful confrontation between Eddie and his mother, Katherine. Eddie demands that Katherine sign the court-ordered release papers. Katherine pleads to keep her daughter, but Eddie persuades her otherwise. Eddie's "independence" is, ironically, not equated with having the freedom to travel the world with his friend Mike; rather, it is circumscribed by his sister's *dependence* on him. His commitment to Theia and to life on the reservation breaks the cycle of self-destruction in the family, imbuing him with the characteristics of adulthood.

Independence

The play opens with Eddie and his sister playing games, which are intended to create a sense of calm that contrasts with what is happening in Eddie's home. A fight between Eddie's mother and her sometimes-boyfriend ensues.

From the play's opening it is evident that Eddie must protect his younger sister from the violence in his household. Throughout the play, Katherine and Lenny's relationship creates stress. Their drunken brawls are relentless and provide Eddie with a motivation to leave. The only outlets for Eddie and his friends on the reservation are drunken parties that last through the night.

Alcoholism plays a large role in the drama. Katherine and Lenny drink throughout the play. Lenny even steals Katherine's money (little though there is) for liquor. Such conditions may be perceived as stereotypical, and the play has come under considerable criticism for its depictions of alcoholism. Yellow Robe defends the play against such claims. In an interview by Paul Rathbun in *Native Playwrights' Newsletter*, Yellow Robe describes his play in relation to other so-called stereotypical portrayals:

> We have [Katherine], the mother, who's screaming and yelling, whose language is hard; the younger sister Theia is attacked. But this is a slice of life, and does it make it theater? To a certain extent, yes, because, for instance, Eugene O'Neill's *Long Day's Journey into Night* has characters where the mother is a morphine addict, the younger son has tuberculosis, the older brother is going through alcoholism, [and] the father has never 'fessed up to anything.[9]

Yellow Robe is referring to clichés about the Irish in O'Neill's play, in which alcoholism and the harshness of life are central to the plot. Yet O'Neill's play is rarely criticized for stereotyping the Irish. Yellow Robe rebuts the criticism of his representation of Native life: "As far as attacking the stereotype" of alcoholism goes, he says, "we have a generation that doesn't understand why these stereotypes exist, and why they are bad." He adds the following:

> If you trace the history of alcoholism among Native Americans, you have to look first at the whole process of drinking as a tool, an economic tool. It was used to gain economic favor from Indian tribes.
>
> [. . .]
>
> Another thing, too, about stereotypes. . . . I try to present characters first. Yes, they fall into stereotypes. . . . [But] in *The Independence of Eddie Rose* when Eddie finally says no to his mother, "No," he's not going to walk the same path, that's one of the hardest things to do, especially within that cycle. Part of breaking the system of this destructive cycle is being able to say "no."
>
> One of the things that always amazes me about *Eddie Rose*, about reactions among Native American tribes, is that whenever you deny the problem of alcoholism on your reservation, you are also denying the fact that today, someone is going to die from alcoholism. You are denying the truth that "Yes, there is a drinking problem."

Yellow Robe continues, saying that "if we don't do something about this denial, then we are in trouble."[10]

At the beginning of the play, Eddie himself is in a state of denial, which manifests itself in avoidance, as he looks for ways to escape and achieve "independence." For Eddie, independence does not simply mean an escape from the reservation. It is, rather, a complex notion involving issues of identity, place, home, and security. In his book *Native Pragmatism: Rethinking the Roots of American Philosophy*, Scott L. Pratt reminds us that "invasion by European Americans undermined the places of Native people, not because whites sought a place to live in America, but because they did so in a way that undermined the sustaining relations of place."[11] Eddie's sense of place (or home) is fundamentally disrupted by domestic violence and alcoholism; his aimlessness is symbolic of the struggle of Native peoples to secure their roots. While other minorities and oppressed ethnic groups in the United States (such as African Americans and Chicanos) can look abroad for some sense of solace and connection, Native Americans live on the very land that is their native home but have been deprived of many of their former rights and traditional practices. In an effort to reconnect with the land, Eddie listens to his Aunt Thelma's stories of the past and mourns at his dead grandmother's gravesite, where his ancestral connections might provide him with some semblance of identity and comfort. "Aunty Thelma," as she is called in the play, values modesty over materialism and humility over grandiosity. She fears the disintegration of her heritage, and remains on the reservation in the hope that it will sustain and nurture connections to a rooted past. She becomes aware of Eddie's guilt at the thought of leaving the reservation but at the same time understands that the reservation in its current state offers young men and women little in life.

Mike pulls Eddie in another direction. He views Seattle as a place free of poverty, social ills, and high suicide rates. Eddie's uncertainty as to whether to accompany him is a result of his adolescent idealism and his inner withdrawal from the seemingly insurmountable problems he faces. As James Hardin indicates in discussing the historical transition of the bildungsroman, the new type of narrative "falls into two opposite types, that of abstract idealism, in which the hero is active and confronts the world, on the one hand, and that of disillusion and reflection, on the other, in which the protagonist withdraws into himself in the conviction that any attempt to assert oneself will result in defeat and humiliation."[12] Eddie Rose oscillates between confrontation and disillusionment, idealism and withdrawal. His relationship with Mike represents his assertion of control over his life as he plots Mike's escape from jail and their journey to Seattle. But the time Eddie spends at his grandmother's gravesite is also a sign of withdrawal. Alone, he hides cans of food in the brush beside the grave's tombstone in preparation for his journey with Mike, and he begins speaking to her: "Grandma? Watch these for me, please? I'll be back for them. Thank you for doing this for me. I hope at last you can hear me. I wish you were here. I know you can help me" (54).

But when Eddie returns at the end of act 1, the cans have been stolen, leaving him without food for his trip. It can be suggested that Eddie's grandmother did not want him to leave the "rez"; the theft might be a

spiritual signal of the grandmother's intentions. The end of the act epitomizes Eddie's humiliation and disillusionment.

> *The graveyard. Eddie enters. He goes to the headstone and sits. He takes*
> *out a small plastic bag with pot in it [given to him by Mike]. He takes out*
> *some papers that are with the weed, rolls himself a number, takes out some*
> *matches and lights up. He kicks back and takes a big toke. He coughs a*
> *little.*
>
> You weren't shitting there, Mike. It is good. Thank you, Grandson.
> Hey, Grandma, you know what that stink guy said . . . (*He faces the head-*
> *stone, and realizes something has changed. The paper sack he had left is*
> *gone. The wrappers he used to cover his canned goods are on the ground.*
> *He looks around*). Oh shit. How . . . who . . . (*He puts out the joint and*
> *places it back in the bag*). Grandma. I thought you were going to watch
> this stuff for me. I asked you. You probably didn't hear me, like everyone
> else. (*He hears a dog barking. He stands and picks up a rock and throws it*
> *at the dog*). Damn stink dog. (72)

Eddie's despair is made evident by two facts: his speaking into a void and his
use of the term "stink dog." The first is obvious; Eddie is isolated, his voice
echoes into nothingness. Second, the word "stink" pervades the play; characters use it to describe objects, animals, and people. It reflects cynicism as
well as a familiar scent. At the halfway point in the story, Eddie's internal
despair is rendered theatrically by the image of a saddened and confused
sixteen-year-old sitting onstage by himself. It is a poignant moment, made
more so by the silence, which is broken only by a lone dog barking in the
distance.

In the next act, Eddie encounters more than abstract idealism; he comes
in direct contact with his faith in Native traditions. Thelma represents such
traditions; her character signifies a past connected to rituals and action
defining a Native way of life. She finds Eddie at the gravesite. He expresses
his feelings of loneliness and alienation to her: "I come here to talk with
Grandma. Some of my friends are here. I come to talk with them. I tell
them, too, but they don't hear me. I'm all alone, Aunty Thelma. I have no
one. Sometimes, certain days, I wish I was with them. I just want to be like
them" (74). Thelma advises Eddie. She insists that he find his sister and
take her away from Eddie's mother and Lenny. She offers something more:

a small, but powerful, Native ritual. She takes Eddie to the grave, places sage in a bowl, and prays.

> (*She lights the sage with a match. The flames go out. Thelma fans the smoke.*)

THELMA: Here. I want you here. (*Points to a place near the bowl.*) Now, wash yourself in the smoke.

EDDIE: What?

THELMA: Wash up. (75)

The act of washing can appear clichéd when read. But in performance, the enactment is essential to the drama, as it demonstrates the significant physical impact of prayer. Steeling himself with new-found strength, Eddie leaves Thelma at the graveyard and tries to wrest his sister away from his mother. However, his effort comes late. Before Eddie has a chance to save Theia, Katherine attempts to throw Lenny out of the house. In the ensuing fight, Lenny seeks revenge for Katherine's rejection. He ends the scene by going into the bedroom offstage and assaulting Theia.

In the play's final scene, Eddie comes to take Theia away from the home. Theia has been hospitalized as a result of the assault. Eddie tries to persuade his mother to sign the release papers.

KATHERINE: What . . . what are these? (*She slowly reaches up and takes the papers.*)

EDDIE: That first one there . . . That's a complaint against Lenny. They have him and will hold him, but you have to sign so they can get him to court. You have to sign there, on the—

KATHERINE: Papers. Those dumb son of a bitches. They think these mean something. This is going to change anything. Oh God. (*She looks up at Eddie*). Why . . . why the hell did they give me all these damn papers? (*She waves them like a fan*). See. Eddie. See. You see. This is what I go through when I try to get help for us. They give me all these damn papers. What good are they? (93)

There is merit to Katherine's skepticism. The use of "papers" in the play is symbolic, representing the legacy of broken agreements, false treaties, and meaningless signatory documents that are all-too-familiar to

Native Americans. Based on the historical record, "papers" are empty signifiers.

Eddie, however, must overcome the force of Katherine's argument if he is to take responsibility for his sister's well-being. In his book *Phantom Formations: Aesthetic Ideology and the Bildungsroman*, Marc Redfield contends that the genre requires an "exemplary" figure that shoulders responsibility.[13] By choosing to remain on the reservation, forgoing his youthful idealism, and by accepting social responsibility, Eddie indeed seems to have embraced this role. When his mother reminds him of all that she has done for him, he replies:

> I thought you would change. And you didn't. You may never change . . . may never change (*Looks at her but she turns away. He waits, and then she looks at him*). I feel sorry for Lenny, and for everybody who was in this house, but I don't feel it. So I think it. That's what I do. And I would sit here and look, and then nothing changed. Nothing moved. Just us. And soon we were moving around and around, always on the same path, never really going anywhere. (95)

This speech marks a realization for Eddie that life must change, or he and Theia will be carried along in the same cycle of violent destruction as his mother.

It is worth comparing Eddie's words with those of Black Elk, who speaks of a revelation, or an awakening, in the face of despair:

> And as I looked . . . and wept, a strange light leaped upward from the ground close by—a light of many colors, sparkling, with rays that touched the heavens. Then it was gone, and in the place from whence it sprang an herb was growing and I saw the leaves it had. And as I was looking at the herb so that I might not forget it, there was a voice that woke me, and it said: "Make haste! Your people need you!" . . . Then the daybreak star came slowly, very beautiful and still; and all around it there were clouds of baby faces smiling at me, the faces of the people not yet born.[14]

While Eddie avoids Black Elk's romantic imagery, he does express the necessity of change. In the face of loss and destruction of Native ways, Eddie, like Black Elk, comes to terms with the revelation of a moral imperative. Katherine, too, comes to terms with herself, in a small way, at the end. She finally relents and signs the papers. Eddie offers his mother the locks of his

Aunt Thelma's braided hair, signifying a moment of great change. Eddie says:

> Mom. Mom. Here. (*Holds the braids out*). These were Aunty Thelma's. (*He takes a book of matches.*) I'm going to burn mine. I want you to have the other and please burn it, Mom. (*Eddie hands her a braid.*) And later . . . I'm going to pray for you . . . and Theia. Aunty Thelma says she knows some people who can help Theia. They'll help you, too, if you want them to. I don't want any more bad things happening to you, her or me. (*Pause*) At least try and heal one of our cuts. (96)

As the curtain comes down, Eddie *"reaches out and helps [Katherine] steady her hand"* while she burns the braid (97).

In his book *The Apprenticeship Novel*, Randolph P. Shaffner lists over three dozen characteristics of the bildungsroman. Five are worth quoting, since they also relate to Yellow Robe's protagonist in *The Independence of Eddie Rose*: the idea that living is an art of growth and education; the belief that a young person can adapt in the art of life; the notion of choice; the prerequisite of potential for mastering one's destiny; and the development of an affirmative attitude toward life as a whole.[15] Correspondingly, Eddie Rose's life becomes a symbol for coping with the world. He also confronts the world and adapts to his environment throughout the play. He realizes, in the end, that making choices is a necessary part of coming-of-age. At the conclusion, he emerges as a mature adult. (In a production I directed, Eddie wore his baseball cap backward until the last moment, echoing the symbolism in *The Catcher in the Rye*.)[16] Eddie adopts an optimistic, yet realistic, attitude toward life as a whole. His faith in himself is not without doubt, nor is he innocent of the fact that life ahead poses difficulties. Yet, as the play demonstrates, he has taken the first steps toward self-realization and responsibility. Yellow Robe's Eddie Rose is a paradigmatic bildungsdrama protagonist, effectively couched in a Native American milieu.

CHAPTER 11

Feathers, Flutes, and Drums

Images of the Indigenous Americans in Chicano Drama

JORGE HUERTA

ESTELA PORTILLO TRAMBLEY'S *Day of the Swallows*, first published in 1972, and Luis Valdez's *Mummified Deer*, first produced in the year 2000 and published in 2005, are two plays that frame the evolution of a Chicano dramaturgy that shows a fascination with and respect for the Chicanos' Indigenous roots. Further, these two plays affirm the Chicano as Native American. Indeed, the Indio (Native American) has been an almost constant presence in the plays of many of the Chicana and Chicano playwrights who have followed in Valdez's and Portillo Trambley's pioneering footsteps. Best known as the founder of the Teatro Campesino (the Farm Workers' Theater) in 1965, Valdez has also been called the "Father of Chicano Theater." If Valdez is the "Father," Portillo Trambley is certainly the "Mother of Chicana playwrights." As well as being Portillo Trambley's first play, *Day of the Swallows* is, significantly, also the first play by a Chicana to be published. I credit these two individuals with breaking the ground for an entire generation of theater artists who are writing plays about the Chicana/o experience today. In this essay I hope to show the distinctions and similarities between Valdez's and Portillo Trambley's visions of the Chicana/o's Indigenous roots.

Although not all Chicana/o playwrights employ Indigenous symbols or themes, many do. As descendants of a Mexico that extended through much of the western United States (including Texas and California), the Chicanos often write about themselves as "foreigners in their own land," a people with a fractured, postmodern identity that is more Mexican than Anglo and more Indio than Spanish. In fact, Mexico is always seen as a mestizo (mixed) nation—Indio rather than Spanish—in the Chicana/o's visions of herself/himself. Sometimes Indigenous characters physically appear, but at other times the Indio is imagined through the use of Indigenous music, flutes and drums that provide a background or undercurrent to the action of the play.

In some instances the Indio is offstage, as in Cherríe Moraga's *Giving Up the Ghost* (1982), in which the male Indio character figures prominently in the narrative although we never see him.[1] In Edit Villareal's contemporary adaptation of *Romeo and Juliet*, retitled *The Language of Flowers* (1991), the action takes place on the Mexican Day of the Dead, an Indigenous custom that is practiced to this day.[2] Likewise, Octavio Solís's *Man of the Flesh* (1988), an adaptation of the Don Juan plays, takes place on the Day of the Dead and again invokes Indigenous mythologies.[3] An example of a play that takes place in both the present and the colonial past is Josefina Lopez's *Unconquered Spirits* (1997). In this play Lopez compares a contemporary Chicana's struggles with those of an Indian woman during the conquest.[4] These are but a few examples of plays that remind the audience of the Chicanos' Indigenous heritage.

In Estela Portillo Trambley's *Day of the Swallows* the Indio appears as the "noble savage," a masculine figure that she contrasts with the superfeminine central character whose connection with her Indigenous roots is through images that only she can see and feel. In Valdez's *Mummified Deer*, the Indio appears as an eighty-four-year-old Yaqui woman and as various Yaqui characters, in a separate reality that only she and the audience see. In this paper I investigate these two plays as distinct, yet similar, representations of the Indio in Chicano drama. Portillo Trambley's play offers a female vision of Indio nobility set in a nineteenth-century realm, while Valdez's play provides a male, twenty-first-century image of the Indio as metaphor for the Chicana/o's erased history in the United States. Together, the plays demonstrate both a thematic and an aesthetic evolution from poetic realism to poetic fantasy.

Valdez and Portillo Trambley are U.S.-born Chicanos of the same generation. She was born in El Paso, Texas, in 1936, and he was born in Delano, California, in 1940. The Southwestern desert is always present in Portillo Trambley's writings, while Valdez's plays either reflect the fecundity of California's Central Valley or take place in an urban setting. Both playwrights share the belief that Native Americans reflect a oneness with and an understanding of the earth, *La Tierra, Nuestra Madre*.

Portillo Trambley, who passed away in 1998, is regarded by most

Chicana/o critics and scholars as the woman who inspired and opened the doors for all the Chicana writers who followed her. Best known as a novelist and short-story writer, Portillo Trambley left us some very important statements about the Chicano and, especially, the Chicana condition. She often wrote Native American characters into her scenarios that depicted both ancient and contemporary images. Concurrently, Luis Valdez has written about the Indigenous cultures of America since the late 1960s. His primary fascination was with pre-Columbian civilization, and he included Aztec and Maya figures in his early *mitos* (mythical plays).

In 1981 Portillo Trambley said to an interviewer, "I hope . . . [Chicanos] still relate to seasons and to plants and to colors and to the wind, and to the Indian in them, or the element that is closest to the earth."[5] Several years earlier, Valdez had written a poem, "Pensamiento Serpentino" ("Serpentine Thought"), evoking the Maya as the Chicanos' spiritual, cultural, scientific, and political ancestors. He wrote: "El Indio BAILA [the Indian dances] / He DANCES his way to truth / In a way INTELLECTUALS will / Never understand."[6] Valdez is not being anti-intellectual, but he is stating unequivocally that one cannot rationalize miracles. For both of these playwrights, the world of the Indio is full of miracles: the miracle of life and the mystery of death permeate these two plays.

Day of the Swallows is written in a style that I would describe as poetic realism, due to the often heightened language and the romantic setting. The playwright follows an Aristotelian model in which all of the action takes place in one setting, in the course of a day. However, despite this realistic mode of representation, the play is grounded in the playwright's belief in nature gods. Although the characters in the play are Roman Catholics, the playwright combines Christian ritual with Indigenous myth; the power of unseen spirits permeates the world of the central character, Doña Josefa.

The playwright describes Doña Josefa as "a tall, regal woman about thirty-five. Her bones are Indian's; her coloring is Aryan."[7] Thus, Doña Josefa is a mestiza, a woman in touch with both her Indigenous and her Spanish cultural and spiritual roots. Although everyone perceives her as devoutly Roman Catholic, Doña Josefa has other forces that speak to her: her "magicians," or magical powers that we do not see. The tension between her Christian devotion and her magicians symbolizes a life force that only Josefa can reconcile. In the metaphorical struggle between the old gods and the newer Christian faith, the Indigenous gods win, immortalizing Josefa in an animistic belief in an afterlife.

Day of the Swallows takes place in Doña Josefa's nineteenth-century parlor, a refuge from the harsh world of men. The action of the play begins the morning before the Day of San Lorenzo, when the virgins of the town wash their hair in the lake "and bathe in promise of a future husband," a ritual tradition that will honor Josefa this year (207). But Josefa will never participate in the ritual, for her destiny has been sealed long before this day. From the moment the play begins we know that something is terribly wrong in Josefa's household. Alysea, a young woman who has lived with Josefa since being rescued from a bordello, is obviously very upset and nervous as she begins her daily chores. But Josefa maintains her composure as other characters come into their refuge. Though a pillar of the community, she is hiding some dark secret, and as the action unfolds we discover that the previous night Josefa had cut out the tongue of David, the boy who lives with them, because he witnessed her and Alysea in an act of passion. The boy represents the outside world of "*¿qué dirá la gente?*—what will people say?"—and Josefa's immediate response to the horror on the boy's face is to cut out his tongue while the terrified and confused Alysea holds him down.

After confessing to the parish priest, her only male friend, Josefa decides that she has no other recourse but to commit suicide. In the final climactic scene of the play, Josefa, defeated in this world but not in the realm of her magicians, the light and the lake, dons her white gown and becomes one with these powers by drowning herself. The mental picture is powerful and characteristic of the playwright's Indigenous imagery as she describes the return of Josefa's spirit following her suicide: "the almost unearthly light streaming through the windows gives the essence of a presence in the room" (245). In the words of Louise Detwiler, who comments on the moment as expressing Indigenous traditional belief, "Josefa has returned," as she had predicted she would.[8]

Detwiler carefully articulates the basis for Portillo Trambley's vision. She believes that by "tapping into the collective consciousness of her Indigenous heritage in the midst of the prevailing patriarchal consciousness of the Roman Catholic legacy . . . ," Josefa represents "a nexus between animism and Roman Catholicism."[9] Further, Detwiler feels that "Joséfa identifies with an animistic symbol system while she rejects the patriarchal symbols of Roman Catholicism."[10] In other words, the playwright has created a world in which Indigenous, female powers prevail. Detwiler sees Josefa's belief in the "Earth as Mother" as a direct contrast to the Judeo-Christian concept of God the Father. In her words: "Through the worship of fertility goddesses, that is, life-giving symbols, Joséfa creates a universe that offers her those things that the life-taking patriarchal cosmology surrounding her within the community lacks: sexual passion, life, freedom, sisterhood and rebirth."[11]

Nature is a constant presence in this play. The playwright's upbringing in the desert and her fascination with Indigenous concepts can be read in Portillo Trambley's stage directions as she describes the desert that we cannot see onstage. She writes: "The tierra [land] of Lago de San Lorenzo is within memory of mountain sweet pine. The maguey thickens with the ferocity of chaotic existence. Here the desert yawns. Here it drinks the sun in madness."[12]

This play is arranged in a series of scenes between Josefa and other characters, each one contributing her/his own tone to the rising tension. With the exception of the priest, the male characters represent confrontations. But Josefa's real nemesis is the only full-blooded Native American in the play, Eduardo, who tells Alysea that he is taking her away to "a wilderness . . . mountain, pines. My Squaw . . . living and loving in the open" (216). Eduardo does not know about the women's relationship or the truth about David's injury, but he is in love with Alysea and knows that he has to live on the land with her to be truly happy.

Eduardo, the Indigenous man, provides a link between Josefa and La Tierra, inspiring the most poetic dialogue in the play. In the conversation between Eduardo and Josefa, the playwright equates the native people with the land and the poetry that Mother Nature can inspire. But Eduardo is also a man, and Josefa flatly declares that she is not interested in the love of a man: "I did not want the callous Indian youth . . . with hot breath and awkward hands . . . a taking without feeling . . . no, not that! I wanted so much more . . ." (222). Yet there is also a mystical/sexual tension and connection between Josefa and Eduardo. It is in her first and only meeting with him that Josefa describes her magicians:

> There by the lake, I felt the light finding its way among the pines . . . to me . . . It took me . . . then . . . perhaps it was my imagination . . . it said

to me: 'We are one . . . make your beauty . . . make your truth.' Deep, I felt a burning spiral . . . it roared in my ears . . . my heart . . . [Pause] It was too much to bear . . . so I ran and ran until I fell, opened my eyes, and found myself calmly looking up at the stars . . . sisters of my love! The moon had followed me; it lay a lake around me, on the grass . . . [ellipses are the playwright's]. (222)

Thus, although the Indian male may have been a threat to Josefa's sense of sexual beauty, he also represents her Indigenous roots. Eduardo symbolizes the best and the worst of humanity in Josefa's world, for he is Nature personified as Man. And yet Josefa tells Eduardo: "You are easy to fall in love with," for he is the rebel Indian she would like to be (200). Eduardo has had his way with the wife of the hacienda owner and will now take Alysea away from the barrio and into a natural surrounding, where she will be ostensibly free of the colonizing Spaniards' control. Eduardo's "temple" is the forest, in the same way that Josefa believes in nature gods. Both Josefa and Eduardo worship in the same temple, although their gods may be distinct.

Luis Valdez, who has had the longest career and who has generated more critical interest than any other living Chicana/o playwright or director, is the focus of the second part of this chapter. Best known in theater circles for his play *Zoot Suit*, Valdez's 1987 film *La Bamba* diverted the playwright's focus to the film industry for several years. But the theater is in Valdez's blood, and fourteen years after his last play, *I Don't Have to Show You No Stinking Badges!*, first produced in 1986,[13] he wrote and directed *Mummified Deer*.

Valdez first began to think about what would become *Mummified Deer* in 1984, when he read a newspaper article about the discovery of a sixty–year-old fetus in the womb of an eighty-four-year-old woman. Over the years, as he continued to think about that image, he determined that he would write a play centered on the character of an old Yaqui woman who had been carrying a fetus in her womb for sixty years. As he prepared to open the play in San Diego, California, in the year 2000, he told an interviewer: "I immediately saw her in a hospital bed, surrounded by her family."[14] He told me that he based the central character on his own Yaqui grandmother, though, of course, she had not carried a mummified fetus in her womb.[15] For Valdez, the mummified fetus became a metaphor for the Chicanos' Indio heritage, seen through the lens of his own Yaqui background.

Like Portillo Trambley, Valdez understands that the desert is full of life; one only has to look for it. After a reading of the play, he told a group, "The non-Indio looks at the desert and sees nothing; the Indio looks at the desert and sees life everywhere."[16] Valdez's description of the setting for this play is reminiscent of the imagery in Portillo Trambley's poetic narrative:

> Metaphorically, the sterility of the hospital must belie a profound fecundity, like the great Sonoran desert. The walls must speak across time and space with ancient petroglyphs, shadows, transparencies, lightning and thunder; at other times, with the miasma of veins and muscles vibrating with every heartbeat. This is a womb of birth and death, full of the memories, fears and dreams of generations.[17]

While the main action of the play is framed by a narrative to the audience that takes place in the present, or 1999, Valdez situates his play in the year 1969. This was the beginning of the Chicano movement, a time when Chicanas and Chicanos were questioning the power structure and demanding better conditions in the schools, in the workplace, on the streets, and in the courts. This was also an era of deepening Chicano/a interest in their Indio roots. Chicanos knew that they owed their culture to Mexico, but beyond that mestizo nation they were more interested in what the Native Americans on both sides of the manmade national border had to say to them.

The almost surreal image of a woman carrying a fetus for sixty years kept haunting Valdez as he searched for a way to express the Chicano's history through theater and ritual. And as he began to picture the eighty-four-year-old Yaqui woman on her hospital bed, he also imagined a Yaqui deer dancer as her alter ego, a vibrant reminder of her own past and that of her people. The deer dancer thus becomes an integral part of Valdez's play, a symbol of the mummified fetus in the old woman's womb.

The old Yaqui woman, named Mama Chu by her children, slips in and out of consciousness as her family members debate what to do after having been told of the fetus in her womb. Mama Chu's granddaughter, Armida, is a graduate student in cultural anthropology at Berkeley, and thus she crosses into the world of academia in her search for her Native

American roots. Armida frames the action, introducing the main character and giving the last words about her, as in a classroom, when the play ends. During her journey, Armida learns that scholars cannot tell her who she really is. Mama Chu raised Armida because her mother had committed suicide and, as Armida questions her aunt and uncle about the past, the truth of the family's history is slowly revealed.

The play goes back and forth in time and place, with Mama Chu's hospital bed as the central image. The action moves fluidly through time, a time that is measured not in minutes or hours, but in heartbeats. Through the flashbacks to Mama Chu's past, we are introduced to the history of her family and learn of her strength in the face of relocation and enslavement by the Diaz government just prior to the Mexican Revolution. Mama Chu's visions are dreams or nightmares that she experiences while under sedation, and Valdez ingeniously contrasts her surreal visions with the real characters, her family members discussing her condition and history. The audience also learns a great deal about the fate of the Yaqui, a people who survive to this day and who celebrate a syncretic form of Christianity and native beliefs often symbolized in the Deer Dance.

The deer dancer appears in Mama Chu's visions, unseen by the other characters. She calls the deer dancer Cajeme, the name of a legendary Yaqui rebel who fought against the Mexican government in the nineteenth century. Cajeme lingers in Mama Chu's mind, either as one of her children or as representative of her people in general. At one point she sees him as vulgar—an erotic, lustful Indio—at other times he becomes her child. He is a symbol of her Yaqui past, a past that she has attempted to repress, as is illustrated by the fetus in her womb. Cajeme represents her inner thoughts, her fears, her Yaqui blood and being—and, for me, Mama Chu represents all mestizos in their internal colonization and cultural confusion.

The play was first produced at the San Diego Repertory Theatre in early April 2000, directed by Valdez and starring Alma Martínez as Mama Chu. Later that year, the playwright revised the play and directed it in the Teatro Campesino's playhouse in San Juan Bautista, California. Ms. Martínez again played Mama Chu and corresponded with me about the play and her character. As the central character, who is constantly onstage, perhaps Ms. Martínez knows the play, and certainly her character, better than anybody else. When I asked her what she thought Cajeme represented, she answered me thus: ". . . Cajeme . . . is both my beloved son and the lasting memory of my dead husband. . . . His death is my physical death and, his life, is the life of the memory of the Yaqui's way of life as it was." She continued: "The characters have now become divided into two camps, those that 'want [Cajeme's] flesh and those that want his spirit,' colonizers and revolutionaries. He is, to Mama Chu, above all a son, a man, a symbol of freedom, purity and pre-conquest liberation. As long as he is in my womb he is all of that which is why I fight, to my death, to try to preserve his incubation/mummification."[18]

In a monologue delivered by Mama Chu toward the end of the play, we discover that she was present on the day in which the Díaz government attacked the Yaqui people, massacring men, women, and children without mercy. She was carrying her dead husband's child and escaped death only to be raped, sold into slavery, and then shipped to Yucatán. After this horrific experience, she prayed to God not to let her child be born a slave or, worse, to be killed and fed to the dogs (58–59). Her wish is granted, and so her "children" realize that they are not her real descendants, since she could not have borne them with the mummified fetus in her womb. The Big Question thus becomes: "What will become of the family?" The final scene takes place in the present. Mama Chu, who is now dying at the "ripe old Yaqui age of 114," is joined by both her family and her ghosts. The family does not dissolve but, hopefully, learns and grows from its past.

The revised version of *Mummified Deer* was more accessible than the original production, which was more complex because it featured Yaqui ceremonial dancers—Pascolas, Fariseos, and Chapayekas—representative of a culture and of rituals not recognizable outside of Yaqui territory. Due to its representation in various folkloric dance companies, the Deer Dance is perhaps best known among the uninitiate, but beyond visual recognition most audience members do not know what, exactly, the deer dancer represents. Thus, Valdez complicated his vision by adding both the deer dancer, originally called Yaqui, and the other ceremonial dancers.

Perhaps Valdez realized that he was confusing his audience, since the ceremonial dancers are no longer present in the second, published version of the play. The playwright also changed the name of the deer dancer from Yaqui to Cajeme, although few in the audience would recognize the name of this legendary rebel. While Cajeme appears to Mama Chu as a symbol of her Yaqui heritage, the mestizos are represented by the raggle-taggle circus troupe that her daughter ran away with. As Mama Chu relives her past, we see grotesqueries of the circus contrasted with the traditional quality of the deer dancer. Valdez uses this juxtaposition to confront both his Indio past as well as his roots in Western European popular entertainment like the Mexican circus and the early *carpas*, or tent shows.

Ultimately, Portillo Trambley's vision of the Indio is a generalized trope of noble savage and nature gods without specific references to a particular tribe or time period. Indeed, one can read *Day of the Swallows* as a nineteenth-century period piece set somewhere in the Southwestern desert. Valdez's representation is much more specific in both time and place, managing to weave its way through various historic periods without confusion. Also, the construction of the two plays is very distinct: the first is a realistic portrayal, and the second a surreal vision of the Chicano's distorted postmodern, internally colonized condition. The dysfunctional family in Valdez's play is a microcosm of the relationship between the Yaqui, mestizo, and Chicano; and Armida, the Chicana, is representative of Valdez's own generation of activists who are in search of their past.

In *Day of the Swallows*, Doña Josefa describes her visions and passions to other characters, while in *Mummified Deer* the audience sees the visions in Mama Chu's mind, because Valdez wants to demonstrate the contrasts between the Yaqui and mestizo cultures. Thus, the Mexican circus clown, named Cosme Bravo, appears as a counterpoint to Lucas Flores, Cajeme's historical adversary. Mama Chu recognizes Cosme as the man who raped her and sent her into slavery, but nobody will believe her as he entices her "daughter" to join the circus. Cosme represents the *torocoyori*, whom Mama Chu describes as: "a turn-coat Yaqui, who was slaughtering his own people like a rabid dog at the service of his Yori [Mexican] masters" (59). Every culture has its *torocoyori*, the playwright suggests, and the cultural violence rendered by them has often been dramatized by Chicana and Chicano playwrights.

Mama Chu represents the past, while Armida, now a middle-aged Dr. Flores, represents the future. In the final moments of the play, Armida asks:

Dear God . . . Is it so outrageous to believe that the mummified fetus like an ancient kernel of millennial corn soaked with the waters of divine mercy and luck might yet spring to life, that something sacred and alive might come from all that suffering . . . Is it a pipe dream to believe that the mummy's tomb is no less than the womb of time, and that our entire family history is but the struggle to find our birth passage to a new world . . . (61, ellipses the playwright's).

When Mama Chu finally does die, the playwright describes the action thus: "Cajeme dances to a climax at the foot of the bed. With his deer head up in triumph, he collapses, lifeless. Black[out]" (62). End of play. Mama Chu has died and taken Cajeme with her. Or does Cajeme die, taking Mama Chu with him? Most importantly, Cajeme dies dancing, with his head held high "in triumph," signifying both the importance of traditional values and the potential for social change. As Lucas Flores, Cajeme's adversary, tells Mama Chu early in the play, "If death is real, anything is possible" (19). It is also important to note that in the poem "Pensamiento Serpentino," quoted earlier, Valdez states three times that we do not die (179–84). Both Mama Chu and Cajeme have endured beyond expectation and will now pass to the next stage of the cosmic Indio vision, as will Doña Josefa. Each has served their purpose, and the revolution will continue.

The final moments of both plays—the image of the triumphant deer dancer and the light streaming into Doña Josefa's parlor—recall Valdez's declaration quoted earlier in this chapter: "El Indio BAILA. / He DANCES his way to truth / in a way INTELLECTUALS will / Never understand."

Both Estela Portillo Trambley and Luis Valdez understand the dance; hopefully, we can, too.

CHAPTER 12

Metamora's Revenge

Bruce McConachie

GIVEN THE AMOUNT OF ENERGY devoted over the last twenty years to interpreting and explaining John Augustus Stone's play *Metamora, or The Last of the Wampanoags* (1829), the historian might be excused for believing that the "revenge" I note in my title refers to irresolvable conundrums left to future scholars by the playwright and Edwin Forrest, the star who commissioned the work. Looking to link Forrest's immensely popular performances of this play to the Jacksonian policy of Indian removal in the 1830s, which killed thousands of members of eastern tribes, historians Donald Grose and Mark Mallet analyzed the play to accuse Forrest of pursuing a racist agenda for personal political gain.[1] Others, notably Jeffrey Mason, Sally Jones, Jill Lepore, and Theresa Strouth Gaul, denied overt racist intent but concluded that Forrest's and Stone's *Metamora* indirectly legitimated racism and Indian removal by portraying a noble-but-doomed savage whose death was rendered inevitable by the march of civilization.[2] Several of these historians broadened their analysis to include Forrest's acting style but continued to make their case primarily on an analysis of the melodrama. Challenging both of these interpretations was a 1999 article by Scott Martin, who stated that the play and Forrest's interpretation of the title role "comprise a rich fabric of interwoven and interacting symbols" open to many readings.[3] Toward the beginning of this flurry of scholarly activity was my own take on Forrest and his star vehicle in 1992, which I developed in *Melodramatic Formations: American Theatre and Society, 1820–1870.*[4] Fifteen years ago, I had nothing specific to say about possible relations among the play, the policy of Indian removal, and white racism but did note the importance of situating the drama's reception in the context of Forrest's charismatic star power and in several strands of Jacksonian ideology.

Settling the possible meanings of *Metamora* for its antebellum audiences (and, implicitly, for American history) is important, because the melodrama had an enormous impact on the "Indian" plays and their stage Indians that populated the American theater from 1830 through the 1870s.[5] During this period, theatrical producers occasionally put Native Americans on the stage as curiosities, but Native Americans neither wrote nor performed in any of the plays that native Americans of European descent produced and enjoyed at their theaters. Most of the plays preceding *Metamora* that featured Native American characters depicted them in European terms as children of nature; a few, however, also showed them as warriors in Indian–white conflicts. After *Metamora*, heroic and occasionally vengeful Indians filled the stage, as playwrights and stars attempted to model their work on the huge success that Forrest was enjoying with his Indian chief. These melodramas included *Carabasset* (1830), *Oralloossa* (1832), *Tecumseh* (1836), *Pontiac* (1836), *Nick of the Woods* (1838), and *Putnam* (1844). The rage for Indian plays died down in the 1840s but revived again after 1865, when yellow journalism and dime novels pumped new conflicts on the frontier for melodramatic thrills. Although these later Indian plays usually attempted more realism and less romantic rhetoric than their predecessors, several also featured a heroic chief. *Metamora*, in other words, cast a long shadow; its popularity has relevance not only for understanding Forrest's huge success in the role but also for understanding the place of the stage Indian in popular American culture.

Given this brief overview of U.S. Indian plays in the nineteenth century, it may seem that those scholars who claim that Forrest's 1829 vehicle helped to incite racism against Native Americans in the antebellum era are correct. Perhaps the scholarship linking *Metamora* to Indian removal is accurate. From my perspective, however, Scott Martin's debunking of the connection between the play and the Jacksonian policy is more persuasive. As he points out, audiences came to the theater primarily to see and hear Forrest, regardless of the play he was performing that night. On the question of motives, although Forrest did consider running for office as a Jacksonian Democrat in the 1830s, the star had no political ambitions when he picked *Metamora* as his first-prize play in 1829. Further, the drama generally maintains the Indian chief's nobility, despite his occasional lapses into savagery, to the end of the play. Besides, as Martin points out, no star would have chosen a vehicle that made him look like a villainous savage to his fans. Nor does Metamora die so that white civilization can advance. Opposing Forrest's chief and his tribe are hypocritical Puritans and rapacious English aristocrats; on several occasions, Stone's script makes Metamora more decent and humane than the villains at war with him. Finally, Martin states that it was unlikely that urban audiences went to the theater expecting to connect *Metamora* with a divisive political policy such as Indian removal. Martin draws on my own and David Grimsted's scholarship to note that antebellum theater managers and stars rarely presented plays with overt political agendas; such shows risked polarizing their audiences. Martin concludes that audiences may have attributed some racist characteristics to Metamora and his tribe, but their reception had little to do with the politics of Indian removal.

In revisiting *Metamora*, I'd like to build on Martin's conclusions but examine a more specific context for Forrest's performances than his article undertakes. In particular, I will situate the reception of Forrest and his play by the star's core audience in New York City between 1840 and 1855—an audience predominantly composed of native-born, male workers. There are several reasons for this choice. First, the attempt to link the cultural-political meanings of *Metamora* to the policies of Indian removal ignores the long-term popularity of the play, which Forrest continued to perform into the 1860s. If audience interest in Indian removal played some role in spectator response in the 1830s, did this interest continue when removal was no longer in the headlines? If not, the historian must ask why the star retained this melodrama in his repertoire and why audiences continued to applaud him in the title role. Forrest's charismatic power in *Metamora* suggests that the policy of Indian removal was far removed from audience involvement in the 1840s and '50s.

Second, spectators in playhouses—not producers, playwrights, or even stars—were the final arbiters of cultural meaning in the nineteenth-century popular theater. Unlike most other scholars in the *Metamora* wars, Martin understands this, but he stops short of putting the star vehicle within a specific time frame and before the historical spectators who occupied the box, pit, and galleries of certain theaters. Forrest toured widely and performed before many kinds of audiences, but there is little doubt that his core audience for performances in urban centers after 1840 was American-born workers. Examining performances in New York theaters between 1840 and 1855 allows the historian to draw on a wealth of evidence that relates the actor to his fans. Forrest's involvement in the Astor Place Riot of 1849 and his record-breaking string of performances following his scandalous divorce trial in 1852 provide a necessary context for understanding his fans' likely interpretation of *Metamora*.

Finally, most scholars have assumed that performances of *Metamora* revealed much about the national identity of the United States in the antebellum era, primarily through the play's construction of a racial Other. An analysis of Stone's text does indeed betray the racialization of Native Americans in this play, as it does in the hundred or so other dramas featuring stage Indians during the period. Given Forrest's core audience for productions of the drama, however, it is difficult to generalize about national racial identity on the basis of *Metamora*'s popularity. The play did not appeal to a broadly representative audience after 1840. Many Americans did not attend the theater, and others who did, including the social elite and those who aspired to elite status, looked down their noses at Forrest in the 1840s and '50s. To be sure, most native-born workers understood themselves as white men and patriots, but they came to their brand of nationalism through an ideology that was not widely shared by citizens in the rest of the country.

The debate about *Metamora* and Indian removal must shift from literary analysis and general cultural values to star power and specific audience perceptions. Within this more relevant historical context, it is apparent that Forrest's core urban audience primarily applauded the national and class antagonisms that fueled the conflicts of Stone's drama. Although racial dynamics were not absent from Forrest's performance of the Indian chief, spectators probably made other meanings out of their enjoyment of *Metamora* between 1840 and 1855, meanings more immediately relevant to their urban, working-class lives.

When Forrest played in New York City in the 1840s through the mid-1850s, the star performed primarily at the Bowery and Broadway theaters, both known for their predominantly working-class attendance. Historian George C. D. Odell reports occasional appearances by Forrest at the Park and at the Chatham (later the National) theaters as well. Although a precise count is impossible, it is likely that Forrest played *Metamora* between sixty and eighty times among these playhouses between 1840 and 1855.[6] More than half of these performances probably occurred at the Broadway, the largest theater in New York for ten years after its construction in 1847.

According to one nineteenth-century theater historian, the Broadway Theatre

> would accommodate 4,500 persons, having seats for 4,000. There was an immense pit to which only men and boys were admitted. The price of admission [to the pit] was twenty-five cents and the seats were plain benches without backs, and on crowded nights the jam used to be terrific. The first and second galleries were called the dress and family circles. Three rows of benches were set apart in the latter for the accommodation of colored persons.[7]

Those "men and boys" on the benches at the Broadway cheered Forrest for sixty-nine performances in 1852, "an engagement unparalleled in the history of the stage," according to one astonished reporter.[8] No doubt many of Forrest's fans in 1852 had participated in the Astor Place Riot three years before, when Tammany Hall rallied loyal Democrats to vindicate their hero against the villainy of William Charles Macready, the English star whom Forrest supporters believed had libeled their hero.

This core group of Forrest fans in New York was predominantly male, native-born, working-class, and traditionalist in orientation. Beginning with Tom Hamblin at the Bowery Theatre in the 1830s, theatrical capitalists in New York were producing entertainment for specifically working-class spectators; by 1840, Gotham workers in search of fun could travel to the Bowery area around Chatham Square for the taverns, dance halls, brothels, and theaters that catered to their tastes and purses. Although Irish immigrants constituted the majority of residents in that neighborhood by 1855, most workers from other areas of the city could easily walk there, and did, for an evening of entertainment. Some Irish Americans probably enjoyed Forrest, but his primary audience seems to have been "American" rather than "Irish" workers—a distinction that carried significant weight in boxing matches, tavern life, and other areas of Bowery culture before the Civil War.

Among native-born workers, primarily the "traditionalists" applauded Forrest. Historians Paul Faler and Alan Dawley define three types of response among workers to the incursions of capitalism after 1820. Neither the "radicals" nor the "revivalists"—workers attracted to unions and churches, respectively—attended the theater in significant numbers.

Rather, it was the "traditionalists," the third and most numerous group of urban workers, who constituted the overwhelming number of workers who enjoyed Forrest on the stage. Most traditionalists in the 1840–55 period labored at preindustrial crafts, worked at home, out of doors, or in small shops, and continued the laboring habits of earlier days, which included frequent breaks for alcoholic refreshment. They sought their social life in taverns, street gangs, political organizations, volunteer fire companies, and other groups where a man proved his honor through stamina and muscle.

Bowery honor anchored the loyalty of its adherents in nation and class. Many native-born workers identified the class distinctions of the rich as a legacy of English oppression and mounted several riots in the antebellum era to protest what they saw as aristocratic pretension. Among these was the Astor Place Riot of 1849, which quickly devolved from a spat between Forrest and William Charles Macready, an English star, into class warfare. As one anonymous account reported, "Macready was a subordinate personage, and he was to be put down less on his own account than to spite his aristocratic supporters. The question became not only a national, but a social, one. It was the rich against the poor—the aristocracy against the people. Forrest's advocates looked upon it as a piece of retributive justice."[9]

Jeering at aristocratic English power, coupled with a desire to defend traditional male prerogatives, also spurred Forrest's fans to defend their hero after his wife successfully sued him for a divorce. From Forrest's point of view, his wife's reputation was more a matter of public honor than private trust. Fearing that some marital scandal involving his English-born wife might tarnish his name, he sued her for divorce. She countersued and won a substantial settlement against him. Stung by what he took as a public humiliation, Forrest mounted his record-breaking string of performances to seek vindication from his loyal supporters, in what he called "the people's court." They, as much as the star's stamina, sustained his sixty-nine-night run, effectively reassuring him that his honor remained intact among Bowery workers. In both episodes, Bowery honor—a mix of fraternal solidarity, muscular aggressiveness, and scorn for the emerging norms of Victorian respectability and domesticity—incited the response of Forrest's fans.[10] The major question, then, is How might Bowery honor have shaped the kinds of meanings and emotions that these same spectators enjoyed when they watched Forrest in *Metamora?*

The ending of Forrest's performances in the 1840–55 period brings this question into sharp focus. By act 5, scene 5, the English have defeated the Wampanoags and fatally wounded Forrest/Metamora, who delivers this final speech before falling to his death:

> My curses on you, white men! May the Great Spirit curse you when he speaks in his war voice from the clouds! Murderers! The last of the Wampanoags' curse be on you! May your graves and the graves of your children be in the path the red man shall trace! And may the wolf and the panther howl o'er your fleshless bones, fit banquet for the destroyers! Spirits of the grave, I come! But the curse of Metamora stays with the white man! I die! My wife! My Queen! My Nahmeokee![11]

The staging of this speech left little doubt about the "white men" that Forrest/Metamora was cursing. Stone's stage directions place the star–Indian chief upstage and elevated on a land bridge overlooking the entire cast of white people, which included some of the "good whites" the hero had helped during the course of the play. Facing the English settlers from his upstage position, Forrest/Metamora was also directing his curse out to the audience. But did the butchers, carpenters, and other "men and boys" in the pit believe that Metamora was cursing them as well? Was Forrest/Metamora the kind of villain you love to hate by this point in the play, a sort of Native American Richard III, whose every utterance incited counteridentifications? Or did traditionalist workers temporarily disassociate themselves from the term "white men" and identify Metamora's revenge, including its scourge of western expansion, as a righteous cause? This final speech left the audience no third alternative. I will argue that the development of the play and its implicit definition of racial difference, coupled with Forrest's stardom and Bowery honor, suggest that only one answer can be given to this necessary question. When Forrest cursed the "white men" on stage and vowed vengeance against western expansion, his core audience in New York roared its approval.

Forrest's initial entrance in act 1 ensured rapt attention and laudatory identification right from the start. No sooner does the English girl Oceana describe her rescue from a panther by Metamora and call the Indian chief "the grandest model of a mighty man," than the superhero bounds on stage, poses for a child-of-nature tableau on the landbridge, and runs off again (207). The entrance was an obvious claptrap, and spectators would have applauded heartily, as much for Forrest's muscular physique as for his charismatic reputation. For many traditionalist workers, the beefcake of their hero probably reminded them of similar strong men they had cheered before, during barroom brawls, fire companies' "musses," and boxing matches, a favorite pastime of traditionalist workers.

Following Metamora's reentrance, Stone gave Forrest ample opportunity to develop the verisimilitude of his role, at least within the parameters of the "white man's Indian." Easterners had seen Indians on parade, occasionally even in theaters, and most knew what to expect from a stage redskin by 1840. Forrest, who had briefly lived with a Choctaw tribe as a young man, developed gestures, vocal inflections, and modes of walking that the audience believed to be uniquely Native American. To Stone's "nativized" dialogue, Forrest added many "hahs" and "humphs" to increase the guttural sounds in his speech. Many critics congratulated Forrest on the realism of his impersonation. As historian Sally Jones notes, Forrest constructed Metamora "to instill a sense of the exotic and of 'otherness,' while at the same time retaining attributes with which the audience would identify."[12]

Forrest's Indian chief was certainly an exotic Other for his spectators, but did this characterization necessarily render his warrior racially inferior? Philosopher Kwame Anthony Appiah's distinction between racism and racialism is relevant here. Like racism, racialism roots difference in nature and insists that unchangeable attributes distinguish various human populations. Racialists, however, believe that the races of the world are not hierarchically ordered; some groups may be variously higher or lower than others over a range of categories, including courage, rationality, empathy, etc., depending on historical and environmental factors. Further, racialists do not propose or support a permanent racial order based on domination and subordination.[13] Rousseau, Diderot, and a few other philosophers of the Enlightenment believed in racialism, and their ideas continued to influence many westerners into the first half of the nineteenth century. Among them was playwright August von Kotzebue, whose *Pizarro in Peru* (adapted by Sheridan for the English stage) influenced Stone's work on *Metamora*. Like Kotzebue's Incan hero Rolla, Stone's Metamora stands above and between the decadent pleasures of the Europeans and the squabbling and savagery of his own tribe. The plots of both plays show striking similarities as well. Both involve a Native American victory against the European invaders early in the action, followed by eventual defeat and the hero's rescue of a helpless victim from the enemy camp. Both plays end in the death of the Native American hero, although Rolla, unlike Metamora, does not curse European expansion. Significantly, Kotzebue racialized both Spaniards and Incas in *Pizzaro in Peru*; both had fixed, unchangeable attributes rooted in their natures that led to various behaviors—some noble, some villainous—throughout the play.

Metamora, deploying a similar ideology of Enlightenment racialism, also characterizes both the English and the Indians as racially distinct. Like Kotzebue's Spaniards, the English are greedy, superstitious, rapacious, and perfidious. Racializing the English was a common practice in the United States during the nineteenth century. For most Americans, including Bowery workers, the English, also known as the Anglo-Saxons, joined the Irish, the Germans, the Jews, and other nationalities and ethnic groups as one of many white races. Stone departs from common American understanding, however, by segregating the English settlers in his play from any link to the founders of the nation. Nowhere in the script does Stone tie these Puritans and aristocrats to present-day Americans; even the "good whites" among the English are caught up in plots and accusations that bind them to the exhausted power struggles of the Old World. Arguably, Stone did cross the line separating racialism from racism in his depiction of the English. His Anglo-Saxons are apparently driven by their nature to enforce their oppressive social discriminations in the New World, where, according to Stone's script, the bounty of nature defies aristocratic hierarchy. All of this was red meat for Bowery traditionalists, who already held racialist or racist views of the English and came to Forrest's performances to watch their hero battle their traditional oppressors.

Following Kotzebue and Rousseau, Stone depicted his Indian chief as a natural man to puncture English pretensions to civilization. For most of the first two acts, Metamora is a lover of nature, a heroic father and husband, and a forbearing leader of his people. Then, after the English threaten to imprison him and steal his people's lands on trumped-up charges, Metamora stabs a traitor from his tribe and tells the astonished English that "the wrath of the wronged Indian shall fall upon you like a cataract" (214). In the next act, he avenges the English threat with a quick and relatively bloodless attack on their settlement. The rest of the play, too, shows the audience a Metamora who is as aggressive as he is noble. Although it is possible to read these actions through a racist lens as evidence of Indian savagery, it is unlikely that his working-class auditors did so. By this point in the action, Stone has made it clear that Metamora's turn to savagery is entirely motivated by English duplicity.

Further, although Forrest played an authentic Indian within the racialist understanding of his working-class audience, it is unlikely that any of them ever willingly suspended their disbelief so far as to forget the actor under the greasepaint. What performance theorist Bert States calls the "self-expressive mode" was endemic among the star actors of the nineteenth-century stage. In this mode, the actor, says States, "seems to be performing on his own behalf," saying, "in effect, 'See what I can do.'"[14] Forrest, in other words, mixed his representation of a real Indian with plenty of reminders to his fans that he had created the character and remained bigger than his chosen role of the evening. The repertory system of starring, of course, in which the luminary performed several roles during her or his two- to three-week stay at one theater, increased audience consciousness of the star's versatility. In the 1840s and early '50s, Forrest typically played Metamora along with six or eight other starring roles when he came to town. As the eponymous hero of *Jack Cade* and Spartacus in *The Gladiator,* Forrest performed other roles in which he defended nature's noblemen against marauding aristocrats. These vehicles, including Stone's script, provided numerous opportunities for virtuosity, from consciously poetic speeches to impressive feats of skill, such as sticking a tomahawk into the stage floor.

The star's charismatic appeal also worked against the tendency of the audience to collapse the star's persona into his Indian role. Regarding Forrest's effect on spectators, a New York reviewer wrote, "Witness the furor of audiences subjected to his control, the simultaneous shouts of applause which follow his great efforts, see the almost wild enthusiasm he kindles in the breasts of his auditors, and who will deny that Mr. Forrest has got the heart, nay, 'the very heart of hearts' of the masses."[15] As this critic and others affirm, audiences wanted to be swept along by Forrest's power; hoping to lose themselves in the reality of a tragic Indian's demise was not the primary appeal of the star's performances.

Finally, the type of vengeance adopted by Forrest's Metamora was fully in accord with Bowery honor. In the rough-and-tumble world of the Bowery, men of honor responded to threats and insults in public with physical violence, meted out individually or with one's compatriots. This was the response of Forrest's followers at the Astor Place Riot, and Forrest himself took this path in answering a purported insult to his honor from an admirer of his wife before their divorce trial. Traditionalist workers applauded many plays in which heroes avenged past wrongs through violence and destruction. *The Gladiator* and *Jack Cade* involved similar situations, and more than a dozen apocalyptic melodramas featured at the Bowery and Chatham theaters in the 1840s also centered on righteous, violent revenge. Like many native-born working-class heroes of the antebellum era, Forrest's Metamora died to defend the traditional rights and honor of his forefathers. Bowery workers knew that glorying in vengeance offended the respectable, but from their point of view Victorian propriety was unmanly. Metamora's revenge did not set the Indian chief apart as an inferior Other; it confirmed his identity as a man of honor.

Although Forrest's Metamora suffered no opprobrium in the eyes of the star's audience as a racialized exotic, the other Indians in his tribe may have. Stone portrayed several Wampanoag warriors as bloodthirsty, superstitious, and cowardly. The English overwhelm Metamora and his tribe at the end of the play, because Kaweshine, an Indian prophet, strikes fear into the Wampanoags and leads the English soldiers to Metamora's stronghold, for example. But did Bowery spectators view Kaweshine as a typical redskin, or did they demonize him as an individual villain, without regard to his apparent race? Because the play avoids a strict white/red dichotomy and does not position its spectators as white men, many traditionalist workers in the audience may not have viewed Kaweshine's treachery as representative Indian behavior. And if they did, they likely saw the racialized English as more treacherous.

In this sense, Stone's drama served primarily as a star vehicle. Compared to its worshipful elevation of Forrest and his Indian chief, *Metamora's* racial dynamics must have been of secondary importance for its audience. Like *The Gladiator* and *Jack Cade*, *Metamora* pits a Jacksonian star, a hero of "the people," against a type of aristocratic oppression to refight the Revolutionary War. In the two other star vehicles, "the people" are Roman slaves and English peasants; in *Metamora*, they happen to be Indigenous Americans. Although "the people" in all three plays are filled with Judas figures who betray their Christlike hero, they remain more worthy than the oppressors they fight against. Metaphorically, these slaves, peasants, and Indians are the American people of the Revolutionary era, yearning for freedom from English tyranny. In the world of these melodramas, they need only a hero to fight (and die) for them.

There are only two races in Stone's play. Had the playwright introduced an African American into *Metamora*, it is unlikely that Stone would have ended his play with his Indian chief cursing "white men"; the term would have drawn attention to the races of all of the characters and undercut the eminence of Forrest's Indian chief. In the immediate context of the drama, however, "white men" simply became a synonym for "English." Indeed, Stone had Metamora use both terms synonymously throughout the play. Similar dramatic construction and social dynamics deemphasized race in the audience response to Forrest's performances of Spartacus in *The Gladiator*. With no black characters on stage, few in the audience ever supposed that Forrest's hero, who fomented a slave rebellion in ancient Rome, was encouraging African Americans to rebel against their masters.

Racialist thinking was ubiquitous in the nineteenth-century American theater, as it was in the culture as a whole, but that does not mean that dramas that deployed racialism necessarily induced their spectators to respond to the play in wholly racial terms. Certainly, Forrest's *Metamora* legitimated racialist categories, but for its working-class traditionalists the drama primarily provided another opportunity to cheer their star and damn the Brits, plus those aristocrats in America who copied English ways. Nationalism and class orientation, not racialist belief, probably channeled most of the response to *Metamora* in New York between 1840 and 1855.

Part IV

Challenging Stereotypes through Film

Performance and "Trickster Aesthetics" in the Work of Mohawk Filmmaker Shelley Niro

KRISTIN L. DOWELL

Native American[1] media experienced an impressive growth over the last thirty years as Native American filmmakers took up the camera to reclaim the screen. Native filmmakers use media to articulate the complexities of contemporary Native life and to counteract the absence of Native perspectives in the mainstream mediascape.[2] Native filmmakers document cultural practices, recuperate community narratives, and sustain cultural memory through their media. Film and video have become salient forms of expression through which Native people negotiate cultural traditions and identities. Film and video have also been employed to challenge and respond to dominant representations of Native Americans. This chapter analyzes Native media as a medium through which Native filmmakers resignify cultural traditions and practices of representation in the borderlands between dominant and Indigenous forms of film/video practice.

I draw upon the metaphor of "borderlands" and border theory as a framework for analyzing the improvisations, cultural play, and border crossing that are characteristic of Native life as well as Native cinema. The space of "borderlands" has been theorized as a site of the negotiation of identity and community where multiple voices and experiences are expressed in complex and often contradictory ways. Artist, scholar, and curator Gerald McMaster (Plains Cree) articulates the concept of borderlands to include the numerous improvisations and innovations that occur within the cultural space between multiple social worlds. He argues, "The border zone is a place for new cultural practices that involve improvisation and the recombination of disparate cultural elements, creating a diverse cultural repertoire. Identity becomes ever stronger, not diffused."[3]

I use this borderlands framework to examine the cinematic space of Native media as a venue through which multiple Native voices and experiences can be presented, contested, and negotiated. Borderlands theory can be useful as a way to account for the improvisation, complexity, polyvalency, and contradiction that Native media offer to contest dominant Hollywood representations that cast Native people as one-dimensional, "vanishing," "barbaric," or "noble savages." Indigenous aesthetics within Native media illustrate the performative strategies that Native filmmakers use to counter dominant stereotypes of Native people with alternative representations of their communities. After first providing a brief historical sketch of the development of Native media and the institutional structures under which this work is produced and circulated, this chapter explores "trickster aesthetics" and humor as a strategy of resistance and cultural survival in the work of Mohawk filmmaker Shelley Niro. I analyze her films *Honey Moccasin* (1998) and *It Starts with a Whisper* (1993) to connect her use of parody and humor with larger Native discourses and theories of a Native "trickster" aesthetic within Native art and literature.

Development of Native American Film and Video

The legacy of dominant forms of visual representation of Native peoples has left a profound absence of positive portrayals of Native life from Native perspectives. Film scholar Jacquelyn Kilpatrick (Choctaw/Cherokee/Irish) discusses the impact of the development of the "Hollywood Indian" on popular representations and conceptions of Indians. She contends, "The history and cultures of Native Americans have been miscommunicated in films, and the distortions have been accepted as truth, with sometimes disastrous results."[4] She argues that stereotypes of Indians historically developed in cultural forms such as the dimestore novel, captivity narratives, and Wild West Shows, and solidified in celluloid through Hollywood's distortions and misrepresentations of Native Americans, consequently impacting public perceptions of Native Americans. Native American projects of self-representation in film, video, and photography critique dominant (mis) representations by creating works that reflect more accurately the complexity and diversity of Native voices, experiences, and histories.

The steady growth of Native American film and video over the last thirty years has coincided with several important technological, historical, and political moments. Advances in technology have made video equipment much more portable and less costly. Moreover, the political activism

during the 1960s and 1970s and the impact of the American Indian Movement (AIM) and Red Power movement challenged the social and political
inequalities facing Native communities. Political activists in these movements recognized the importance of the media to raise awareness of their
activism and stressed the necessity of Native people creating media to tell
their own stories.

During this period institutional organizations such as the Museum
of the American Indian (renamed the National Museum of the American Indian in 1994 when it became part of the Smithsonian Institution)
and governmental funding sources, such as the National Film Board of
Canada and Native American Public Telecommunications,[5] began to
support media production in Native communities by providing funds for
production as well as venues for distribution. Additionally, in the United
States, as governmental regulations regarding gaming on reservations
changed during the 1980s, a few communities began to use casino profits
in the late 1990s to fund Native American films and videos.[6] Many of
these works, however, are made primarily for their own communities and
may be screened only within a community context. Other Native film/
video works are circulated nationally and internationally on both Native
and independent film festival circuits,[7] and some works are broadcast on
public television. The development of the Aboriginal Peoples Television
Network in Canada, which launched in 1999, has created additional visibility, funding, and distribution possibilities for Native film and video.

Native American media are enmeshed in a broader movement of
self-determination and sovereignty among Native communities. Just as
Native activists assert claims of political sovereignty, Native artists are
reclaiming visual space as they use the screen to tell Native stories from
Native perspectives. It is important to recognize that Native filmmakers do not merely replace mainstream cinematic images of Indians with
positive representations but challenge the power hierarchy of dominant
society to represent Native communities. Theorist Stuart Hall addresses
a similar situation with the politics of representation in black British
cinema, asserting, "the cultural politics of black British filmmakers
encompasses first, the question of *access*, to the rights to representation
by black artists and black cultural workers themselves. Second, the *con-
testation* of the marginality, the stereotypical quality, and the fetishized
nature of images of blacks, by the counterposition of a 'positive' black

imagery."[8] Claiming a visual space to create their own representations is a particularly political act for Native peoples who have had a long history of objectification at the hands of non-Native filmmakers. Native artist Hulleah Tsinhnahjinnie (Seminole/Muskogee/Diné) sees the camera in Native hands as a way to expose the problematic dominant representations of Native people. She asserts, "No longer is the camera held by an outsider looking in; the camera is now held with brown hands opening familiar worlds. We document ourselves with a humanizing eye, we create new visions with ease, and we can turn the camera and show how we see you."[9]

The world of Native filmmaking encompasses a wide range of genres, content, and cinematic styles. While documentary film and video production remains a dominant genre, as is evident in the work of George Burdeau (Blackfeet), Sandra Sunrising Osawa (Makah), Barb Cranmer ('Namgis), Annie Frazier-Henry (Lakota-Blackfeet-French), Arlene Bowman (Diné), and Loretta Todd (Métis Cree), other filmmakers choose to make experimental short video, as in the case of Dana Claxton (Hunkpapa Lakota), Nora Naranjo-Morse (Santa Clara Pueblo), Victor Masayesva Jr. (Hopi), and Shelley Niro (Mohawk). There has been a recent growth in the number of feature films by such prominent filmmakers as Gary Farmer (Cayuga), Sherman Alexie (Spokane/Coeur d'Alene), Shirley Cheechoo (Cree), Chris Eyre (Cheyenne/Arapaho), and Zacharias Kunuk (Inuit). The availability of public television funds for Native film production has also influenced the production of documentary videos by Native filmmakers for public television broadcasting. In Canada, government-sponsored support for Native filmmaking, including such programs as the National Film Board's Challenge for Change program in 1969 and the Aboriginal Filmmaking Program in 1996, as well as the development of the Inuit Broadcasting Corporation and the Aboriginal People's Television Network, has helped sustain a vibrant, diverse, and multigenerational community of Aboriginal filmmakers over the last thirty years. For this chapter I have chosen to focus on the work of Mohawk filmmaker Shelley Niro to address the role of "trickster aesthetics" and humor as cinematic strategies in Native film. Niro's work draws heavily upon her photography background, in which she consistently uses humor as a way to destabilize stereotypes of Native people. Her media work is unique in its playfulness, its humor that deconstructs conventional cinematic representations, and its commitment to her Mohawk community, resulting in films that are well received among avant-garde art and cinema circles while appealing to Mohawk and Native American audiences.

Indigenous Aesthetics and Visual Sovereignty

With the rise of Native American media, scholars have examined questions of Indigenous aesthetics and whether these works embody a distinctive alternative aesthetic. Cinema studies scholars Robert Stam and Ella Shohat analyzed the "esthetics of resistance" in terms of the development of oppositional cinema across the world that recognizes that "avant-garde" cinema and cinema that challenges aesthetic convention cannot be claimed by only Euro-American artists and filmmakers. They state:

> This spectrum includes films and videos that bypass formal conventions of dramatic realism in favor of such modes and strategies as the carnivalesque, the anthropophagic, the magical realist, the reflexive modernist, and the resistant postmodernist. These alternative esthetics are often rooted in non-realist, often non-Western or para-Western cultural traditions featuring other historical rhythms, other narrative structures, other views of the body, sexuality, spirituality, and the collective life.[10]

They contend that many aesthetic forms of these oppositional cinemas can be linked to other cultural traditions, such as the move toward oral-inflected narratives that can be seen in such videos as Trinh T. Minh-ha's *Surname Viet Given Name Nam* (1989) or Victor Masayesva's *Itam Hakim, Hopiit* (1984). Anthropologist Faye Ginsburg has also looked at the alternative aesthetics of Indigenous media and has been instrumental in shifting analysis of Indigenous media into a framework of social action. She contends that as a result of the drastic ruptures in the social histories of Indigenous communities, media have been taken up as a way to form and negotiate Indigenous identities. The work of Indigenous media makers in the Chiapas Media Project documenting military and political oppression against Indigenous peoples in the region, the extensive use in Native North America of tribally sponsored community video projects to document oral traditions and life histories of elders, and the video produced with Inuit filmmaker Zacharias Kunuk and the Inuit film collective Iglook Isuma, are all examples of the incorporation of media technologies to document cultural practices and to maintain cultural identities.[11] Ginsburg's work has also been crucial in opening up an analytical space in which Indigenous media practices can be understood as part of the processes of the recuperation of kinship, social memory, and community history.

Ginsburg's concept of *embedded aesthetics*[12] has also been useful in transferring the focus of Indigenous media analysis from the formal qualities of the texts themselves to the social practices in which film and video production is engaged. The concept provides a framework for understanding the ways in which Indigenous media producers evaluate their media practices. Ginsburg analyzes the social circumstances experienced by those involved in Indigenous media production, asserting, "For many Aboriginal producers, the quality of the work is judged by its capacity to embody, sustain, and even revive or create certain social relations, although the social bases for coming to this position may be very different for remote and urban people."[13] The idea of *embedded aesthetics* enables us to recognize different criteria upon which Indigenous productions can be evaluated, criteria not necessarily rooted in the film text itself, but in the Indigenous cultural worlds of the media producers. Ginsburg also notes that this aesthetic practice may be taken up differently by urban Aboriginal producers, who may self-consciously embrace *embedded aesthetics* as a strategic move to situate their work within broader discourses and as a practice through which to negotiate Aboriginal self-representation.

Historian Troy Johnson notes, "Sovereignty is fundamental to this ability to both realize and retain indigenous identities and cultures."[14] Native artists similarly recognize that the maintenance of Native artistic and cultural practices, essential to Native identity, is also a form of sovereignty. Tuscarora artist and scholar Jolene Rickard advocates the work of Native American filmmakers and artists, stating, "Today, sovereignty is taking shape in visual thought as indigenous artists negotiate cultural space."[15] Visual sovereignty can include the incorporation by Native filmmakers of Indigenous aesthetic systems and cultural traditions in their work as well as their reclamation of the right to represent their communities in cinematic and artistic practice.

Trickster Aesthetics

One of the ways in which Indigenous aesthetics have emerged in Native media is through the use of humor and parody. Drawing upon Native literary theory of "trickster discourse," I expand the use of the trickster figure as a metaphor for Native cultural survival to aesthetic strategies in Native media. The trickster is a figure found in oral cultures across the globe and is central in the cultures of Native North America as a prominent figure in traditional stories and folklore. The trickster takes many names and forms across Native communities, including: Glooscap, Manabuzho, Wanabush, Nanabojoh, Nanabush, Weesakejak, Napi, Raven, Hare, Iktomi, and Coyote. Half-fool, half-hero, the trickster is the focus of stories that are at once admonitions, instruction, and entertainment.[16] While the trickster is most often referred to as "he," it is important to note that, as the trickster transgresses boundaries, the gender identity of the trickster figures can also shift. Traditionally, in many Native communities, trickster narratives were used to teach culturally appropriate attitudes and behavior. Trickster narratives often illustrate stories of creation or origin.[17] Scholar Paul Radin asserts: "Trickster is at one and the same time creator and destroyer, giver and negator, he who dupes others and who is always duped himself. He wills nothing consciously. He knows neither good nor evil, yet he is responsible for both. He possesses no values, moral or social, is at the mercy of his passions and appetites, yet through his actions all values come into being."[18]

The trickster and his countless comic adventures have entertained and educated generations of Native peoples, and his influence has left a lasting impact on Native artists who draw inspiration from his curiosity, ingenuity, playfulness, irreverence, and resilience. Art historian Allan Ryan observes, "The Trickster is admired for being a risk taker, rule breaker, boundary tester, and creator/transformer."[19] It is important to note that the trickster is also appealing to Native artists and scholars because he is first and always an active agent. His identity is inextricably bound up in behavior and defined by his performance. It is this active transgression and defiance of boundaries and rules that appeals to Native artists and scholars seeking a metaphor for Native cultural survival and resistance.

The aesthetic of transgression, contradiction, inversion, and dissonant polyphony is also embodied in other cultural practices such as carnival.[20] Stam and Shohat contend, "In the carnival esthetic, everything is pregnant with its opposite, within an alternative logic of permanent contradiction and non-exclusive opposites that transgresses the monologic true-or-false thinking typical of a certain kind of positivist rationalism."[21] In much the same way that the symbolic inversion of social order occurs during carnival, the trickster also reveals the constructed nature of the world through his exploits. Anthropologist Lawrence Sullivan states, "Trickster's character and exploits embody the process of ironic imagination. His dynamism of composition mocks, shatters, and re-forms the overly clear structures of the world . . . in him the double-sidedness of reality reveals itself."[22] The trickster is radical in action and disruptive in social and cultural values.[23]

The nature of the trickster as one who transgresses boundaries and who exposes the constructedness of the world through ironic, and often bawdy, exploits has inspired Native scholars, particularly in regard to postmodern analysis of Native literature. Much of the literature on trickster discourse is indebted to the work of Anishinaabe writer and literary critic Gerald Vizenor. Born in Minneapolis in 1934, Vizenor spent much of his childhood on the White Earth Reservation in northern Minnesota. He is a self-described "mixed-blood"[24] and has discussed his struggle to maintain identity between the Anishinaabe world and the white world. He has applied theories of postcolonialism to Native life and uses the trickster figure throughout his work. Vizenor coined the phrase "trickster discourse" as an alternative trope for analyzing Native narratives in opposition to dominant narratives that cast Native people in tragic terms and construct them as vanishing, alienated, and losing cultural practices. He sees humor and comic narratives as a prominent aspect of Native life that has been neglected by dominant analyses and uses the trickster as a way to capture that sense of playfulness, laughter, and subversiveness. Vizenor contends that the trickster provides imaginative liberation through comic narratives and is an appropriate metaphor for both Native life and literature. He asserts, "Tribal narratives are creative productions rather than social science monologues; the trickster is a comic trope, chance in a narrative wisp, tribal discourse, and an irreversible innovation in literature."[25] Native artists, including Lawrence Paul Yuxweluptun (Salish), Gerald McMaster (Plains Cree), Jimmie Durham (Cherokee), Rebecca Belmore (Anishinabekwe), and Roxanne Swentzell (Santa Clara Pueblo), and filmmakers Shelley Niro (Mohawk), Chris Eyre (Cheyenne/Arapaho), Sherman Alexie (Spokane/Coeur d'Alene), and Nora Naranjo-Morse (Santa Clara Pueblo), have also been inspired by the creative, playful, and transgressive nature of trickster. In the following section I use Vizenor's notion of "trickster discourse" to explore the role of the trickster in the aesthetic and cinematic choices of Shelley Niro.

The Trickster and Humor as Cinematic Strategies

Niro is a prominent artist, scholar, and filmmaker, whose work has been exhibited for over twenty years. She has been active in the development of the burgeoning Native film world, participating in Native film festivals in both the United States and Canada. Her work is distinctive in genre and aesthetic, combining a neo-camp visual style that speaks to a trickster spirit that uses humor to critique dominant perceptions of Native peoples while celebrating the resilience of Native women. Niro grew up on the Six Nations Reserve in Ontario and has been practicing photography for many years and producing film and video since the early 1990s. Her media works are largely experimental in style and open up cinematic space to suggest alternative visions of Native life.[26] Art historian Jennifer Skoda contends, "A transformative nature and biting wit enable Trickster to break conventions and create a space for change."[27] Niro draws upon these trickster qualities to open up a space in her photographs and films to playfully employ invention and creativity to subvert stereotypes of Native people. Her work also challenges gender roles and conventional western ideologies of women's beauty, sexuality, and social roles.

As a trickster, Niro challenges stereotypes of Native women by turning these images upside down to create photographic images that convey the complexities and playfulness of Native life and identity. In photographs such as *The Rebel* (1987) and the *Mohawks in Beehives* (1991) series, Niro subverts gender roles and ideologies of beauty to create visual space for the individuality of Native women. *The Rebel* features Niro's mother lying on top of a car in a pose that mocks the associations of beautiful women in marketing ads for cars. Art historian Allan Ryan argues, "This image undermines both the Indian princess and the earth mother stereotypes. It also challenges prevailing standards of beauty and the marketing strategy of using sexy women to sell sexy cars. Not a bad achievement for one photograph."[28] While Niro uses humor to mock stereotypes through her work, she explains that it is important that she not intentionally create humorous images, because she feels that this would seem artificial. She prefers to take images that "just happen" and enlists the help of her sisters, Bunny, Betsy, and Beverly, who donned an assortment of 1950s fashions and mugged for the camera for the *Mohawks in Beehives* series. *Mohawks in Beehives I* (1991) is a photograph that exudes a sense of confidence and attitude. These women look "cool" and completely in control, and — just as the title of another Niro photograph, *I Enjoy Being a Mohawk Girl* (1992) suggests—they exude pride in their Mohawk identity. At the same time that Niro's work captures a playful and exuberant quality of Native life with humor and laughter, her images celebrate Mohawk and, specifically, Mohawk women's identity. Her work also demonstrates that "conventionalized images are not appropriate for representing the diverse, dynamic people and cultures of Native communities."[29] Niro's photographs and films use laughter and humor as a means of challenging conventional representations of the stoic Indian and to illuminate the quirks and complexities of Native people. Niro uses her photography to create positive images that reflect her experiences with her community. She states, "I use photography as a mirror to myself and also to those around me. In Native people, I see a lot of happiness and an emerging kind of confidence which glows from the inside, of warmth and love."[30]

Niro's work also often addresses the historical trauma and cultural memory of her community, incorporating humor as a strategy to do so. Through the use of humor, inventiveness, and the playful quality of her experimental work, Niro emphasizes culture as a creative process that is always open to reinvention. Niro's film *Honey Moccasin* (1998) captures this sense of the inherent innovation in cultural tradition and the ingenuity of Native cultural survival. *Honey Moccasin* is the story of its title character, a local bar owner on the reserve who becomes a sleuth after the powwow outfits of the elders are stolen. The multilayered film comments on such diverse issues as dissension in Native communities, Native gender identity, the inventiveness of the elders who create innovative powwow regalia, and the persistence of Native cultural survival. Importantly, Niro created this film primarily for a Native audience as she sought to provide characters and situations that Native people could relate to. She explains:

The target audience for *Honey Moccasin* is First Nations, Natives, and Indians. I want them to relate to the situations in this film without trying to find a way in. They're in as soon as the film starts. Most of the characters are Indians. Conflicts and resolutions come from the Native community. The entertainment, the social commentaries, the acts of wackiness all come from this fictional reserve. We are seeing variety, strength, weakness, emotion, and humour in this film.[31]

That Native people are the primary audience is evident in the scene with the character Zachary John (played by actor Billy Merasty [Cree]), the thief of powwow regalia, standing in front of the mirror wearing a jingle dress. This scene references Native knowledge to comment on gender identity, as this scene can be read as an acknowledgment of the traditional role of "two-spirit"[32] people in Native life.

Just as the trickster is a figure that constantly transgresses boundaries and has transformative powers, *Honey Moccasin* asserts that Native peoples have a long tradition of invention and that, as the elders declare in the film after the powwow outfits are stolen, they don't need the outfits to have the powwow. Their inventiveness in the use of unlikely materials such as rubber inner tubes and Froot Loops to create powwow outfits illustrates that Native cultural survival has always involved a sense of constant innovation and improvisation. The powwow itself as a cultural activity involved improvisation and invention across tribal lines to create the social dances performed at this intertribal gathering. The unusual and innovative powwow outfits in *Honey Moccasin* can be read both as a statement about Native cultural survival in the face of assimilation policies and as a broader statement about "culture" and "tradition." This film counters notions of culture as static and unchanging and instead asserts that cultural traditions always involve dynamic reinvention. As Comanche cultural critic Paul Chaat Smith writes, "*Honey Moccasin* imagines a contemporary reserve where someone has stolen every dance outfit, feather, shawl, and piece of decorative beadwork in the entire community. In Niro's world, they are challenged to find new ways to define what it means to be Indian, and they respond with daring and imagination and creativity."[33]

The trickster figure is also woven throughout the narrative by the character of Zachary John, who has stolen the materials for the elders' powwow regalia in a competitive bid for attention and as an expression of alienation from the community. His behavior runs against community norms and serves to alienate rather than integrate him into the community. Like the trickster of oral traditions whose exploits must be corrected by other animals and spirits to restore moral order, Zachary is accepted back into the community only after he has been reprimanded by the elders, returned the stolen items, and apologized to the individuals from whom he stole. Interestingly, in the film this apology is broadcast to the community through the local Native television station, "Native Tongue." By depicting a local Native-run television station within her film, Niro is acknowledging the increasing importance of broadcast communications within Native lives as technologies that are incorporated for local forms of Native self-representation.

In *Honey Moccasin*, "Native Tongue" broadcasting reports local news and community events from Native perspectives in a way that "aboriginalizes television" and becomes a form of empowerment as a powerful venue for Native self-representation.[34] Through the playful depiction of the "Native Tongue" television show in *Honey Moccasin*, Niro reflects the development of network communications throughout Canada and, most notably, the launch of the Aboriginal Peoples Television Network. APTN, which became the world's first national Aboriginal television channel when it was established in 1999, and which is now available on all basic cable service, is run by a board of twenty-one directors from Native communities all over Canada. The station combines over 80 percent Aboriginal Canadian programming with 20 percent international Indigenous programming. APTN is a crucial step for integrating Aboriginal media production within the national Canadian mediascape while increasing opportunities for Aboriginal people and communities to engage in developing practices of self-representation through media production.[35] The emergence of Native broadcasting can be seen as a form of *bricolage*, or appropriating available technologies and practices to serve the cultural needs of Native communities, and it is characteristic of a trickster sentiment.

Another innovative moment in *Honey Moccasin* involves the performance art of Honey's daughter Mabel. Mabel can be read as at least a partially autobiographical figure for Niro. Like Niro, Mabel is an artist and a filmmaker who produces art that she feels is important to her community and yet is "artsy" enough that Native audience members might not "get it." Mabel uses the stage in Honey's bar to present both her films and her performance art for the community. Mabel is an important figure, because she moves between the world of the reserve and the world of dominant society as an artist and a filmmaker who has gone to art school and returns with this knowledge to use it for her community. In her performance piece Mabel appropriates Peggy Lee's popular love song "Fever" to comment on the historical genocide and crimes against Native peoples, especially the painful history of the deadly spread of smallpox (fever) through Native communities after contact. As is clear in several scenes, the community, as audience members, may not always understand the artistic message behind her work, but they applaud her efforts in using the medium of film and art to express their history and community concerns. In the performance piece, Mabel is draped in a tipi-shaped outfit while singing "Fever" as slides of archival images of human genocide and forced assimilation of Native peoples are illustrated on the canvas covering her body. Native author Millie Knapp asserts, "As she sings, Mabel's head sticks up outside a man-sized tipi. Projected images of holocausts like Wounded Knee, Hiroshima, Indian relocations in the United States, sick and dying Indians infected with small pox are projected onto the tipi as she belts out, 'I get a fever that's so hard to bear, You give me fever.'"[36]

This scene illustrates Niro's skillful use of song and parody to discuss historical traumas of Native communities. Moreover, the projected slides inscribe images of past colonial violence onto the body of a contemporary Native person, thus profoundly embodying Native cultural memory and historical narrative.

The use of the body in performance art has been analyzed in terms of popular protests and street art, particularly in Latin America and in Chicano/a art. Performance studies scholar Diana Taylor discusses the use of photographs by political activists in Argentina to protest against the disappearances of children that were rampant in the 1970s and 1980s. She states, "When the Madres took to the street to make the 'disappearance' visible, they activated the photographs, they performed them. . . . The Madres turned their bodies into archives, preserving, and displaying the images that had been targeted for erasure."[37] Similarly, in *Honey Moccasin*, Mabel voices memories that dominant national narratives have sought to erase. Consequently, the symbol of the tipi, which has become associated with the "Hollywood Indian," is reappropriated and utilized to stress the realities of Native history.

Native scholars and artists have noted a trend of using humor as a strategy for cultural survival in both Native art and life. Renowned comedian Charlie Hill (Oneida) explained, "I think it's our humor that has helped us to survive. When the situation is most grim, that's when you see Indian people making jokes about it, just for the survival."[38] Niro, too, "reacts against the flat characterizations of Native people as they are so often portrayed in mainstream cinema. She aims to create a narrative that plays on the kinds of subtleties and nuances that animate traditional Native tales."[39] Her work is proof, as Vizenor asserted, that "for Native people humor is simply a compassionate act of survival."[40]

Another instance wherein Niro deploys the trickster as a means of promoting Native survival is her short video *It Starts with a Whisper* (1993). Made in response to the Quincentennial of Columbus's first voyage to the Americas, *It Starts with a Whisper* follows a young Haudenosaunee woman, Shanna, as she struggles to come to terms with her own Native identity. Shanna's inner conflicts stem from doubts about her self-worth, as she reflects on the disappearance of the Tutelo people in the Great Lakes region years ago. Shanna is surrounded by her "spirit aunties," or matriarchal clowns, which are trickster figures who wear flamboyant clothes and perform outrageously—particularly in their campy performance of a pop song that pokes fun at the trope of the "vanishing Indian." The lyrics slyly declare, "I'm surviving, I'm thriving / I'm doing fine without you / This affair was a crime, but I'll waste no more time / I'm doing fine without you."[41] It is important that Shanna's journey of self-discovery and acceptance of her Native identity takes her to Niagara Falls, a frontier space that was traditional Iroquois land and became a popular tourist attraction in the late 1800s. Niagara Falls is a liminal space, the space in which trickster dwells and thrives, and this space represents a tourist and social space of encounter. Shanna and her "aunties" travel to Niagara Falls to address her questions of Native identity in light of the Quincentennial anniversary.

These spirit aunties who guide Shanna through her journey are quintessential tricksters; their ability to transform their outer appearance without altering the fundamental core of their identity is essential to their survival. As art historian Ruth Phillips notes, "This is the wisdom and the gift they have to pass on to Shanna, but she can accept their wisdom only after her own transformative experience."[42] Niro uses the final scene, in which Shanna and her aunts eat cake in the shape of a globe on New Year's Eve of 1992 while singing a traditional Iroquois song, to assert a theme of resistance and survival. Comanche scholar Paul Chaat Smith declares, "Niro's characters end their journey (and begin out into the next half-millennium) with elaborately choreographed musical numbers that somehow manage to strike the perfect chord. She captures the tough love, humor, absurdity, and honest confusion of being red and alive in the 1990s."[43]

Niro's work, while addressing historical issues of cultural loss and oppression, celebrates the ingenuity of Native women in their strategies of survival that often incorporated resistance through humor. Like trickster, Niro irreverently disregards conventional representations of Native people to assert the resilience of Native cultural life in face of historical trauma and oppression. In its creative invention and playful transgression of boundaries, Niro's work embodies a trickster aesthetic that reimagines cinematic space for the representation of all the complexities, contradictions, and strengths of contemporary Native life.

CHAPTER 14

Speaking Lives, Filming Lives
George Burdeau and Victor Masayesva

Annie Kirby-Singh

> Even as ghosts, the indigenous people of the Americas pervade and
> fill the continent's imaginative spaces, exactly like the winds that
> blow freely over national borders.
> —Victor Masayesva Jr., "Indigenous Experimentalism"

> In your heart when you hear these songs, you're told by the red man
> you sing this song whatever you do.
> —Grandmother, *A Season of Grandmothers*

STORYTELLERS WHO WISH to convey Native stories in media other than
oral tradition face difficult choices, because, as Elaine Jahner has pointed
out, oral traditions are "epistemological realities" that "reflect particular
ways of knowing."[1] Hopi photographer and filmmaker Victor Masayesva
Jr. observes that "each new medium of conveyance . . . poses a tremendous challenge to the tribal person." Storytellers must decide what "is so
important that it must be shared" and, if the audience includes those outside of their specific tribal culture, how best to express their knowledge so
that it will not be misused or misinterpreted.[2]

The challenges facing Native writers who wish to convey the "epistemological realities" of their particular oral traditions in written literature
have received extensive critical attention. Less critical interest, however,
has been afforded to the development of Native American film and video.
As early as 1976, Blackfeet director George Burdeau was filming a series of
videographies of eastern Washington, Idaho Panhandle, and western Montana Native cultures as part of "The Real People" project.[3] Since then, film

and video have become widely utilized tools for expression and negotiation of Native American discourse.[4]

Masayesva and Burdeau create films arising out of very different personal and tribal histories. Masayesva, born in the traditional Hopi village of Hotevilla, has spent most of his life immersed within a Hopi community and perspective. Steven Leuthold notes the "intensely local focus" of Masayesva's films, the majority of which concentrate on a depiction of Hopi life and culture.[5] Contrastingly, Burdeau, the first Native American to become a member of the Directors Guild of America, was born and raised in Oklahoma, away from his Blackfeet tribal heritage, and has spent much of his career working on films that deal with a wide variety of tribal cultures.[6] A number of congruent themes become apparent in Masayesva's and Burdeau's works, for example, the endurance and continuing importance of storytelling traditions and a culturally cohesive oral tradition in contemporary tribal cultures, the importance of tribal relationships with specific landscapes, and the accumulation of knowledge and wisdom through a lifetime of immersion in and interaction with storytelling traditions. Where the two directors differ is in the perspective from which they articulate these prevalent concerns. Masayesva tends to approach his themes from within a Hopi-centric milieu, most conspicuously in his early works, while Burdeau often takes a more inclusive approach that is both pan-tribal and cross-cultural in its orientation.

Masayesva asks, "What's different about Native filmmakers? Why do we even insist on being the storytellers?" and proposes the following answer to his own question: "A Native filmmaker has the accountability built into him. . . . as an individual, as a clan, as a tribal, as a family member."[7] Masayesva identifies in Hopi culture a characteristic secretiveness, an understanding of "the value of silence and unobtrusiveness. . . . As a Hopi, you cannot violate the silences, just as you would not intrude on ceremony. . . . Refraining from photographing certain subjects has become a kind of worship."[8]

This raises important and difficult questions for filmmakers who, like Masayesva, originate from communities that have been subject to excessive and intrusive anthropological and ethnological study. Hopi photographers and filmmakers endeavor to explore ways of committing images to film that do not infringe the community's collective understanding of the limitations of cultural disclosure. As a result, Masayesva, in his early films, shifts away from an ethnological focus on the "interpretation of Hopi-ness by and for outsiders" and concentrates instead on privileging a Hopi audience.[9]

Hopiit (1980) presents a montage of images of contemporary Hopi life expressed through their relationship with the seasons, including children dancing a Deer Dance in winter and a woman and child making blue paste for corn cakes in spring.[10] The film opens with prayer feathers blowing in the breeze, symbolically communicating, according to Beverly Singer (Santa Clara Pueblo), good wishes to the audience.[11] An old man, speaking in Hopi, is sitting by a window, looking out toward the sun, as the shadow of a dancer fades in and out of focus.[12] Other images include children sliding on corn ears in the back of a pickup truck while eating watermelons, a sustained shot of barely moving peach blossoms, and a woman stacking ears of blue corn. Masayesva presents these images as integral and reciprocal components of contemporary Hopi life.[13]

Significantly, for the non-Hopi viewer, no explanation is provided of the images and activities presented in the narrative. Masayesva provided, on his Web site at the time, a list of comments made about *Hopiit* by panelists and jurors at the American Film Festival:

- This looks like a home movie—no narration is provided thus leaving the viewer totally bewildered as to what one is viewing.
- Poor because the viewer does not know what is being explained.
- No narration. Visuals do nothing to explore the subject.
- Too much dialogue with no translation.
- *Too idiosyncratic for broad understanding*; conceits were either overdone or the result of poor technique; whichever, the end result was diminished.[14]

Such remarks, of course, underscore precisely the point Masayesva was making. *Hopiit* is intended for a predominantly Hopi audience, who require no explanation of the imagery and symbolism contained in the film, in the same way that communities sharing a body of oral tradition do not need to have stories explained, because shared community knowledge provides all the context that is needed.

In *Itam Hakim, Hopiit* (We Someone, the Hopi) (1984), Ross Macaya,

a tribal elder of the Bow clan, recounts, in the Hopi language, various episodes in both his personal history and the communal tribal history.[15] Like
Hopiit, this film does not attempt to explicate or analyze Hopi culture for
the benefit of a non-Hopi audience, instead relying on the shared body
of knowledge incumbent in a Hopi audience. Furthermore, as Elizabeth
Weatherford has noted, the narrative structure parallels "Hopi patterns for
instruction" through the developmental "unfolding" of information.[16]

Like *Hopiit*, the film includes footage of a captive eagle that will be
sacrificed to obtain feathers for use in prayer.[17] Explicit explanation of this
and other Hopi-centric images is neither provided nor required. Masayesva's Hopi-centered narratives, according to Kathleen M. Sands and Allison Sekaquaptewa Lewis, express a common Hopi "dream," the "cultural
sensibilities" of which are collectively understood to a degree that enables
them to be "complete as they are received into the minds and imaginations
of Hopi viewers," even though they may appear incomplete or inadequate
to non-Hopi viewers.[18]

Masayesva acknowledges the significance of a shared body of myth,
legend, and memory and points out the "cobwebby (*wishapiwta*)" nature
of such deeply embedded knowledge. He recalls hearing a story from his
grandmother about famine and starvation, a story similar to that which
was delivered by Mr. Macaya and recorded by Masayesva on video. Masayesva himself had created a poem and photograph born from the same
communal story: "There was a lot we ate that year / In the wintertime we
ate our children."[19] Another Hopi storyteller provided a further "cleaned-
up" recording of the story, based on Mr. Macaya's version, to be shown on
television. Masayesva perceives this cumulative experience of storytelling
as being "what defines and refines the indigenous aesthetic. Not only is
it the accumulative experience of one individual, but it gets passed on to
everyone with whom he or she comes into contact, clinging like sticky
cobwebs."[20]

In this way, Masayesva's Hopi narratives, poems and photographs, his
grandmother's stories, and Mr. Macaya's stories all function as culturally
meaningful experiences within a culturally charged setting that depends
on the "cobwebby" sharing of communal knowledge and experience for
its meaningfulness. Furthermore, by refusing to explicate Hopi culture
for non-Hopi viewers, the films reflect back onto non–Native American
audiences a sense of "otherness," challenging Euro-American audiences

to acknowledge and reexamine deeply embedded Eurocentric cultural assumptions about identity and discourse. Ironically, the challenges extended by Masayesva to the dominant discourse resulted in an increased level of European and Euro-American interest in his work, prompting the translation of *Itam Hakim, Hopiit* into English through a combination of dubbing and subtitles.[21] Masayesva mediated this apparent act of conciliation by incorporating the implications of increased Euro-American interest in his work as a central theme of subsequent films.

For example, in *Siskyavi: The Place of Chasms* (1989), Masayesva explores the tensions between Hopi and non-Hopi pedagogy and epistemology, employing a narrative structure that combines documentary, oral literature, and live animation, in a manner partially accessible to non-Hopi viewers.[22] The film opens with a grandmother telling, in English, the story of how the Flute Clan came to Wálpi, emphasizing the importance of oral tradition and signifying Masayesva's increased willingness to engage with a non-Hopi audience. The film recounts the experiences of a group of Hopi high school students who travel to the Smithsonian Institution in Washington, D.C., to study and analyze Hopi pots. Masayesva contrasts their experience to that of one of their classmates, who stays at home and learns about pottery making and Hopi culture from her grandmother.

The students at the Smithsonian receive systematic instruction in the scientific procedures used to date and analyze the pots, contrasting sharply with the more holistic teaching and learning relationship between the grandmother and granddaughter. As the grandmother instructs her granddaughter in the techniques for extracting, preparing, and working the clay, she also recounts Hopi stories and explains important rituals. This includes a baby-naming ceremony during which the baby's head is washed with a corn and suds mixture made in a pot fashioned by the baby's grandmother. This sequence is significant, because it places the Hopi pot within a cultural context infused with value and meaning, contrasting with the pots in the museum, which are disconnected from the cultural context that gives them meaning and value.[23] Masayesva's use of animated sequences of patterns based on Hopi design, interwoven throughout the narrative, underscores the interpretation of the pots as constituent parts of a vibrant cultural identity. Significantly, despite the clinical environment in which they receive their instruction, the students at the Smithsonian comment that the pots are "examples of what our life is made of," implicitly under-standing the pots as integral components of their cultural fabric.

Many Native American storytellers specifically avoid explaining the meanings of their stories, conferring the responsibility upon their listeners to find their own meaning in the story. As Susan Berry Brill de Ramírez notes, storytelling in the oral tradition, "although meaningful, is never-theless aporetic, leaving the listeners . . . to find the truth and meaning for themselves."[24] Correspondingly, Masayesva makes no overt editorial judgment on the respective merits of the different pedagogical systems, rather conferring upon *Siskyavi*'s audience the responsibility to engage interactively with the narrative and draw their own conclusions.

In the feature-length documentary *Imagining Indians* (1993), which further develops Masayesva's willingness to engage with a non-Hopi au-dience, he deconstructs Hollywood's stereotypical Indian and subverts common assumptions about the relationships between written and oral discourse.[25] The framing story is about a Native American woman visiting her non-Indian dentist for a tooth extraction. The dentist, whose surgery is decorated with posters from so-called Indian movies, has a disturbing enthusiasm for *Dances with Wolves* and plans to establish his own "higher consciousness" resort for "spiritual" people to attend weekend Indian-style seminars. The relationship between the loquacious Euro-American dentist and the mute Native American patient highlights perceived inequalities between the discourses of the colonizers and the colonized, assumptions that Masayesva then proceeds to undermine.

At various stages during the film, Native American interviewees re-count their experiences with non-Native filmmakers. A man who worked as an extra on *Dances with Wolves* criticizes the conditions under which the movie company expected the extras to perform. Interspersed with his interview are visual excerpts from newspaper articles reporting his com-plaints and the movie company's responses. Another interviewee criticizes the makers of *Thunderheart* for their failure to address concerns relating to the authenticity and appropriateness of material used. As she speaks, of-ficial press releases from the movie company, stating their desire to be re-spectful and pointing out the support they have received from prominent members of the Native American community, scroll across the bottom of the screen.

At first glance, it would seem that Masayesva is providing an even-handed examination of the issues surrounding the appropriation of Native American culture by Euro-American filmmakers, simply juxtaposing conflicting opinions without imposing editorial comment. However, the power play between discourses is considerably more complex, because the medium of film ensures that those opinions delivered verbally have significantly more impact than those represented in writing, undermining the assumed authority of written discourse. The interviewees, speaking in the present moment, are able to make active choices about content, deciding how they will contribute to the "story" told by the film.[26] The written excerpts not only are passive and rooted in the past, but are subject to varying degrees of control by Native Americans, from the interviewees, whose choice of subject indirectly influences the choice of written extracts, to Masayesva, who directly selects which extracts should be included and in what form they appear on screen.

In the final sequence, the dental patient rises from her chair, wrests the drill from the dentist's hand and turns it on the camera lens, as examples of George Catlin's nineteenth-century Indian portraits fragment and dissolve into dust. As Weatherford has pointed out, the camera lens does not just represent an abstract collective of non-Native filmmakers but is literally the lens through which Masayesva himself is shooting the film, indicating that his critical assessment of movie makers and the responsibilities entailed in making films about Native Americans extends as much to himself and other Native filmmakers as it does to non-Natives.[27]

Masayesva regards the medium of film as a force for "radical empowerment" and argues that "experimental films and videos can be defined by the degree to which they subvert the colonizer's indoctrination and champion indigenous expression in the political landscape."[28] Masayesva recalls an incident following a recording session with Mr. Macaya, who later suggested that they record certain elements he had omitted from his story that day and splice them back into the sequence. Masayesva recalls that this was the point when he realized that Mr. Macaya had become an active participant in the filmmaking process, rather than a passive subject:

> These are the moments when collaboration between the camera and the subject truly begins. The participants become engaged in circular time, in which space is no longer separated forever into past and present but becomes

unified in community time—when the elders pass on their knowledge to the new generation of knowledge holders, when patient camera technique and the relating of minutely observed events ensures survival.[29]

Masayesva's observation about Mr. Macaya's transformation from subject to participant is significant in understanding the relationship between the interactive, culturally meaningful practice of storytelling and the collaborative and interactive process of film and video making in Native American communities. Where, in Masayesva's narratives, this transformation is most frequently articulated within an intensely Hopi-centric milieu, in the films of Burdeau the transformational process is most often expressed in a broader context that includes not only different Native American cultures, but also extends an invitation into the collaborative storytelling process to non-Indian audiences.

Like Masayesva, Burdeau is a fervent believer in the potential of film and video as means for Native peoples to make their voices heard and to tell their stories in new ways. Jacquelyn Kilpatrick notes Burdeau's work as a teacher at the University of Washington and as a director of the American Indian Film Institute in Santa Fe and describes his attitude toward learning as "a Native approach based on traditional ways of working together, creating a circle of community that shares a creative vision."[30]

A Season of Grandmothers (1976) begins with an origin story about how a special person, who created beauty, happiness, and laughter and ceremonies in the old world, was saved for the new world.[31] The special person was a grandmother. Old women from various Northwestern plateau cultures tell stories about their lives, including the impact on tribal dances following conversion to Catholicism and the shooting of one woman's family by a game warden who claimed they had killed too many deer. A voice-over narrated in English explains the importance of grandmothers:

> Here are the mothers of our own mothers. Their stories have been told time and again. Blood from every grandmother and grandfather back flows in every vein of our children's bodies. The blood of grandmothers flows warm, strong in our hearts now. Grandmothers teach us how to make our fingers dance, creating worship and ceremonial clothes, weaving ears of corn as if weaving time. And long ago when corn was first eaten she sits and sings and shows us how to bead designs from bitter roots and shooting stars. Grandmother is guardian of the sacred. She teaches

us how to respond to rhythms of the moon, to seasons of the salmon. She teaches us how to dance in ancient movements of time and space. Because she has lived, been nurtured by sun, the shadow of grandmother is her very own, her moccasins touch the earth. Now, if we all live right with one another, we too can be so privileged to live among grandmothers and grandfathers. You see, Indians are alive. We are here, we are now, and we live in seasons and this is winter, our season of grandmothers.

A Season of Grandmothers, in which stories, ceremonies, and knowledge symbolically flow from the blood of grandfathers and grandmothers into the veins of their grandchildren, posits a "special" kind of knowledge connecting across a number of tribal cultures—in this case knowledge about the special qualities of grandmothers—and reinforces an enduring Native presence on the American continent. To a viewer familiar with Indians only through one-dimensional Hollywood portrayals, the experience of listening to and watching the grandmothers talk about their lives is powerful and affecting. Burdeau has stated that the grandmothers featured in the film taught him much about the art of filmmaking by showing him that "the real power of creativity lies in people and their relationships with each other and the natural world."[32]

This emphasis on the creative wisdom of elders and an interconnected universe is typical of Burdeau's films. For example, his Emmy Award–winning film *The Pueblo Peoples: First Contact* (1990) draws the audience's attention to the wisdom of a respected tribal elder, Zuni House Chief Mecalita Wystalucy.[33] As Mr. Wystalucy tells a Zuni origin story, his words are translated into English by Conroy Chino, a television newscaster who is a member of Acoma Pueblo and the film's narrator/presenter.[34] With a lingering shot of Mr. Wystalucy's age-wrinkled face, Burdeau intimates that Mr. Wystalucy's wisdom is the result of a lifelong immersion in Zuni oral tradition and that wisdom is a condition that accumulates over time, residing in the stories that are the fabric of Pueblo culture.

The narrative throughout maintains an emphasis on relationality. The Pueblo people's special relationship to the landscape is emphasized by Chino, who states, "The story of my people and the story of this place are one single story. No man can think of us without thinking of this place." Leuthold notes Burdeau's frequent use of dissolves to indicate a sense of interconnectedness between the Pueblo people and their art, intercutting images of people with images of objects or architecture. A portrait of a Pueblo Indian dissolves into an Anasazi bowl, which then dissolves to a photograph of three more Pueblo Indians. As Leuthold notes, the "bowl's circular form exactly encompasses the pyramidal form of the three Indians, formally expressing the close integration between art and life in traditional Pueblo cultures."[35]

The origin story told by Mr. Wystalucy and translated by Chino is alternately faded in and out with a more "conventional" version of Zuni history provided by scholars Joe S. Sando (Jemez Pueblo) and Alfonso Ortiz (San Juan Pueblo). At first, it seems that the two histories are unconnected. Mr. Wystalucy speaks of a giant who could not be killed. The scholars recount the arrival in Zuni of Estevanico, the Moroccan slave who, as part of Fray Marcos de Nisa's expedition, was imprisoned and eventually killed by the Zuni. Estevanico took with him to Zuni a sacred gourd for power, but the Zuni were not afraid of him and broke the gourd. As Mr. Wystalucy's story continues, describing how the Sun Father told the people that the giant's heart was in the gourd rattle that he held in his hand, the audience comes to understand the symbolic link between Mr. Wystalucy's version of the Zuni origin story and the story of Estevanico's arrival in Zuni in 1539. The result of this convergence is an emphasis on the dynamic and adaptable nature of Zuni storytelling, whereby the Zuni origin story has evolved to mediate the shocking consequences of the arrival of the Spanish in Zuni territory.

The endurance and vitality of oral tradition is also a crucial element of *Backbone of the World* (1997), which was filmed on the Blackfeet reservation in Montana and was for Burdeau a return to the cultural and spiritual home of his people.[36] One of Burdeau's primary motivations was to provide "a voice" for the sacred treaty land Badger Two-Medicine, which was threatened by proposals for oil and gas extraction. The film opens with the voice of a tribal elder explaining the importance and difficulty of storytelling. Her generation learned the stories from their grandmothers, and her role is to pass the stories along to her grandchildren. The narrator tells the legend, in her native language, of Scarface, who received the gift of the Sun Dance on behalf of the Blackfeet people. A male narrator translates her words into English. The combination of storytelling through the male and female narrators and Burdeau and his film crew stresses the communality of storytelling and the "authorless" origination of the story.

They are all conveyors but not originators of the story, which forms part of the body of Blackfeet oral tradition.

The Scarface legend not only frames the narrative and establishes the importance of oral literature to Blackfeet culture and identity but also engages the audience in an active and reciprocal role by extending to them the opportunity to become part of the collaboration, and their responses to the stories dialogically become an integral part of the storytelling process. Burdeau wished to engage not only with members of the Blackfeet community but also with those promoting oil explorations in the region and also wanted to raise awareness of these issues among liberal PBS viewers. Darren Kipp, one of the videographers, remarks that the sacred experience of Badger Two is not confined to the Blackfeet but is "a human issue," particularly in terms of "defending the cultural rights of all peoples." The narrative, therefore, invites the audience to consider the threat to Badger Two within the context of what is sacred in their own particular cultures.

Burdeau and his videographers include themselves within their own narrative on a number of occasions. Footage is included of the crew discussing a technical problem that occurred when they were filming a group of old women talking and obtained a visual but no audio recording. They decide to include the silent images of the old women talking, which are run concurrently with the discussion about the technical fault. During another scene, when an interviewee pauses to consider an answer, Burdeau is heard to say, "Give me a wider shot," and the camera pans around to him, members of his crew, and technical equipment, recording them in the act of receiving her story. This approach emphasizes the filmmakers' role as part of a storytelling community, bound together by shared cultural values and understanding.

Personal testimony, tribal memory, and communal history also provide important voices within the narrative and reveal the frictions and ambiguities of filmmaking in Native communities. As Burdeau films a ceremony, honoring those who died in the Baker Massacre of 1869, he muses on the problems of using film as a tool to represent and interpret the experience of a colonized culture, questioning whether it is "appropriate even to shoot" the ceremony. The combination of modern and traditional methods of storytelling parallels the interweaving of ancient legends and contemporary stories that signify the Blackfeet experience but also places Burdeau in the role of elder or mentor teaching his skills to the young videographers, providing them with a new way of telling their stories.[37]

In summary, both Masayesva and Burdeau resist colonialism by reinforcing Native "survivance" through a vibrant and enduring storytelling tradition. Masayesva's challenge is to mediate Hopi tradition through a medium historically used as a colonizing tool against Native cultures. As such, he places strict limitations on access into his narratives for outsiders, either by presenting esoteric, Hopi-centric narratives or by undermining the perceived epistemological authority of the dominant culture. Burdeau adopts a more inclusive methodology, inviting his audiences to engage with his narratives on a more participatory level, encouraging a more empathetic understanding, on the part of non-Native viewers, of the challenges facing contemporary Native cultures.

In the same way that Masayesva notes the transformation of Mr. Macaya from passive subject to active participant, Burdeau believes that new technology is the key to "creating a system by which we can once again effectively communicate, not only in our own individual communities, but also in our regional and national communities, and to the world at large."[38] The films of both Masayesva and Burdeau, whether tribal-centric or cross-cultural in orientation, confirm that film and video have become essential tools in the enduring struggle for Native Americans to tell their own stories on their own terms.

Notes

Introduction

1. "General Assembly Adopts Declaration on Rights of Indigenous Peoples," http://www.un.org/News/Press/docs/2007/ga10612.doc.htm.

2. Simon Critchley, *Infinitely Demanding: Ethics of Commitment, Politics of Resistance* (London: Verso, 2007), 107.

3. Ibid., 109–10.

4. Richard Hill, "Introduction," *Native American Expressive Culture* [special double issue], *Akwe:kon Journal* 11, nos. 3 and 4 (fall/winter 1994): 6.

5. W. Richard West Jr., "Foreword," *Native American Dance: Ceremonies and Social Traditions* (National Museum of the American Indian, Smithsonian Institution, with Fulcrum Publishers, 1992), x.

6. Birgit Däwes listed seventy-nine Native North American theater companies and locations in 2006. Däwes, *Native North American Theater in a Global Age: Sites of Identity Construction and Transdifference* (Heidelberg: Universitätsverlag, 2006), 464–66.

7. See also ibid., 117–72.

8. Ibid., 27.

9. For example, Mimi Gisolfi D'Aponte, ed., *Seventh Generation* (New York: Theatre Communications Group, 1999); Hanay Geiogamah and Jaye T. Darby, eds., *Stories of Our Way: An Anthology of American Indian Plays* (Los Angeles: UCLA American Indian Studies Center, 1999); Jaye T. Darby and Stephanie Fitzgerald, eds., *Keepers of the Morning Star: An Anthology of Native Women's Theater* (Los Angeles: UCLA American Indian Studies Center, 2003); and Monique Mojica and Ric Knowles, eds., *Staging Coyote's Dream: An Anthology of First Nations Drama in English* (Toronto: Playwrights Union of Canada Press, 2003).

10. Jacquelyn Kilpatrick, *Celluloid Indians: Native Americans and Film* (Lincoln and London: University of Nebraska Press, 1999), xv.

Chapter 1. Inventing Native Modern Dance

1. Rosalie Jones, "Native Modern Dance: Beyond Tribe and Tradition," *Native American Dance: Ceremony and Social Traditions*, ed. Charlotte Heth. (Washington, DC: National Museum of the American Indian, Smithsonian Institution, with Starwood Publishers, 1992), 169–84.

2. Jeffrey Huntsman, Introduction, *New Native American Drama: Three Plays*, ed. Hanay Geiogamah (Norman: University of Oklahoma Press, 1980), xii.

3. Hanay Geiogamah, personal interview, Southern California Indian Powwow, Orange County, July 2002.

4. Daniel Gibson, ed., "They're Dancing in Canada," *Indian Artist*, winter issue, 1998.

5. Cate Montana, "Aboriginal Arts Program Exploding," *Indian Country Today*, June 21, 2000.

6. Ibid.

7. Rosalie May Jones, "The Blackfeet Medicine Lodge Ceremony: Ritual and Dance-Drama," master's thesis, University of Utah, 1968.

8. This essay is dedicated to Lee Udall, who gave me the gift of expanding my professional horizons, and to Lloyd Kiva New, who gave generations of Native youth the opportunity to become artists.

Chapter 2. Old Spirits in a New World

1. Chief Robert Joseph, in Bruce Grenville, Robert Joseph, and Peter MacNair, *Down from the Shimmering Sky: Masks of the Northwest Coast* (Seattle and Vancouver, BC: University of Washington Press and Vancouver Art Gallery, 1998), 18.

2. Alexandra Harmon, *Indians in the Making: Ethnic Relations and Indian Identities around Puget Sound* (Berkeley: University of California Press, 1998), 249.

3. Ned Blackhawk, quoted by Sherman Alexie, in "Generation Red," *Seattle Weekly*, February 15 , 1995, 18. Alexie, a Spokane/Coeur d'Alene Indian who grew up on the Spokane Indian Reservation in eastern Washington, is internationally known through his poetry, novels, short stories, and films. He is now a self-described "urban Indian" living in Seattle. In 1995 Ned Blackhawk, a Western Shoshone from Detroit, was a twenty-three-year-old PhD student of history at the University of Washington. He earned the PhD in 1999 and now teaches History and Indian Studies at the University of Wisconsin–Madison.

4. Claude Lévi-Strauss, *The Way of the Masks* (Seattle and London: University of Washington Press, 1988), 5–7.

5. Sylvia Modelski, "Translator's Note," in ibid., v.

6. Jean-Paul Sartre, "The Ethics of Authenticity," *Being and Nothingness: An Essay on Phenomenological Ontology* (1943), trans. Hazel E. Barnes (New York: Washington Square Press, 1966). Sartre's discussion of authenticity first appears here but also runs throughout many of his later works.

7. Dean MacCannell, "Staged Authenticity," in *The Tourist: A New Theory of the Leisure Class* (New York: Shocken Books, 1976), 91–108. See also Christopher Balme, "Staging the Pacific: Framing Authenticity in Performances for Tourists at the Polynesian Cultural Center," *Theatre Journal* 50 (1998): 53–70.

8. James Clifford, "Of Other Peoples: Beyond the 'Salvage' Paradigm," in *The Politics of Representations*, ed. Hal Foster (Seattle: Bay Press, 1987), 121.

9. Lévi-Strauss, *Way of the Masks*, 8.

10. Among Franz Boas's numerous works on the Northwest Coast Indians are *The Social Organization and the Secret Societies of the Kwakiutl Indians*, Report of the National Museum (1895); *The Decorative Art of the Indians of the North Pacific Coast*, Bulletin of the American Museum of Natural History, vol. 9 (1897), 123–76; *The Kwakiutl of Vancouver Island*, Memoirs of the American Museum of Natural History, vol. 8 (1909), 307–515.

11. Edward S. Curtis, *The North American Indian*, 20 vols., Cambridge: The University Press, 1907–30.

12. Lévi-Strauss, *Way of the Masks*, 8.

13. "First Nations Territories of the Pacific Northwest: Condensed History of the Northwest Coastal People," http://www.northwest-connection.com/Pages/nations.htm. Also see at http:///www.snowwowl.com/peopleinuit3.html.

14. Edward Said, *Orientalism* (New York: Vintage Books, 1979).

15. Bill Holm, *Northwest Coast Indian Art: An Analysis of Form* (Seattle and London: University of Washington Press, 1965).

16. George F. MacDonald, "Pathways to Heaven: Journeys of the Soul in Northwest Native Cultures," lecture and slide presentation, Burke Museum of Natural History and Culture, Seattle, November 6, 2003. MacDonald was director of the museum at this time.

17. Michael Taussig, *Mimesis and Alterity: A Particular History of the Senses* (New York: Routledge, 1993), xviii.

18. See, for example, Chief Robert Joseph, 18–35, and Peter MacNair, 36–185, in *Down from the Shimmering Sky: Masks of the Northwest Coast*, by Bruce Grenville, Robert Joseph, and Peter MacNair (Seattle and Vancouver, BC: University of Washington Press and Vancouver Art Gallery, 1998). See also photos of a closed and open Nuxalk sun transformation mask, figures 74A and 74B, 98–99.

19. Caroline Mary Budic, "Wolf Ritual Dances of the Northwest Coast Indians," master's thesis, University of Washington, 1964, p. 86.

20. Franz Boas, *The Social Organization and the Secret Societies of the Kwakiutl Indians*, Report of the National Museum (1895), Washington, 491.

21. Clellan Ford, *Smoke from the Fires: The Auto-biography of a Kwakiutl Chief* (Handon, CT: Archon, 1971), 110.

22. "Special Events," at U'mista Cultural Society, http://www.umista.org/kwakwakawakw/events.php, italics mine. This official Web site of the U'Mista Cultural Society further explains: "Featuring traditional Kwakwaka'wakw dances, performances by First Nations youth representing various tribes within our language group are presented throughout July and August. All dances and songs are presented with pride and have our Elders' approval, and remain unchanged since our Creator gave them to us." Native people were said to have *u'mista* when they were lucky enough to be returned home by their white captors. "The return of our treasures from distant museums is a form of u'mista."

23. Edward S. Curtis, writer/ director of the film, originally titled *In the Land of the Headhunters: A Drama of Primitive Life on the Shores of the North Pacific* (United States and Canada: Seattle Film, 1914). Restoration by Bill Holm, George Quimby and David Gerth as *In the Land of the War Canoes*. Songs and dialogue performed by contemporary Kwakwaka'wakws (Seattle: University of Washington Press, 1972).

24. Mary Elizabeth Fullerton, "Reception and Representation: The Western Vision of Native American Performance on the Northwest Coast," PhD diss., University of Washington, 1986, p. 58.

25. Edward Curtis sought "Indianness" in both his films and his photographs of Native Americans across the United States and Canada. The photos are collected in twenty volumes of *The North American Indian*, 1907–1930.

26. *In the Land of the War Canoes*, dir. Bill Holm. Film retitled for 1972 restoration, with newly recorded soundtrack, including dialogue and songs by contemporary Kwakwaka'wakws.

27. Mary Elizabeth Fullerton, "Reception and Representation: The Western Vision of Native American Performance on the Northwest Coast," 199–204.

28. Budic, "Wolf Ritual Dances," 109.

29. Samuel A. Barrett, "Introduction," *Masks of the Northwest Coast*, ed. Robert Ritzenthaler and Lee A. Parsons (Milwaukee: Milwaukee Public Museum, 1966), ii.

30. Boas describes the ethnographic exhibits at the 1893 Chicago World's Columbian Exposition in "A World's Fair: Ethnology at the Exposition," *Cosmopolitan* 15 (September 1893): 607–9.

31. Brochure, *Seattle's Tillicum Village*, 2005–6.

32. Katie N. Johnson and Tamara Underiner, "Command Performances: Staging Native Americans at Tillicum Village," in *Selling the Indian: Commercializing and Appropriating American Indian Cultures*, ed. Carter Jones Meyer and Diana Royer (Tucson: University of Arizona Press, 2001), 45.

33. Jean-Paul Sartre, "The Ethics of Authenticity," in *Being and Nothingness: An Essay on Phenomenological Ontology* (1943) (New York: Washington Square Press, 1966).

34. John R. Jewitt, "Primary Forms of Material Culture: Living and Eating" (1824), in *Indians of the North Pacific Coast: Studies in Selected Topics*, ed. Tom McFeat (Seattle and London: University of Washington Press, 1992), 15.

35. Ibid., 14.

36. "Tour Description," Tillicum Village Web site, www.tillicumvillage.com, 6.

37. Ibid., 8.

38. Johnson and Underiner, "Command Performances," 53.

39. Alexie, "Generation Red," 19.

40. Johnson and Underiner, interview with Bill Hewitt, May 1995.

41. MacCannell, "Staged Authenticity," 91–95. The concepts of "front space" and "back space" were first developed by Erving Goffman in *Relations in Public: Microstudies of the Public Order* (New York: Basic Books, 1971) and *Behavior in Public Places: Notes on the Social Organization of Gatherings* (New York: Free Press, 1963).

42. Charles H. Burke, directive to the Bureau of Indian Affairs (1921), quoted in *The Sacred: Ways of Knowledge, Sources of Life*, by Peggy V. Beck, Anna Lee Walters, and Nia Francisco (Tsaile, AZ: Navajo Community College Press, 1992), 154–55.

43. Ibid., 155.

44. Boas was adamantly opposed to this alleged "science" of social Darwinism.

45. Burke, quoted in *The Sacred*, 158

46. Alexie, "Generation Red," 19.

47. Ibid., 18.

48. Dwight Conquergood, "Performance Theory, Hmong Shamans, and Cultural Politics," in *Critical Theory and Performance*, ed. Janelle Reinelt and Joseph Roach (Ann Arbor: University of Michigan Press, 1992), 43.

49. Lloyd J. Averill and Daphne K. Morris, *Northwest Coast Native and Native-Style Art: A Guidebook for Western Washington* (Seattle and London: University of Washington Press, 1995). Averill and Morris note that there are thirty-three manhole covers ("hatchcovers") within the city of Seattle, which in the 1960s commissioned three distinguished Native artists, including Nathan Jackson of the Tlingit Nation. See description and photo, 63 and 64.

Chapter 3. Owners of the Past

1. This chapter is a revised version of my article "Readbacks or Tradition? The Kluskap Stories among Modern Canadian Mi'kmaq," *European Review of Native American Studies (ERNAS)* 16, no.1 (2002): 9–16.

2. There are many ways to spell Glooscap (Gloscap, Gluskap, etc.). I have chosen the spelling Kluskap.

3. In many of the traditional North American Indian stories there is a difficultly defined character known as the trickster. In the trickster, two more or less opposite roles are combined. The stories show an immoral character that breaks taboo, is thievish, sexually active, and antisocial, and that continuously cheats those around him. But he can also be described in positive terms as a culture hero. As such, he defeats monsters, steals the fire, and creates the landscape through transformations. The trickster as culture hero has never been an object of worship. Traditionally, he was not looked upon as a god but more as a character in a mythical time. The place of his dwelling varies in different traditions. Many stories tell of his disappearance in the past, nevermore to interfere in people's lives. For information about Kluskap as trickster and culture hero, see Anne-Christine Hornborg, *A Landscape of Left-Overs: Changing Conception of Place and Environment among Mi'kmaq Indians of Eastern Canada*, Lund Studies in History of Religions, vol. 14 (Sweden: Almqvist and Wiksell International, 2001), or Hornborg, "Kluskap—as Culture Hero and Global Green Warrior: Different Context for the Canadian Mi'kmaq Culture Hero," *Acta Americana* 9 (2001): 1.

4. Fisher (238) writes that this motif, "hero chases a beaver which gets away," is widely spread among the Mi'kmaq, Passamaquoddy, Penobscot, Maliseet, Ojibwa, and Menomini. Margaret Fisher, "The Mythology of the Northern and Northeastern Algonkians in References to Algonkian Mythology," in *Man in Northeastern North America*, ed. Frederick Johnson, *PPFA* 3 (1946): 226–62. Cf. Mi'kmaq stories about Kluskap chasing a beaver in Silas T. Rand, *Legends of the Micmacs* (New York: Longmans, Green, 1971 [1894]); Charles G. Leland, *The Algonquin Legends of New England or Myths and Folk Lore of the Micmac, Passamaquoddy, and Penobscot Tribes* (London: Sampson Low, Marston, Searle and Rivington, 1884); Frank G. Speck, "Some Micmac Tales from Cape Breton Island,"

Journal of American Folklore 28 (1915): 59–69, Elsie Clews Parsons, "Micmac Folklore." *Journal of American Folklore* 38 (1925): 55–133; and Wilson D. Wallis and R. Sawtell Wallis, *The Micmac Indians of Eastern Canada* (Minneapolis: University of Minnesota Press, 1955).

5. *Micmac Maliseet Nation News*, no. 2 (1992), 26.

6. *Cape Breton Post*, Sept 26 , 1989.

7. Ernest S. Burch Jr., "The Future of Hunter-Gatherer Research," in *Key Issues in Hunter-Gatherer Research*, ed. Ernest S. Burch Jr. and Linda J. Ellanna (Oxford: Berg, 1994), 444.

8. Silas T. Rand, *A Short Statement of Facts Relating to the History, Manners, Customs, Language, and Literature of the Micmac Tribe of Indians in Nova Scotia and P. E. Island* (Halifax: James Brown & Son, 1850); and Rand, *Legends of the Micmacs*.

9. Rand, *A Short Statement*, 28.

10. Ibid., 29.

11. Rand, *Legends of the Micmacs*, 1971 [1894], 76.

12. Ibid., 154.

13. Leland, *Algonquin Legends of New England*, iv.

14. Ibid., v.

15. Ibid., 2.

16. Ibid.

17. Rand, *Legends of the Micmacs*, 14.

18. Leland, *Algonquin Legends of New England*, 253.

19. Ibid. (footnote); cf. Thomas C. Parkhill, *Weaving Ourselves into the Land: Charles Godfrey Leland, "Indians," and the Study of Native American Religions* (New York: State University of New York Press, 1997), 57.

20. For Leland it was of great importance to document the Algonkin legends, since he saw a deep bond between them and the North American continent itself. Through the stories, the settlers could take part in this bond and gain a feeling for home in a landscape in which they still felt alien: "And I venture to say from the deepest conviction that it will be no small occasion of astonishment and chagrin, a hundred years hence, when the last Algonkin Indian of the Wabano shall have passed away, that so few among our literary or cultured folk cared enough to collect this connected aboriginal literature" (Leland, in Charles Godfrey Leland and John Dyneley Prince, *Kulóskap the Master: And Other Algonkin Poems* [New York: Funk and Wagnalls, 1902], 15).

21. In "Tradition, but What Tradition and for Whom?" *Oral Tradition* 6, no. 1 (1991): 104–24, Ruth Finnegan describes how, previously, the anthropologist's project was to document the "traditional" story and focus on the "original" form.

22. Alfred G. Bailey, *The Conflict of European and Eastern Algonkian Cultures 1504–1700* (Saint John, N.B.: Publications of the New Brunswick Museum, 1937), 135.

23. Ibid., 188.

24. An early name, first applied in the sixteenth century for the present-day U.S. mid-Atlantic coastline, was Arcadia. The French version, l'Acadie or Acadia, later became the name of the easternmost French colony in the New World.

25. Other scholars (e.g., Wilson D. Wallis and Ruth Sawtell Wallis, 321) say that centuries of culture contacts have made it impossible to draw any sharp limits between the cultures at all.

26. Rand, *Legends of the Micmacs*, 228.

27. William Elder, "The Aborigines of Nova Scotia," *North American Review* 112 (1871): 16. Silas Rand, *Legends of the Micmacs*, 23.

28. Parsons, "Micmac Folklore"; Speck, "Some Micmac Tales from Cape Breton Island"; and Wallis and Wallis, *Micmac Indians of Eastern Canada*. Although he did not write it down before 1955, Wilson did most of his collection in 1911–1912.

29. Wallis and Wallis, *Micmac Indians of Eastern Canada*, 318.

30. Isabelle Knockwood, *Out of the Depths: The Experience of Mi'kmaq Children at the Indian Residential School at Shubenacadie, Nova Scotia* (Nova Scotia: Roseway, 1992), 14.

31. When Speck collects stories among the Penobscot, Kluskap is again represented as a transformer of the landscape. Now it is the local place names from this tribe that appear in the texts and thus get their explanations. Franklin G. Speck, "Penobscot Tales and Religious Beliefs," *Journal of American Folklore* 48, no. 187 (1935): 6.

32. Speck, "Some Micmac Tales from Cape Breton Island," 59–60.

33. Parsons, "Micmac Folklore," 87.

34. Ibid., 85.

35. Wallis and Wallis, *Micmac Indians of Eastern Canada*, 306.

36. Ibid., 305.

37. Ibid., 481.

38. Philip K. Bock, *The Micmac Indians of Restigouche: History and Contemporary Description* (Ottawa: National Museum of Canada, 1966), 85.

39. For a more careful study of this period, see Hornborg, *Landscape of Left-Overs*.

40. Kay Hill, *Glooscap and His Magic: Legends of the Wabanaki People* (Toronto: McClelland and Stewart, 1963), *Badger the Mischief Maker* (Toronto: McClelland and Stewart, 1965), *More Glooscap Stories: Legends of the Wabanaki Indians* (Toronto: McClelland and Stewart, 1970); cf. Parkhill, op. cit., 25.

41. These two movies were reviewed by Alvin H. Morrison, "Glooskap (1971), Glooscap Country (1961)," *American Anthropologist* 78, no. 4 (1976): 957–58.

42. Parkhill, *Weaving Ourselves into the Land*, 28.

43. Personal communication with Sten Eirik (1998), who was one of the actors in the play.

44. Later on, two Mi'kmaq joined the actors and even got roles in the play.

45. *Cape Breton Post*, March 26, 1989.

46. Information recorded by the Sacred Mountain Society (Mi'kmaq traditionalists) from meetings, papers, and interviews on the radio, since, as the information sheet states, "no brochures or printed details about the project have been made available although such has been promised."

47. *Chronicle Herald*, April 21, 1990, B3.

48. *Network News: Nova Scotia Environmental Network*, no. 2 (July/August 1992), 5.

49. Anne-Christine Hornborg, *Landscape of Left-Overs*, 291 (meeting transcribed from a videocassette recording, March 1992, privately held).

50. Letters to Mi'kmaq traditionalist Sulian Stone Eagle Herney from the Nova Scotia Department of Education, Nova Scotia Museum.

51. Stephen A. Davis and Brian Preston, eds., *Curatorial Report Number 77: Archaeology in Nova Scotia 1989 and 1990* (Nova Scotia Museum: Department of Education, 1993), 89–90.

52. *Micmac Maliseet Nation News* no. 5 (1994), 17.

53. Alf Hornborg, "Environmentalism, Ethnicity and Sacred Places: Reflections on Modernity, Discourse and Power," *Canadian Review of Sociology and Anthropology* 31, no. 3 (1994): 252.

54. *Network News: Nova Scotia Environmental Network*, no. 2 (July/August 1992), 4, italics added. By referring to "the elders," the speaker gains authority among Yupiit. Cf. Calvin L. Martin, *The Way of the Human Being* (New Haven and London: Yale University Press, 1999), 110.

55. Alf Hornborg, "Environmentalism, Ethnicity and Sacred Places," 252.

56. Sulian Stone Eagle Herney, *Micmac Maliseet Nation News*, no. 2 (1992). Cf. Martin, *Way of the Human Being*, 155, who says that there is a tendency that modern readers might depict the Native (in this case the Yupik) stories as a kind of childish entertainment, as if they had nothing to say about real life: "the majority of us regard the native stories as mere juvenile entertainment. We, in our ontology, see no familiar or verifiable reality in these stories."

57. *Micmac News*, April 19, 1991, 3, italics added.

58. Sulian Stone Eagle Herney, *Network News. Nova Scotia Environmental Network*, no. 2 (July/August 1992), 4.

59. Hornborg , *Landscape of Left-Overs*, 286.

60. Rita Joe, *Song of Eskasoni* (Charlottetown, P.E.I.: Ragweed Press 1991 [1988]), 40.

61. Ibid.

62. Parsons, 87.

63. Rita Joe's poem was originally published in 1988, and the plans for a quarry were announced in 1989.

64. The examination was made in October 1989. Ruth Whitehead was one of the "Museum staff" (Ruth Whitehead, personal communication, 2000).

65. Davis and Preston, *Curatorial Report Number 77*, 89–90; also Whitehead, personal communication, 2000.

66. *Cape Breton Magazine*, no. 53 (Jan. 1990).

67. In the foreword to Ruth Whitehead, *The Old Man Told Us* (Halifax: Nimbus, 1991), Peter Christmas (Micmac Association of Cultural Studies) writes: "By expertly and ingeniously interleaving written and oral excerpts, Ms. Whitehead has provided the Micmac with a more level field of human history." He also writes, at the end: "*The Old Man Told Us* will be an excellent foundation for your introduction into our society. It will spark your interest to seek further knowledge."

68. Rita Joe, *Lnu and Indians We're Called* (Charlottetown, P.E.I.: Ragweed, 1991), 28.

69. Eleanor Johnson, "Mi'kmaq Tribal Consciousness in the Twentieth Century," in *Paqtatek*, ed. Stephanie Inglis, Joy Manette, and Stacey Sulewski (Halifax: Garamond Press, 1991), 26.

70. Ibid., 14.

71. S. Dalby, "Globalization and the Natural Environment: Geopolitics, Culture and Resistance." Draft paper for presentation to the International Roundtable on the Challenges of Globalization at the University of Munich, March 1999, 10.

Chapter 4. The Pocahontas Myth and Its Deconstruction

1. Neal McLeod, "Coming Home through Stories," *International Journal of Canadian Studies* 18 (Fall 1998): 51.

2. This essay is based on a paper that I gave at the 23rd American Indian Workshop "Ritual and Performance" at Trinity College, Dublin, in March 2002. An early version of this essay was published in Mark Shackleton and Veera Supinen, eds., *First and Other Nations* (Helsinki: Renvall Institute Publications, 2005).

3. Philip L. Barbour, ed., *Complete Works of Captain John Smith in Three volumes*, vol. 2 (Chapel Hill: University of North Carolina Press, 1986), 151. John Smith wrote, in fact, three different accounts of being captured, all of which are contradictory, and only the last one makes reference to *Pocahuntas*, as Smith calls her.

4. There has been speculation among historians as to John Smith's reasons for adding the Pocahontas rescue story to his accounts from the Jamestown colony. Some claim that Smith wanted to ride on the wave of Pocahontas's success in the English court on her 1616 visit; others say that Smith simply had a tendency to add boastful stories to his journals to enhance his reputation as a brave and successful adventurer (also among the fairer sex). In many of his travel accounts, John Smith seems to reveal "a peculiar talent for being 'offered rescue and protection in [. . .] greatest dangers'" by various "'honorable and vertuous Ladies'" as Philip Young puts it in his article on Pocahontas, "The Mother of Us All" *(Kenyon Review* [summer 1962]).

5. Helen C. Rountree offers very interesting perspectives on Smith's rescue story's significance and Pocahontas's life in her article "Pocahontas: The Hostage Who Became Famous," in Theda Perdue, ed., *Sifters: Native American Women's Lives* (New York: Oxford University Press, 2001).

6. Helen C. Rountree writes in ibid. that Pocahontas was not really a "princess" in the European sense, because of a different system of succession to the seat of power in the Powhatan system.

7. See ibid., 14–28.

8. Young, "Mother of Us All," 395–6. Young traces the history of Pocahontas depictions in literature in his article.

9. Ibid., 399.

10. James Nelson Barker, *The Indian Princess; or La Belle Sauvage: An Operatic Melo-Drame in Three Acts* (New York: Da Capo Press, 1972), 40.

11. Ibid., 52.

12. Arthur Hobson Quinn, ed., *Representative American Plays: From 1767 to the Present Day* (New York: Appleton-Century-Crofts, 1953), 175.

13. Ibid., 175.

14. Ibid., 191.

15. Raymond William Stedman, *Shadows of the Indian: Stereotypes in American Culture* (Norman: University of Oklahoma Press, 1982).

16. Homi K. Bhabha, *The Location of Culture* (London: Routledge, 1994), 68, referring to stereotypes in 1950s Hollywood films, in his essay "The Other Question: Stereotype, Discrimination and the Discourse of Colonialism." In this essay, Bhabha suggests that both fetishism and voyeurism are important elements in building stereotypes in colonial discourse.

17. As Philip Young calls Pocahontas in his article of the same name in *Kenyon Review* 94 (summer 1962).

18. Leslie Fiedler, *The Return of the Vanishing American* (New York: Madison Books, 1968), 75, my italics.

19. Jacquelyn Kilpatrick, "Race in Contemporary American Cinema: Part 5: Disney's 'Politically Correct' Pocahontas," *Cineaste* 21, no. 4 (1994): 36.

20. However, there is serious doubt as to the accuracy of this portrait of her, since her picture is likely to have been altered to suit the conventions of the time, giving her lighter skin and more European-looking features.

21. In the first Disney film, it was John Smith, and not John Rolfe, that Pocahontas "falls for."

22. Kilpatrick, "Disney's 'Politically Correct' Pocahontas," 36.

23. Ibid.

24. 29 May 2006, http://www.powhatan.org/pocc.html.

25. Ibid.

26. Helen C. Rountree has done a wonderful job of tracing historical evidence of the Powhatan girl in her book *Pocahontas's People: The Powhatan Indians of Virginia through Four Centuries* (Norman: University of Oklahoma Press, 1990).

27. See Helen Gilbert and Joanne Tompkins, *Post-colonial Drama: Theory, Practice, Politics* (London: Routledge, 1996), 204.

28. El Teatro Campesino was founded in 1965 by Chicano dramatist Luis Valdéz for political action to improve the living and working conditions of American Chicanos and Chicanas: in Valdéz's words, "to replace the lingering negative stereotype of the Mexican in the United States with a new positive image created through Chicano art, and to continue to dramatize the social despair of Chicanos living in an Anglo-dominated society," quoted from Marsue Cumming, ed., *Theatre Profiles* 3 (1977), in C.W.E. Bigsby's *A Critical Introduction to Twentieth-century American Drama, Volume 3: Beyond Broadway* (Cambridge: Cambridge University Press, 1990), 363.

29. Confronting stereotypes was also a feature in African American theater of the 1960s. See Bigsby, *Critical Introduction.*

30. This included such events as the occupation of Alcatraz in 1964 and 1969, the Trail of Broken Treaties in 1972, and perhaps most notably, the events at Wounded Knee on the Pine Ridge reservation in 1973 and, amid these events, the birth of the American Indian Movement, AIM.

31. Hanay Geiogamah, *New Native American Drama: Three Plays by Hanay Geiogamah* (Norman: University of Oklahoma Press, 1980), 62–65.

32. See *Canadian Theatre Review* 68 (Fall 1991): 54–63.

33. Ibid., 56.

34. See Daniel David Moses and Terry Goldie, eds., *An Anthology of Canadian Native Literature in English* (Toronto: Oxford University Press, 1998), 326–340.

35. Ric Knowles, "Translators, Traitors, Mistresses, and Whores: Monique Mojica and the Mothers of the Métis Nation," in *Siting the Other: Marginal Identities in Australian and Canadian Drama*, ed. Marc Maufort and Franca Bellarsi (Bern, Brussels, and New York: P.I.E.–Peter Lang, 2001), 247–66.

36. Bhabha, *Location of Culture*, 66.

37. Ibid., 77–78.

38. Rappahannock is one of the Powhatan tribes, closely related to Pocahontas's people. http://www.powhatan.org/history.html.

39. Moses and Goldie, *Anthology of Canadian Native Literature*, 511–12.

40. Ibid., 512.

41. Monique Mojica, *Princess Pocahontas and the Blue Spots* (Toronto: Women's Press, 1991), 13.

42. Ibid., 60.

43. Paula Gunn Allen, *The Sacred Hoop: Recovering the Feminine in American Indian Traditions* (Boston: Beacon Press, 1986), 268.

44. Mojica, *Princess Pocahontas*, 20.

45. Ibid., 14.

46. Ibid.

47. Bhabha, *Location of Culture*, 67.

48. Mojica, *Princess Pocahontas*, 18.

49. Ibid., 19.

50. Ibid.

51. This is a familiar scene from many cartoons and films in which the Indian Princess kills herself for the sake of her white lover. Interestingly, even Disney suggestively leaves his princess standing on a precipice at the end of *Pocahontas* (1995), as she watches John Smith set sail for England. Naturally, being a Disney feature, the heroine does not commit suicide.

52. The Indian Princess and Amazon Queen images of the early colonial period (sixteenth and seventeenth centuries) often symbolized the actual physical, geographical territory of the Americas, offering an obvious phallic image of penetrating the "virgin" land.

53. The colonial Pocahontas story reveals what Rayna Green calls the "Indian woman's dilemma": "To be 'good,' she must defy her own people, exile herself from them, become white" (Rayna Green, "The Pocahontas Perplex: The Image of Indian Women in American Culture," in *Unequal Sisters: A Multicultural Reader in U.S. Women's History*, ed. Ellen Carol DuBois and Vicki Ruiz [London: Routledge, 1990], 18).

54. Idioms such as "Hija de La Chingada," "La Chingada" being the common nickname used for Malinche, meaning "the fucked one."

55. Paula Gunn Allen, *The Sacred Hoop: Recovering the Feminine in American Indian Traditions* (Boston: Beacon Press, 1986), 158.

56. McLeod, "Coming Home through Stories," 51.

57. Mojica, *Princess Pocahontas*, 26.

58. Ibid., 27.

59. Ibid.

60. Blue spots have been considered a sign of "Indian blood," which, as Mojica says in the play, was something that mothers checked for in newborn babies: "When I was born, my mother turned me over to / check for the blue spot at the base of the spine— / the sign of Indian blood. / When my child was born, after counting the fingers / and the toes, I turned it over to check for the blue / spot at the base of the spine. / Even among the half-breeds, it's one of the last / things to go" (20).

61. Barbour, 151.

62. Mojica, *Princess Pocahontas*, 28.

63. Ibid., 29.

64. Ibid., 27.

65. Ibid., 29.

66. See especially Bhabha's essay "Of Mimicry and Man," in *The Location of Culture*, 85–92.

67. Mojica, *Princess Pocahontas*, 28.

68. Gloria Anzaldúa, *Borderlands/La Frontera: The New Mestiza* (San Francisco: Aunt Lute, 1987), 78.

69. Ibid.

70. The trickster figure appears in many Native American artists' and writers' work (originating in many traditional stories) and often represents freedom and independence through humor. It is impossible to pinpoint the trickster's position or to try to hold him/her captive. Often the trickster can change shape and gender and can create real turbulence, as in Thomas King's *Green Grass Running Water* (New York: Bantam Books, 1993).

71. Mojica, *Princess Pocahontas*, 49.

72. Ibid.

73. Ibid.

74. Mimi Gisolfi D'Aponte, "Native Women Playwrights: Transmitters, Healers, Transformers," *Journal of Dramatic Theory and Criticism* volume 14 (Fall 1999): 103. The idea of "comic rhythm" is originally presented by philosopher Suzanne Langer in her work *Feeling and Form* (New York: Charles Scribner's Sons, 1953).

75. Mojica, *Princess Pocahontas*, 59.

76. "Word warriors" is a term used by Paula Gunn Allen in her book *The Sacred Hoop* for Native American writers and literature and their important role in fighting colonialism.

77. Ann Haugo, "Colonial Audiences and Native Women's Theatre: Viewing Spider-woman Theater's *Winnetou Snake Oil Show from Wigwam City*," *Journal of Dramatic Theory and Criticism* 14 (Fall 1999): 131.

78. Mojica, *Princess Pocahontas*, 60.

Chapter 6. Acts of Transfer

1. Regarding this phrase, Peter Nabokov writes, "It is the innately democratic virtue of much oral tradition that its multiple versions 'enrich the listener's experience,'" (*A Forest of Time* [Cambridge University Press: University of California, Los Angeles, 2002], 47–48). Nabokov points out that this phrase also serves as a cross-reference to "native glosses and commentaries" that "usually require an intimate awareness of the community's different, perhaps contradictory microhistories to interpret."

2. An ethos is "a value system governing collective behavior," seen as crucial to ensuring the survival of the group (Delores Huff, *To Live Heroically* [Albany: State University of New York Press, 1997], 70). As Huff observes, the fact that this value system is not always practiced on an individual basis does not diminish its regulatory power over a group's religious, family, economic, and political systems.

3. Diana Taylor, *The Archive and the Repertoire* (Durham: Duke University Press, 2003).

4. Ibid., 19, 18.

5. Ibid., 19.

6. As Taylor points out, this is not to say that one can speak of "uninterrupted or authentic practices—as if there were such a thing—transmitted from one generation to the next ("Scenes of Cognition: Performance and Conquest," *Theater Journal* 56, no. 3 (2004): 371, 21). However, "even though the embodiment changes, the meaning might very well remain the same," *Archive and the Repertoire*, 20.

7. I define Native theater as the intersection of Indian social space with Western theater formats and conventions to create Indian theatrical space. My reference to (Indian) social space is adapted from Henri Lefevbre, *The Production of Social Space*, trans. Donald Nicholson Smith (Cambridge, MA: Blackwell, 1999). Indian theatrical space exists at the material level of enactment by Indian theater artists and the habitus of Native actors and audiences; at the symbolic level, as referents drawn from tribal spatial practice (which need not be mimetic); and at the material/discursive level of critical reception, artistic praxis, and the like.

8. Taylor, *Archive and the Repertoire*, 2.

9. Taylor, "Scenes of Cognition," 21.

10. *Foghorn* is published in *New Native American Drama: Three Plays by Hanay Geiogamah* (University of Oklahoma Press: Norman, 1980), 46–82.

11. Phyllis Brisson reports she was especially taken by Maggie Geiogamah's acting

in the piece—"I knew I wanted to do something like that" (tape-recorded interview by author, Dec. 4, 2004, Los Angeles, California).

12. Ibid. Gerald Bruce Miller, Keith Conway, and Marie Antoinette Rogers exemplify the fluid and nomadic work life of Native actors. As mentioned, Miller originally hailed from Washington state and moved back to the area permanently to work with Red Earth. Conway took up residence in Seattle for a number of shows. Marie Antoinette Rogers performed with REPAC in their very first play, *Raven*, before taking a role in *Body Indian*, at Geiogamah's behest. Geiogamah also made numerous trips to Seattle. REPAC staged two of Geiogamah's plays in all—*Body Indian* and *Coon Cons Coyote*, and each time it did, it brought in the playwright (Donald Matt, telephone interview, Oct. 23, 2005).

13. Matt interview.

14. *Raven* program, October 1975, Inigo Theater, Seattle University, Red Earth scrapbook.

15. Frieda Kirk, tape-recorded interview by author, Dec. 4, 2004, Los Angeles, California.

16. *Raven* program, Inigo Theater.

17. Matt interview.

18. Luci Tapahonso, quoted by Peter Nabokov, *Forest of Time*, 40.

19. Ibid.

20. Louis Owens, *Other Destinies: Understanding the American Indian Novel* (University of Oklahoma Press: Norman, 1992), 10. "The emphasis in storytelling falls . . . not upon the creative role of the storyteller but upon the communal nature of the stories, with the 'outcome' of each story already being known to the audience."

21. Matt interview. Frieda Kirk was part Klamath, but she was also half Sioux. Matt was Flathead, another Washington tribe, but an inland tribe, not a coastal tribe.

22. Taylor, "Performance and Conquest," 371.

23. Lorraine Hale, *Native American Education: A Reference Handbook* (Denver: ABC Clio, 2002), 85. Hale writes that, traditionally, education is a community-based activity for tribes in which children progress at their own pace "through direct experience and hands-on activity-oriented learning." Taylor similarly recognizes the pedagogical aspects of performance: "The term, performance, suggests both a praxis and an episteme" ("Performance and Conquest," 364).

24. *The Oxford Concise Dictionary*, 9th ed. (New York: Oxford University Press, 1995), describes the gavotte as a "medium-paced French dance popular in the eighteenth century," 561.

25. Matt interview.

26. Edward Bruner, quoted by Dwight Conquergood, "Performance Theory, Hmong Shamans, and Cultural Politics," in *Critical Theory and Performance*, ed. Janelle G. Reinelt and Joseph R. Roach (Ann Arbor: University of Michigan Press, 1992), 51.

27. Bruce Miller wrote *Changer* for a state arts grant (interview by telephone with author, Jan. 6, 2005). It was adapted from a Skokomish creation story, dealing with "'the time of capsizing' during which Dukweebaht, the changer, was sent to change the world" (unpublished manuscript, Red Earth scrapbook, 1). *Coon Cons Coyote* is published in

Stories of Our Way, ed. Hanay Geiogamah and Jaye T. Darby (Berkeley and Los Angeles: University of California Press, 1999), 357–444. Geiogamah insists he hardly changed any aspects of the poem "Coon Cons Coyote," which poet Jerome Rothenberg freely adapted from a literal translation of the Nez Perce epic (telephone interview, June 11, 2005). NATE's transculturations came in the staging of the play and the addition of Native repertoires—specific tribal songs, pratfalls, dances, and ritual occasion, like the feast that ends the play. The text and repertoire of *Coon Cons Coyote*, and Miller's script *Changer*, all possessed abundant scatological and sexual references and a polyvalent sexuality. They bore witness to what Gerald Vizenor calls "the erotic shimmer" of the oral tradition (Gerald Vizenor, quoted by Jace Weaver in *Other Words* [Norman: University of Oklahoma Press, 2001], 246).

28. According to Brisson, from the moment Miller joined the group, he brought with him a delight in improvising during performance (interview with author by telephone, Jan. 6, 2005). Gina Gray performed in Miller's play *Changer* when it was staged at the Institute of American Indian Art in Santa Fe. She recalls, "Whatever was on the page was not what came out of that man's mouth. It was a combination of cartoons and storytelling [. . .] he was so animated with his face and body language" (personal interview, July 21, 2005).

29. Kirk interview. Kirk also observes that in *Coon Cons Coyote*, REPAC made costuming choices, such as adding flowered sunglasses to Coyote, that seemed to upset non-Indians, who expected traditional stories always to be serious, high-minded, and fixed in the past.

30. Jean and John Comaroff, quoted in Circe Sturm's *Blood Politics* (Berkeley and Los Angeles: University of California Press, 2002), 23. While this statement seems obvious, it is important to note that Native habitus is not single but multiple and is complexly layered. It is shot through with numerous influences—family, personal, regional, national, geographic, and the like—which are constantly in flux, and subject to historicization. Expectations about Native habitus may promote internal stereotyping on the part of Indian people toward other Indians, expressed in the indictment of someone who "acts white." At the other end of the spectrum are judgments offered up by (mostly) white movie casting agents, and often based upon the latest Indian movie, about what kinds of physical movement and what kinds of accents look or sound "Indian." Members of the American Indian Theater Company of Oklahoma ran into this type of discrimination on a frequent basis during the 1970s Indian-movie wave, according to J. R. Mathews (tape-recorded interview by author, Sept. 4, 2004, Miami, Oklahoma).

31. Culturally active Native spectators' ability to read tribal habitus is itself a product of a habitus and, as such, part of the unique cultural lens Indian audiences bring to the theater.

32. When *Raven* opened, there were only a few Indian spectators present, primarily friends and family of the actors. However, news of the show quickly spread, until Indians made up half the house (Phyllis Brisson, interview by author by telephone, Jan. 6, 2005).

33. Ibid. Brisson explains, "People were curious to see what we were doing."

34. Peggy Phelan, quoted by Camille F. Forbes, "Dancing with Racial Feet," *Theater Journal* 56 no. 4: 608. Phelan refers to this as the principle of "representational visibility."

35. Henry Bial says that, because published reviews are often used to reconstruct historical performance, theater historians, like the actor, assume a "strategic naïveté" toward their work. One aspect of this naïveté involves operating as if the critic is, indeed, an especially aware and educated viewer, while accounting for the critic's idiosyncracies, "biases and blind spots" ("The Play Review as a Means of Querying Difference, or How I Learned to Stop Worrying and Love the Performative," in *Querying Difference in Theatre History*, ed. Scott Magelssen and Ann Haugo [New Castle: Cambridge Scholars, 2007], 26).

36. Pamela Jennings, review of *Raven* by Nick DiMartino (Red Earth Performing Arts Company, Seattle), *Seattle Times*, September 1975, Red Earth scrapbook. Jennings was probably not privy to Miller's influence on the set and costume design. She does, however, qualify Di Martino's adaptation as demonstrating "some understanding" of the Indian legends of the Pacific Northwest Coast.

37. Bial, "Play Review as a Means of Querying Difference," 27.

38. Donald Grat, review of *Raven* by Nick DiMartino (Red Earth Performing Arts Company, Seattle), *Northwest Arts*, September 1975, Red Earth scrapbook.

39. C.W.E. Bigsby, quoted by Sally Ann Heath, "The Development of Native American Theater Companies in the Continental United States," PhD diss. (Boulder: University of Colorado), 144. Bigsby applied this term to the ethnic, political, and experimental theaters of the period.

40. Paula Gunn Allen, "The Sacred Hoop: A Contemporary Perspective," *American Indian Theater in Performance: A Reader*, ed. Hanay Geiogamah and Jaye T. Darby (Berkeley and Los Angeles: University of California Press, 2003), 51.

41. Jennings, review of *Raven*, n.p.

42. Ibid.

43. Geiogamah, *Body Indian*, 7.

44. Ibid.

45. Ibid., 8.

46. Hanay Geiogamah, telephone interview, June 11, 2005.

47. Miller is listed as having played the lead role of Bobby Lee in the La MaMa production (Geiogamah, *New Native American Drama*, 4). In REPAC's show, however, he was cast in the supporting role of Howard. According to Geiogamah and Matt, Miller had a smaller role because he was simultaneously touring with another REPAC show. Geiogamah (June 11, 2005) thinks it was *Changer*. Matt (Oct. 23) thinks it was *Coon Cons Coyote*.

48. Geiogamah interview.

49. Geiogamah, *Body Indian*, 8.

50. Eduardo Duran and Bonnie Duran, *Native American Postcolonial Psychology* (Albany: State University of New York Press, 1995), 28.

51. Ibid., 28. This perception was so strong during the seventies that one popular prevention poster at the American Indian Theater Company, where I worked, bore the slogan, "Drinking won't make you more Indian."

52. American Indians, who own allotments and do not farm the whole portion themselves, will often lease their lands to neighboring farmers or ranchers who must bid on

the land. While the leasers can talk to the Indian owners directly, the leases are executed by the realty agency arm of the tribe.

53. Geiogamah, *Body Indian*, 18, 22.

54. There are a number of stories concerning the origins of 49s. Lilly Williams attributes the dancing style (people, including men and women, linking arms and dancing in a circle facing inward) to Indian veterans' experiences in World War II, watching the Frenchwomen do the can-can. Round dances are performed in a circle, and they are one of the few kinds of tribal dances in which Plains men and women make physical contact, the Two Step and Snake Dance being two others (interview by author by tape recorder, 14 March, 2004).

55. Brisson Dec. 4, 2004 interview.

56. Geiogamah interview.

57. Kirk interview.

58. Brisson Dec. 4, 2004 interview.

59. Roberta Unamuno, introduction to *The Colour of Theatre: A Critical Sourcebook in Race and Performance*, edited by Roberta Unamuno (London: Athune, 2000), 9.

60. Kirk interview.

61. Brisson Dec. 4, 2004 interview.

62. Ibid.

63. Taylor, "Performance and Conquest," 358.

64. Ibid., 365.

Chapter 7. Embodiment as a Healing Process

1. Some of the material on Shirley Cheechoo has been published in Shelley Scott, "A Path with No Moccasins: Embodiment as a Healing Process," *alt.theatre: Cultural Diversity and the Stage* 2, no. 3 (Jan. 2003): 9–10.

2. Djanet Sears, "Naming Names: Black Women Playwrights in Canada," in *Women on the Canadian Stage: The Legacy of Hrotsvit*, ed. Rita Much (Winnipeg: Blizzard, 1992), 97.

3. Ibid., 102.

4. Quoted in Daniel David Moses, "Write about Now: A Monologue in Changing Lights," *Canadian Theatre Review* 65 (winter 1990): 48.

5. Jordan Wheeler, "Voice," in *Aboriginal Voices: Amerindian, Inuit, and Sami Theater*, ed. Per Brask and William Morgan (Baltimore, London: Johns Hopkins University Press, 1992), 39. According to Drew Hayden Taylor in "Storytelling to Stage: The Growth of Native Theatre in Canada," *TDR* 41, no. 3 (fall 1997): 149, traditional Native storytelling does not usually involve much overt conflict, at least not in the way of the European dramatic process, and is therefore sometimes accused of being nondramatic.

6. Tomson Highway, "On Native Mythology," in *Canadian Theatre History: Selected Readings*, ed. Don Rubin (Toronto: Copp Clark, 1996), 420–23. Reprinted from *Theatrum* 6 (spring 1987): 421.

7. Barbara Godard, "Listening for the Silence: Native Women's Traditional Narratives,"

The Native in Literature, eds. Thomas King, Cheryl Calver, and Helen Hoy (Oakville, ON: ECW Press, 1987), 137.

8. This monologue was performed by George Leach as part of a show called *Mortality*, conceived and directed by Ross Manson, which premiered at the Theatre Centre in Toronto in January 2002.

9. Quoted in Marjorie Beaucage, "Strong and Soft: Excerpts from a Conversation with Muriel Miguel," *Canadian Theatre Review* 68 (fall 1991): 7.

10. Margo Kane, "From the Centre of the Circle the Story Emerges," *Canadian Theatre Review* 68 (fall 1991): 29.

11. The name Debajehmujig is Cree/Ojibway for "telling of tales" or "first storytellers." See Shannon Hengen, "Tellers of Tales," *Canadian Theatre Review* 106 (spring 2001): 35.

12. It was produced by PAS Cultural Exchange Arts with the Association for Native Development in the Performing and Visual Arts. It has also been performed for CBC Morningside Drama and at a "Celebration of Native Women Playwrights" at Miami University in Oxford, Ohio, sponsored by their theater department and the Native American Women Playwrights Archive. The play has been published by The Talent Group in Toronto, and also in a collection of plays called *Canadian Mosaics* (1995), edited by Aviva Ravel. Quotes from reviews are from the published texts.

13. Kim Morrison, "A Look into Real Life," *Meliorist*, September, 30, 1999, 17. In September 1999, Shirley Cheechoo gave two performances of *A Path with No Moccasins* at the University of Lethbridge. As part of her residency at Lethbridge, Cheechoo also gave a public talk, participated in a Fine Arts Council conference of high school teachers, and screened her short film *Silent Tears*.

14. Quoted in Andrew Clark, "Celluloid Sorceress," *Maclean's*, January 31, 2000, 73.

15. Shirley Cheechoo, *A Path with No Moccasins* (Toronto: Talent Group, 1991), 5.

16. Ibid., 46.

17. Gary Farmer, "Introduction," in ibid., 8.

18. Catherine Graham, "Theatrical Bodies and Everyday Life," *Canadian Theatre Review* 109 (winter 2002): 3.

19. Daniel David Moses and Terry Goldie, eds., "Preface: Two Voices," *An Anthology of Canadian Native Literature in English* (Toronto: Oxford University Press, 1992), xvii.

20. Varela, Francisco J., Evan Thompson, and Eleanor Rosch, *The Embodied Mind: Cognitive Science and Human Experience* (Cambridge: MIT Press, 1991), quoted in Graham, "Theatrical Bodies and Everyday Life," 3.

21. Michelle Newman, "body/absence/body: Symptomatologies," *Canadian Theatre Review* 109 (winter 2002): 21.

22. Ibid.

23. Quoted in ibid.

24. Godard, "Listening for the Silence," 184.

25. Agnes Grant, "Introduction," in *Our Bit of Truth: An Anthology of Canadian Native Literature* (Winnipeg: Pemmican Publications, 1990), ix.

26. Quoted in Charlotte Meares, "Indian Play Dances to the Beat of All Drummers," press kit materials.

27. Rosalie Jones, press kit materials and class lectures, University of Lethbridge, Lethbridge, Alberta, January 22–26, 2002.

28. Ibid.

29. Jones founded her company, Daystar: Contemporary Dance-Drama of Indian America, in 1980. In 1996 she began writing the script for *No Home but the Heart*, with the idea that it would be a solo performance; in 1998 it was workshopped in Grand Rapids, Michigan; in 1999 it premiered in Santa Fe; in September of 2000 it was performed in upstate New York; in January of 2002 it was performed at the University of Lethbridge with dancers Sid Bobb, Penny Couchie, and Geraldine Manossa. It has also been presented as a lecture/demonstration in Banff, Calgary, and Dublin.

30. Jones lectures, University of Lethbridge, Lethbridge, Alberta, January 22–26, 2002.

31. Beth Herst, "Review," *Canadian Theatre Review* 98 (spring 1999): 66–67.

32. Ibid., 68.

33. After a lengthy development process, *Princess Pocahontas and the Blue Spots* was first fully produced at the Theatre Passe Muraille Backspace in co-production with Nightwood Theatre, February 9 to March 4, 1990, directed by Muriel Miguel, and was published by the Women's Press (Toronto) in 1991.

34. Ric Knowles, *The Theatre of Form and the Production of Meaning: Contemporary Canadian Dramaturgies* (Toronto: ECW Press, 1999), 207.

35. Ibid., 208.

36. Mojica played: Princess Buttered-on-Both-Sides; Contemporary Woman #1; Malinche; Storybook Pocahontas; Pocahontas/Lady Rebecca/Matoaka; Deity/Woman of the Puna/Virgin; Marie/Margaret/Madelaine; Cigar Store Squaw; and Spirit Animal. Alejandra Nunez played: The Host; The Blue Spots; Contemporary Woman #2; Troubador; Ceremony; The Man; Spirit-Sister; and Musician.

37. Knowles, *Theatre of Form*, 149.

38. Monique Mojica, "Stories from the Body: Blood Memory and Organic Texts," *alt.theatre: Cultural Diversity and the Stage*, 4, nos. 2 and 3 (May 2006), 16–20. For more on her recent work, see also Monique Mojica, "Of Borders, Identity and Cultural Icons: A Rant," *Canadian Theatre Review* 125 (winter 2006), 35–40. Turtle Gals disbanded in 2008.

39. See the last chapter in S. E. Wilmer, *Theatre, Society and the Nation: Staging American Identities* (Cambridge: Cambridge University Press, 2002).

40. Elvira and Hortensia Colorado, "Artistic Statement," in Kathy A. Perkins and Roberta Uno, *Contemporary Plays by Women of Color: An Anthology* (London, New York: Routledge, 1996), 79–80. For further information on Spiderwoman Theater, see pp. 297–99 in the same book.

41. Spiderwoman Theater, "Winnetou's Snake Oil Show from Wigwam City," *Canadian Theatre Review* 68 (fall 1991): 56.

42. ViBrina Coronado, "Here Is Gone and I Could Not Hear It: Using Coatlicue Theatre

Company's Open Wounds on Tlaltecutli to Compare Performance Studies and Theater Methodologies," *Journal of Dramatic Theory and Criticism*, 14, no. 1 (fall 1999), 152.

43. Ann Wilson, "Bored to Distraction: Auto-Performance and the Perniciousness of Presence," *Canadian Theatre Review* 79/80 (fall 1994): 36.

44. Elizabeth Theobald, "Their Desperate Need for Noble Savages," *TDR*, 41, no. 3 (fall 1997): 142.

45. Moses, "Anthology," xxi.

Chapter 8. The Hearts of Its Women

Author's Note: This article grows directly out of my experience working and talking with Monique Mojica on an anthology of First Nations plays, *Staging Coyote's Dream: An Anthology of First Nations Drama in English* (Toronto: Playwrights Canada, 2003). I am currently working with her on volume 2 of that anthology, and I also worked with her on the board of directors of Turtle Gals Performance Ensemble. I am also grateful to Monique Mojica, Jani Lauzon, and Michelle St. John for supplying me with an unpublished draft of *The Scrubbing Project* and for giving me permission to use it here. Finally, I am indebted to Christine Bold for her comments on an earlier version of the paper, which were, as always, extremely helpful. I am grateful for research funding from the Women and Change program of the Social Sciences and Humanities Research Council of Canada. This essay was first published in Sherrill Grace and Albert-Reiner Glaap, ed., *Performing National Identities: International Perspectives on Canadian Theatre* (Vancouver: Talon, 2003), 245–64. Much has changed since then, but I have made only minor revisions here that do not reflect changes that were made in the 2006 production of *The Scrubbing Project*, Monique Mojica's departure from Turtle Gals in 2006, the company's folding in 2008, changes in her personal situation, or any of her subsequent work. I have also resisted the temptation to address work that has been done since 2003 in which there are representations of rape and residential schools. The essay, nevertheless, retains its integrity, and I felt it best not to tamper with it.

1. Tomson Highway, *Dry Lips Oughta Move to Kapuskasing* (Saskatoon: Fifth House, 1989), 95–101.

2. Monique Mojica, *Princess Pocahontas and the Blue Spots: Two Plays* (Toronto: Women's Press, 1991), 60.

3. Ibid., 58.

4. Drew Hayden Taylor, "Native Themes 101," *NeWest Review* 25, no.4 (2000): 17, 18.

5. Suzanne Fournier and Ernie Crey, *Stolen from Our Embrace: The Abduction of First Nations Children and the Restoration of Aboriginal Communities* (Vancouver: Douglas and McIntyre, 1998), 50. According to Stolo scholars Fournier and Crey (61), by the 1930s almost 75 percent of all Native children in Canada between the ages of seven and fifteen were attending residential schools. As is well documented, these schools were frequently the sites of "rape, sexual assault, induced abortion, and sexual/psychological abuse" (Kim Anderson, *A Recognition of Being: Reconstructing Native Womanhood* [Toronto: Second City, 2000], 93). See also Roland Chrisjohn, Sherri Young, and Michael Maraun,

The Circle Game: Shadows and Subsistence in the Indian Residential School Experience in Canada (Penticton, BC: Thetis, 1997); and Assembly of First Nations, *Breaking the Silence: An Interpretive Study of Residential School Impact and Healing as Illustrated by the Stories of First Nations Individuals* (Ottawa: Assembly of First Nations, 1994).

6. "Marianne's Park: A Project on Cultural Memory" is an interdisciplinary project of the Centre for Cultural Studies at the University of Guelph in collaboration with Guelph-Wellington Women in Crisis, funded by a Strategic "Women and Change" grant from the Social Sciences and Humanities Research Council of Canada. Collaborators in the project are Cawo Abdi, Belinda Leach, Christine Bold, Sly Castaldi, Sabina Chatterjee, Ric Knowles, Christine Lenze, Jodie McConnell, and Lisa Schincariol. Its first book-length publication is Cultural Memory Group (Christine Bold, Sly Castaldi, Ric Knowles, Jodie McConnell, and Lisa Schincariol), *Remembering Women Murdered by Men: Memorials across Canada* (Toronto: Sumach Press, 2006). See also The Cultural Memory Group, "'In Memory of Theresa Vince': Research, Activism, and Feminist Memorializing," *Topia: Canadian Journal of Cultural Studies* 13 (Spring 2005): 121–34; Christine Bold, Ric Knowles, and Belinda Leach, "How Might a Women's Monument Be Different?" *Essays in Canadian Writing* 80 (fall 2003): 17–35; and Christine Bold, Ric Knowles, and Belinda Leach, "Feminist Memorializing and Cultural Countermemory: The Case of Marianne's Park," *Signs: Journal of Women in Culture and Society* 28, no.1 (fall 2002): 125–48.

7. Marie Savard, "Contempt Will Have Had Its Day," in *The Montreal Massacre*, eds., Louise Malette and Marie Chalouh (Charlottetown, P.E.I.: Gynergy Books, 1991), 105.

8. Caffyn Kelley, "Creating Memory, Contesting History," *Matriart* 5, no.3 (1995): 8. The quotation is inscribed on the "Marker for Change" at the Vancouver Women's Monument in Thornton Park, Vancouver. In addition to the Cultural Memory Group, *Remembering Women*, 29–55, the best accounts of the Vancouver Women's Monument are found in Kelley; in Sharon Rosenberg, "Standing in a Circle of Stone: Rupturing the Binds of Emblematic Memory," in *Between Hope and Despair: Pedagogy and the Remembrance of Historical Trauma*, ed. Roger Simon, Sharon Rosenberg, and Claudia Eppert (New York: Rowman and Littlefield, 2000), 75–89; and in *Marker of Change: The Story of the Women's Monument*, dir. Moira Simpson, (1998, Moving Images videocassette). See also the *Woman's Monument Design Competition Guidelines*, ftp://ftp.alternatives.com/library/womanabuse/monument/txt.

9. Simpson, *Marker of Change.*

10. Kelley, "Creating Memory, Contesting History," 8.

11. *The Woman's Monument, Design Competition Guidelines,* my emphasis.

12. Margaret B Wilkerson, "Music as Metaphor: New Plays of Black Women," in *Making a Spectacle: Feminist Essays on Contemporary Women's Theatre*, ed. Lynda Hart (Ann Arbor: University of Michigan Press, 1989), 61. For a similar discussion in a Canadian context, see Ann Wilson, "Beatrice Chancey: Slavery, Martyrdom and the Female Body," *Siting the Other: Re-Visions of Marginality in Australian and English-Canadian Drama*, ed. Marc Maufort and Franca Bellarsi (Brussels: Peter Lang, 2001), 267–78.

13. Helen Gilbert and Joanne Tompkins, *Post-colonial Drama: Theory, Practice, Politics* (London: Routledge, 1996), 213.

14. Ibid.

15. A third "rez" play, *Rose*, was published by Talonbooks in Vancouver in 2003 but has to date received only an amateur production, in January 2000 at the Graduate Centre for the Study of Drama, University of Toronto.

16. Gilbert and Tompkins, *Post-colonial Drama*, 214.

17. Ibid., 215. The danger of this type of Native-woman-as-land trope is apparent from Cree/Métis author Kim Anderson's (*A Recognition of Being: Restructuring Native Womanhood* [Toronto: Second Story Press, 2000], 100–5) account of the "roots of a negative female image" for First Nations women, which begins as follows:

> In both western and Indigenous frameworks, Native women have historically been equated with the land. The Euro-constructed image of Native women, therefore, mirrors western attitudes toward the earth. Sadly, this relationship has typically developed within the context of control, conquest, possession and exploitation. The Euro-Canadian image of Native women has been constructed within this context and has evolved along with the evolving relationship of European people to this continent. (100)

18. Highway, quoted in Judy Steed, "Tomson Highway: My Way," *Toronto Star*, March 24, 1991, D2.

19. "Ann-Marie MacDonald Interview," interview by Rita Much, *Fair Play: 12 Women Speak*, ed. Judith Rudakoff and Rita Much (Toronto: Simon and Pierre, 1990), 143.

20. See Marie Annharte Baker, "Angry Enough to Spit but with Dry Lips It Hurts More than You Know," *Canadian Theatre Review* 68 (1991): 88–89.

21. See Terry Eagleton, *William Shakespeare* (Oxford: Blackwell, 1986), 97.

22. George Ryga, *The Ecstasy of Rita Joe and Other Plays* (Toronto: New Press, 1971), 130.

23. Paula Gunn Allen, *The Sacred Hoop: Recovering the Feminine in American Indian Traditions* (Boston: Beacon, 1986), 51–52.

24. Yvette Nolan, *Annie Mae's Movement* (Toronto: PUC Play Service, 1999), 41–42. The women named are Gloria Miguel, Lisa Mayo, and Muriel Miguel (of Spiderwoman Theatre), Monique Mojica, Joy and Teena Keeper (actors working out of Winnipeg), Margo Kane, Maria Campbell (playwright and author of *Halfbreed*), Beatrice Culleton (author of *In Search of April Raintree*), Minnie Two Shoes (a journalist contemporary of Annie Mae Aquash), April Raintree (a fictional character created by Beatrice Culleton), and visual artist Colleen Cutchell (at Brandon University, Manitoba). A revised version of the play that toured Canada, Australia, and New Zealand in 2006–8 was published in Toronto by Playwrights Canada Press in 2006.

25. Ibid., 41.

26. Marie Clements, "The Unnatural and Accidental Women," *Canadian Theatre Review* 101 (2000), 60. The play has since been published in a revised version in the Mojica and Knowles anthology *Staging Coyote's Dream*, and by Vancouver's Talonbooks in 2005.

27. Marie Clements, *Now Look What You Made Me Do*, in *Prerogatives: Contemporary Plays by Women* (Winnipeg: Blizzard, 1998), 13.

28. Helen Thomson, "Aboriginal Women's Staged Autobiography," in *Siting the Other: Re-visions of Marginality in Australian and English-Canadian Drama*, ed. Marc Maufort and Franca Bellarsi (Brussels: Peter Lang, 2001), 23. Thomson is quoting Hooten, *Stories of Herself When Young: Autobiographies of Childhood by Australian Women* (Melbourne: Oxford University Press, 1990), 313.

29. Ibid., 23.

30. Margo Kane, "Moonlodge," in *An Anthology of Canadian Native Literature in English*, ed. Daniel David Moses and Terry Goldie (Toronto: Oxford University Press, 1992), 286–87.

31. Shirley Cheechoo, *Path with No Moccasins*, in *Canadian Mosaic: 6 Plays*, ed. Aviva Ravel (Toronto: Simon and Pierre, 1995), 28. Subsequent quotations from the play are cited parenthetically in the text.

32. Sandra L. Richards, "Snapshots of 'The Great Homecoming': Memorializing the slave trade in Ghana." Lecture, University of Guelph, Nov. 10, 2002.

33. Mojica, *Princess Pocahontas*, 58. Subsequent quotations from *Princess Pocahontas and the Blue Spots* and *Birdwoman and the Suffragettes*, which together compose Mojica's *Princess Pocahontas and the Blue Spots: Two Plays* (see n. 2), will be cited parenthetically in the text.

34. James Young, *The Texture of Memory: Holocaust Memorials and Meaning* (New Haven: Yale University Press, 1993), 5.

35. For an exploration of the interconnectedness of these roles, see Ric Knowles, "Translators, Traitors, Mistresses, and Whores: Monique Mojica and the Mothers of the Métis Nations," in *Siting the Other: Re-visions of Marginality in Australian and English-Canadian Drama*, ed. Marc Maufort and Franca Bellarsi (Brussels: Peter Lang, 2001), 247–66, reprinted in Rob Appleford, ed., *Aboriginal Drama and Theatre* (Toronto: Playwrights Canada, 2005), 106–23.

36. Anderson, *Recognition of Being*, 26.

37. Ibid., 101.

38. Ibid. Anderson is citing Elizabeth Cook-Lynn, *Why I Can't Read Wallace Stegner and Other Essays* (Madison: University of Wisconsin Press, 1996), 145.

39. Ibid., 101–2.

40. Allen, *Sacred Hoop*, 51–183; Mojica, *Princess Pocahontas*, 59.

41. For "re-membering" used in this context, see Laguna-Pueblo scholar Paula Gunn Allen, *Sacred Hoop*, 11.

42. Lisa Mayo, Gloria Miguel, and Muriel Miguel, *Reverb-ber-ber-rations*, *Women and Performance* 5, no. 2 (1992): 189, reprinted in a revised version in Mojica and Knowles, *Staging Coyote's Dream*. I am indebted for this observation to Kate Higginson's unpublished essay, "Re-membering the Indian Princess as Ancestral Grandmother in the Work of Monique Mojica" (University of Guelph, 19 December 2000).

43. Turtle Gals (Jani Lauzon, Monique Mojica, and Michelle St. John), *The Scrub-

bing Project, 5th draft (unpublished, December 2000), 24. Subsequent quotations from the play will be cited parenthetically in the text. The revised version of the script—which will be published in 2008 by Playwrights Canada Press in volume 2 of Mojica and Knowles, eds., *Staging Coyote's Dream*—includes different versions of the scenes cited here, and in one case replaces "I Am Sad Still" with a comparable "massacre" poem, "Paco and the Shoes."

44. Music by Richard Greenblatt, lyrics by Lauzon, Mojica, St. John, and Greenblatt.

45. Cecelia Rodriguez, trans., Details of the Acteal Massacre. *Indigenous Revolutionary Clandestine Committee–General Command of the Zapatista Army of National Liberation*, http://flag.blackened.net/revolt/mexico/ezln/1997/ccri_acteal_details_dec.html.

46. *Mexico: The Acteal Massacre One Year On and Still No Justice*, "International Secretariat of Amnesty International," http://www.zmag.org/Bulletins/pacteal.htm.

47. The effect of the monologue is cumulative. The full text appears in chapter 5. Slightly different versions of the monologue are published in The Cultural Memory Group's *Remembering Women*, 211–13, and in Judith Thompson, ed., *She Speaks: Monologues for Women* (Toronto: Playwrights Canada, 2004), 206–8.

Chapter 9. "People with Strong Hearts"

1. Jace Weaver, *Other Words: American Indian Literature, Law, and Culture* (Norman: University of Oklahoma Press, 2001), 302–3.

2. Joseph Bruchac, "The Gift Is Still Being Given," in *Smoke Rising: Native North American Literary Companion*, ed. Janet Witalec (Detroit: Visible Ink, 1995), xix.

3. Terminology proves problematic in discussions of the descendants of the Indigenous peoples of what is now called the Americas. The specific name for each people or nation is preferred, which I endeavor to use whenever possible. Often the use of "American Indian" or "Native American" or "Indian" or "Native" varies according to the writer, and between the United States and Canada, and sometimes they are used interchangeably. Throughout this chapter, I generally try to use the term used by the author under discussion, and use "Native" more generally, respectful of the limitations. For a thoughtful discussion of these issues, see Duane Champagne, preface to *The Native North American Almanac: A Reference Work on Native North Americans in the United States and Canada*, ed. Duane Champagne (Detroit: Gale Research, 1994), xvii–xix.

4. See Stephen S. Cornell, *The Return of the Native: American Indian Political Resurgence* (New York: Oxford University Press, 1988), especially 106–218; and Paul Chaat Smith and Robert Allen Warrior, *Like a Hurricane: The Indian Movement from Alcatraz to Wounded Knee* (New York: New Press, 1996), especially 18–59, 96–149, and 177–279.

5. Hanay Geiogamah, "The Native American Theater Ensemble (1972–1975)," unpublished manuscript, 1980, 14. I am indebted to Hanay Geiogamah for this manuscript and its thoughtful overview of the history of the early development of NATE, and for numerous interviews and conversations about his work.

6. For an overview of the early history of the American Indian Theater Ensemble, see Kent R. Brown, "The American Indian Theatre Ensemble," *Players* 48, no. 3 (Febru-

ary–March, 1973): 126–31. See also Ann Haugo, "American Indian Theatre," in *The Cambridge Companion to Native American Literature*, ed. Joy Porter and Kenneth M. Roemer (Cambridge: Cambridge University Press, 2005), 189–204.

7. Initial members (in alphabetical order) included: Richard Camargo, Comanche; Monica Charles, Clallam; Timothy Clashin, Navajo; Keith Conway, Blackfeet; Geraldine Keams, Navajo; Deborah Key, Cheyenne; Jane Lind, Aleut; Grace Logan, Osage; Gerald Bruce Miller, Skokomish-Yakima; David Montana, Papago; Marie Antoinette Rogers, Mescalero Apache; Robert Shorty, Navajo; Deborah Finley Snyder, Colville; Bernadette Track, Taos Pueblo; Michael Trammel, Shawnee-Delaware; and Phil Wilmon, Cherokee (Geiogamah, "Native American Theater Ensemble," 26–28).

8. Geiogamah, "Native American Theater Ensemble," 3.

9. Ibid., 4.

10. Mimi Gisolfi D'Aponte, introduction to *Seventh Generation: An Anthology of Native American Plays*, ed. Mimi Gisolfi D'Aponte (New York: Theatre Communications Group, 1999), xvi.

11. In describing this inheritance, Geiogamah continues: "Coming from our elders, from our mothers and fathers, from our artists and storytellers, from our medicine people and spiritual leaders, our stories become the fabric and patterns of our culture. Our culture protects us and heals us, and out of this rich and complex inheritance, we gain strength to do all the other work we find before us" (Hanay Geiogamah, "Self-Interview," in *Here First: Autobiographical Essays by Native American Writers*, ed. Arnold Krupat and Brian Swann [New York: Modern Library, 2000], 151).

12. Hanay Geiogamah, "The New American Indian Theater: An Introduction," *American Indian Theater in Performance: A Reader*, ed. Hanay Geiogamah and Jaye T. Darby (Los Angeles: UCLA American Indian Studies Center, 2000), 163.

13. Jace Weaver, *That the People Might Live: Native American Literatures and Native American Community* (New York: Oxford University Press, 1997), 43. For clarity, throughout the text the word *communitism* will appear without quotation marks, with the understanding that it is Jace Weaver's term.

14. *Body Indian* and *49* are in Hanay Geiogamah, *New Native American Drama: Three Plays* (Norman: University of Oklahoma Press, 1980). All subsequent references to these plays are in the text.

15. Daniel Heath Justice, "Conjuring Marks: Furthering Indigenous Empowerment through Literature, *American Indian Quarterly* 28, nos. 1 and 2 (winter/spring 2004): 7. For an overview of these issues, see also 3–11 in this essay and the rest of this special issue; Shari Huhndorf, "Literature and the Politics of Native American Studies," *PMLA* 120, no. 5 (October 2005): 1618–27; Devon Abbott Mihesuah and Angela Cavender Wilson, eds., *Indigenizing the Academy: Transforming Scholarship and Empowering Communities* (Lincoln: University of Nebraska Press, 2004); Christy Stanlake, "JudyLee Oliva's *The Fire and the Rose* and the Modeling of Platial Theories in Native American Dramaturgy," *Modern Drama* 48, no. 4 (winter 2005): 819–41; Robert Allen Warrior, *Tribal Secrets: Recovering American Indian Intellectual Traditions* (Minneapolis: University of Minnesota Press, 1995; and Jace Weaver, "More Light than Heat: The Current

State of Native American Studies," *American Indian Quarterly* 31, no. 2 (spring 2007): 233–55.

16. Paula Gunn Allen, Introduction to *Studies in American Indian Literature: Critical Essays and Course Designs*, ed. Paula Gunn Allen (New York: Modern Language Association of America, 1983), xii.

17. Paula Gunn Allen, *The Sacred Hoop: Recovering the Feminine in American Indian Tradition* (Boston: Beacon Press, 1992), first published in 1986; and *Off the Reservation: Reflections on Boundary-Busting, Border-Crossing Loose Canons* (Boston: Beacon Press, 1998), esp. 132–78.

18. Gunn Allen, *The Sacred Hoop*, 88. See also 86–98 for further discussion of *House Made of Dawn*, and 118–26 for *Ceremony*.

19. Weaver, *That the People Might Live*, 43. As a European American scholar, I find Paula Gunn Allen's and Jace Weaver's critical approaches to be particularly helpful.

20. Ibid., 45.

21. Ibid.

22. Weaver, *Other Words*, 304.

23. Weaver, *That the People Might Live*, 43.

24. Daniel Heath Justice, Review of Jace Weaver, *Other Words: American Indian Literature, Law, and Culture, American Indian Quarterly* 26, no. 2 (spring 2002): 325.

25. Weaver, *That the People Might Live*, 164.

26. Ibid., 45.

27. Brown, "The American Indian Theatre Ensemble," 126–31.

28. La MaMa Experimental Theatre Club Press Release, "American Indian Theater Company Ready for New York Opening" (Oct. 10, 1972) 2, cited in Geiogamah, "Native American Theater Ensemble," 32–33.

29. Mildred P. Mayhall, *The Kiowas* (Norman: University of Oklahoma Press, 1962), 255–69.

30. Cornell, *Return of the Native*, 40–67; Benjamin R. Kracht, "Kiowa Religion in Historical Perspective," *Native American Spirituality: A Critical Reader*, ed. Lee Irwin (Lincoln: University of Nebraska Press, 2000), 240–46; Rose Stremlau, "'To Domesticate and Civilize Wild Indians': Allotment and the Campaign to Reform Indian Families, 1875–1887," *Journal of Family History* 30, no. 1 (July 2005): 265–86.

31. Weaver, *That the People Might Live*, 38.

32. Vine Deloria Jr., "Knowing and Understanding: Traditional Education in the Modern World," *Spirit and Reason: The Vine Deloria, Jr., Reader*, ed. Barbara Deloria, Kristen Foehner, and Sam Scinta (Golden, CO: Fulcrum, 1999), 139.

33. Kenneth Lincoln, "Indians Playing Indians," *MELUS* 16, no. 3 (fall 1989–90): 92.

34. Annamaria Pinazzi, "The Theater of Hanay Geiogamah," in *American Indian Theater in Performance: A Reader*, 181. This chapter is based on an English translation of "Postfazione," in *Hanay Geiogamah Teatro* (Roma: Castelvecchi, 1994), 147–77.

35. Deloria Jr., "Knowing and Understanding," 140–41.

36. Jeffrey Huntsman, "Introduction," in *New Native American Drama: Three Plays by Hanay Geiogamah* (Norman: University of Oklahoma Press, 1980), xiv.

37. Ibid., xv.

38. C.W.E. Bigsby, *A Critical Introduction to Twentieth-Century American Drama*, 3: *Beyond Broadway* (Cambridge: Cambridge University Press, 1985), 370.

39. Pinazzi, "Theater of Hanay Geiogamah," 181.

40. Weaver, *That the People Might Live*, 164.

41. Lincoln, "Indians Playing Indians," 94.

42. Lincoln, "Indians Playing Indians," 93.

43. Geiogamah, "Native American Theater Ensemble," 90–93.

44. This section is based on a more in-depth discussion of *49* by the author entitled, "'Come to the Ceremonial Circle': Ceremony and Renewal in Hanay Geiogamah's *49*," *American Indian Theater in Performance: A Reader*, 195–223.

45. See Cornell, *Return of the Native*, 40–67; Vine Deloria Jr., *God Is Red: A Native View of Religion*. 2nd ed. (Golden, CO: Fulcrum, 1994), 236–53, 267.

46. For a discussion of the traditions of dreams and visions amongst various tribes, see Lee Irwin, *The Dream Seekers: Native American Visionary Traditions of the Great Plains*, Civilization of the American Indian series, vol. 213 (Norman: University of Oklahoma Press, 1994), 240.

47. Howard L. Harrod, *Renewing the World: Plains Indian Religion and Morality* (Tucson: University of Arizona Press, 1987), 172.

48. Ibid., 25.

49. Jeffrey Huntsman elucidates these key distinctions: "Fundamental to many, if not most, Native American ritual events are two beliefs that have few direct counterparts for Euro-Americans. The first is the concept of nonlinear time—time that may be viewed cyclically from one perspective and eternally from another. The second is the concept of a dimensionless sacred place, the center of the universe and the locative counterpart of the ever-present time. The two concepts are congruent, in a sense identical, for each point in time or space is infinitely large, extending outward from the sacred event to include all creation, yet located around the event in a way that precisely fixes the position and assures the security of the participants" (Jeffrey Huntsman, "Native American Theatre," *Ethnic Theatre in the United States*, ed. Maxine Schwartz Seller [Westport, CT: Greenwood Press, 1983], 359). See also Gunn Allen, *Sacred Hoop*, 147–54.

50. Kenneth Lincoln, *Native American Renaissance* (Berkeley: University of California Press, 1985), 84–85.

51. Jaye T. Darby, "Re-Imagining the Stage: Tradition and Transformation in Native Theater," in *The Color of Theater: Race, Ethnicity, and Contemporary Performance*, ed. Roberta Uno with Lucy Mae San Pablo Burns (London: Continuum Press, 2002), 68.

52. Weaver, *That the People Might Live*, 20.

53. Gunn Allen, *Sacred Hoop*, 151.

54. Geiogamah, "Native American Theater Ensemble," 90.

55. Lincoln, *Native American Renaissance*, 53.

56. Irwin, *Dream Seekers*, 121–22.

57. Black Elk, from *The Sixth Grandfather: Black Elk's Teachings Given to John G. Neihardt*, ed. Raymond J. DeMallie (Lincoln: University of Nebraska Press, 1984), 296.

58. For a historical account of this period, see Cornell, *Return of the Native*, 40–67; and Lee Irwin, "Freedom, Law, and Prophecy: A Brief History of Native American Religious Resistance," in Kracht, *Native American Spirituality*, 295–316. From a performance perspective, see also Jacqueline Shea Murphy, *The People Have Never Stopped Dancing: Native American Modern Dance Histories* (Minneapolis: University of Minnesota Press, 2007), 1–107.

59. David Martínez, "The Soul of the Indian: Lakota Philosophy and the Vision Quest," *Wicazo Sa Review* 19, no. 2 (fall 2004): 104.

60. Irwin, *Dream Seekers*, 167.

61. Deloria Jr., "Knowing and Understanding," 139.

62. Lincoln, *Native American Renaissance*, 45.

63. Weaver, *That the People Might Live*, 15.

64. Deloria Jr., "Traditional Technology," in *Spirit and Reason*, 134.

65. C.W.E. Bigsby, *Modern American Drama, 1945–1990* (Cambridge: Cambridge University Press, 1992), 336.

66. Huntsman, "Introduction," xxii.

67. Lincoln, *Native American Renaissance*, 53.

68. Jack W. Marken, rev. of *This Song Remembers: Self-Portraits of Native Americans in the Arts*, ed. Jane B. Katz; and Hanay Geiogamah, "New Native American Drama: Three Plays," *American Indian Quarterly* 5, no. 4 (November 1979): 379.

69. For their inspiration and insights at various stages of this work, I wish to thank Hanay Geiogamah, Paula Gunn Allen, Arif Amlani, Pamela Grieman, Ann Haugo, Jane Lind, Don Moccasin, Joanne Snow-Smith, Stephen Wilmer, Ken Wade, and Albert White Hat. My sincere gratitude also goes to the W. K. Kellogg Foundation, the Fund for the Improvement of Postsecondary Education (FIPSE), U.S. Department of Education, and Ford Foundation for their generous support of Project HOOP (Honoring Our Origins and Peoples), of which this scholarship forms a part.

Chapter 10. Coming-of-Age on the Rez

1. Marc Redfield, *Phantom Formations: Aesthetic Ideology and the Bildungsroman* (Ithaca: Cornell University Press, 1996), 55.

2. William S. Yellow Robe Jr., interviewed by Paul Rathbun, quoted from *American Indian Theater in Performance: A Reader*, ed., Hanay Geiogamah and Jaye Darby (Los Angeles: UCLA American Indian Studies Center, 2000), 349.

3. All quotes from William S. Yellow Robe Jr., *The Independence of Eddie Rose* (written in 1986), *Seventh Generation: An Anthology of Native American Plays*, ed. Mimi Gisolfi D'Aponte (New York: TCG, 1999), 39–97. Future references will be listed in the text.

4. Henry and Mary Garland, eds., *The Oxford Companion to German Literature* (New York: Oxford University Press, 1986), 87.

5. For a history of its German origins, see Todd Kontje, *The German Bildungsroman: History of a National Genre* (Columbia, SC: Camden House, 1993).

6. James Hardin, "Introduction," *Reflection and Action: Essays on the Bildungsroman*, ed. James Hardin (Columbia: University of South Carolina Press, 1991), x, xi–xii, xiii. Hardin builds his definition from Jürgen Jacobs and Markus Krause, *Der deutsche Bildungsroman: Gattungsgeschichte vom 18 bis zom 20 Jahrhundert* (Munich: Beck, 1989), 20. For another interesting study of the bildungsroman in English, see Michael Minden, *The German Bildungsroman: Incest and Inheritance* (Cambridge: Cambridge University Press, 1997).

7. Kontje, *German Bildungsroman*, 1, 2.

8. "Bildungsroman wird er heißt dürfen . . . weil er des Helden Bildung . . . darstellt; zweitens aber auch weil er gerade durch diese Darstellung des Lesers Bildung" (Karl Morgenstern, "Ueber das Wesen des Bildungsromans" [1820], in *Zur Geschichte des deutschen Bildungsromans*, ed. Rolf Selbman [Darmstadt: Wissenschaftliche Buchgesellschaft, 1988], 64).

9. Yellow Robe, *American Indian Theater in Performance*, 348.

10. Ibid., 349–50.

11. Scott L. Pratt, *Native Pragmatism: Rethinking the Roots of American Philosophy* (Bloomington: Indiana University Press, 2002), 228.

12. Hardin, "Introduction," xv.

13. Redfield, *Phantom Formations*, 54.

14. Black Elk, quoted in John G. Neihardt, *Black Elk Speaks* (Lincoln: University of Nebraska Press, 1979), 186–87.

15. Randolph P. Shaffner, *The Apprenticeship Novel: A Study of the "Bildungsroman" as a Regulative Type in Western Literature with a Focus on Three Classic Representations by Goethe, Maugham, and Mann* (New York: Peter Lang, 1984), 18.

16. The production took place as part of Yale University's undergraduate theater studies program in 1998.

Chapter 11. Feathers, Flutes, and Drums

1. Cherríe Moraga's *Giving Up the Ghost* is published in Cherríe Moraga, *Heroes and Saints & Other Plays* (Albuquerque: West End Press: 1994), pp. 1–35.

2. Edit Villareal's *The Language of Flowers* has not been published to date.

3. Octavio Solís, *Man of the Flesh*, in *Plays from South Coast Repertory*, vol. 3 (New York: Broadway Play Publishing, 1993), 109–67.

4. Josefina Lopez, *Unconquered Spirits* (Woodstock, IL: Dramatic Publishing, 1997).

5. Quoted in Richard A. Abrams, "Chicana Playwright Struggles with 2 Cultures," *Austin-American Statesman*, December 6, 1981, A24.

6. Luis Valdez, *Early Works* (Arte Público Press, 1990), 177.

7. Portillo Trambley's *Day of the Swallows* is published in the following: Herminio Rios and Octavio Romano-V., eds., *El Espejo* (Berkeley: Quinto Sol, 1972), pp. 149–93; Philip D. Ortego, ed., *We Are Chicanos* (New York: Washington Square, 1973), 224–71; and Roberto J. Garza, ed., *Contemporary Chicano Theatre* (Notre Dame, IN: University

of Notre Dame Press, 1976), 206–45. Further references to this play are cited parenthetically in the text and refer to the version published in Garza.

8. Louise Detwiler, "The Question of Cultural Difference and Gender Oppression in Estela Portillo's *The Day of the Swallows*," *Bilingual Review/Revista Bilingue* (1996), 151.

9. Ibid., 147.

10. Ibid.

11. Ibid., 151.

12. Portillo Trambley, *Day of the Swallows*, 207.

13. Luis Valdez, *I Don't Have to Show You No Stinking Badges!* in Luis Valdez, *Zoot Suit and Other Plays* (Arte Público Press, 1992), 155–214.

14. Quoted in Jennifer de Poyen, "Roots Rockero: Luis Valdez Reaches into His Family History to Create 'Mummified Deer,'" *San Diego Union–Tribune*, October 26, 2000, sec. "Night & Day," 4.

15. Luis Valdez, telephone interview by author, March 15, 2002.

16. Valdez was speaking to the audience at a public reading of an early draft of *Mummified Deer* at the Centro Cultural de la Raza in San Diego, California, prior to the world premiere of the play in 2000. It might be noted that the play was originally titled *The Mummified Fetus*. In the post-reading discussion, which I moderated, the audience generally agreed that the word "fetus" in the title might create unnecessary problems for the producers.

17. Luis Valdez, *Mummified Deer and Other Plays* (Houston: Arte Público Press, 2005), 1. Further references to this play are made parenthetically in the text.

18. E-mail from Alma Martinez to author, March 18, 2002.

Chapter 12. Metamora's Revenge

1. See B. Donald Grose, "Edwin Forrest, Metamora, and the Indian Removal Act of 1830," *Theatre Journal* 37 (May 1985): 181–91; and Mark E. Mallet, "The Game of Politics: Edwin Forrest and the Jacksonian Democrats," *Journal of American Drama and Theatre* 5 (spring 1993): 31–46.

2. Jeffrey D. Mason, "The Politics of Metamora," in *The Performance of Power: Theatrical Discourse and Power*, ed. Sue-Ellen Case and Janelle Reinelt (Iowa City: University of Iowa Press, 1993), 92–110; Sally L. Jones, "The First but Not the Last of the 'Vanishing Indians': Edwin Forrest and Mythic Re-creations of the Native Population," in *Dressing in Feathers: The Construction of the Indian in American Popular Culture*, ed. S. Elizabeth Bird (Boulder, CO: Westview Press, 1996), 13–27; Jill Lepore, *The Name of War: King Philip's War and the Origins of American Identity* (New York: Vintage Books, 1998), 191–226; and Theresa Strouth Gaul, "'The Genuine Indian Who Was Brought upon the Stage': Edwin Forrest's Metamora and White Audiences," *Arizona Quarterly* 56 (spring 2000): 1–27.

3. Scott C. Martin, "Interpreting Metamora: Nationalism, Theater, and Jacksonian Indian Policy," *Journal of the Early Republic* 19 (spring 1999): 98.

4. Bruce A. McConachie, *Melodramatic Formations: American Theatre and Society, 1820–1870* (Iowa City: University of Iowa Press, 1992), 65–118.

5. On the theatrical depiction of Native Americans in the United States, see Eugene H. Jones, *Native Americans as Shown on the Stage* (Metuchen, NJ: Scarecrow Press, 1988).

6. See McConachie, *Melodramatic Formations*, 61–95, 120–22, 141–48, 173–74; Richard Moody, *Edwin Forrest: First Star of the American Stage* (New York: Knopf, 1960), 189–93, 212–39, 298; and George C. D. Odell, *Annals of the New York Stage*, 15 vols. (New York: Columbia University Press, 1927–1949), 5:1–41, 84–120, 165–207, 248–88, 321–67, 412–68; 6: 1–47, 110–47, 197–238, 278–313, 341–79, 424–68.

7. T. Allston Brown, *A History of the New York Stage from the First Performance in 1732 to 1901*, 3 vols. (1903; rpt., New York: Benjamin Blom, 1964), 1:367–68.

8. Quoted in Moody, *Edwin Forrest*, 326.

9. *Account of the Terrific and Fatal Riot at the New York Astor Place Opera House, on the Night of May 10, 1849* (New York: H. M. Ranney, 1849), 19.

10. On Bowery honor and traditionalist workers in the antebellum era, see *Melodramatic Formations*, 119–55, plus Tyler Anbinder, *Five Points: The Nineteenth-Century New York City Neighborhood That Invented Tap Dance, Stole Elections, and Became the World's Most Notorious Slum* (New York: Free Press, 2001).

11. John Augustus Stone, *Metamora, or The Last of the Wampanoags*, in *Dramas from the American Theatre, 1762–1909*, ed. Richard Moody (1966; rpt., Boston: Houghton Mifflin, 1969), 226. All subsequent citations are from this edition of the text.

12. Jones, "The First," 16.

13. Kwame Anthony Appiah, *In My Father's House: Africa in the Philosophy of Culture* (New York: Oxford, 1992), passim. See also George M. Fredrickson, *Racism: A Short History* (Princeton, NJ: Princeton University Press, 2002). For Fredrickson, racists regard ethnocultural differences as "innate, indelible, and unchangeable" (5), support[ing] "a racial order, a permanent group hierarchy" (6), and us[ing] their "power advantage to treat the ethnoracial Other in ways that [they] would regard as cruel and unjust if applied to members of [their] own group" (9).

14. Bert O. States, *Great Reckonings in Little Rooms: On the Phenomenology of Theater* (Berkeley and Los Angeles: University of California Press, 1985), 161.

15. *Albion* (New York), September 2, 1848: [n.p.].

Chapter 13. Performance and "Trickster Aesthetics"

1. Throughout this article I variously use the terms *Native, Native American, First Nations, American Indian,* and *Indian*. Whenever possible, I use the tribal affiliation, and use *American Indian, Native American,* or *First Nations* to speak generally.

2. Arjun Appadurai, "Global Ethnoscapes: Notes and Queries for a Transnational Anthropology," in *Recapturing Anthropology: Working in the Present*, ed. Richard Fox (Santa Fe: School of American Research Press, 1991), 191–210. Appadurai uses mediascape to investigate both the ways in which media technologies are incorporated into

questions of power central to discussions of representation and how media is taken up in the negotiation of identity and expression of locality amidst the global.

3. Gerald McMaster, "Borderzones: The 'Injun-uity' of Aesthetic Tricks," *Cultural Studies* 9, no. 1 (1995): 82.

4. Jacquelyn Kilpatrick, *Celluloid Indians: Native Americans and Film* (Lincoln: University of Nebraska Press, 1999), xv.

5. While not the focus of this essay, it is important to note here the numerous national differences between the United States and Canada in conditions of funding, production, and circulation of Native film/video. These differences are affected by many factors, including the differing official relationships between the U.S./Canadian governments and Native peoples, and that Native people form a larger percentage of the overall Canadian population, which has affected Native visibility and support for Native political activism, the official Canadian policy of multiculturalism, and Canadian policies designed to support Canadian cultural sovereignty.

6. A few recent Native-produced feature-length fictional films have received funding from tribes, including *Naturally Native* (Valerie Red-Horse, 1998), funded by the Mashantucket Pequot tribe, and *Christmas in the Clouds* (Kate Montgomery, 2001), which was executive-produced by the Stockbridge-Munsee Band of Mohican Indians. Many Native directors have asserted that it is crucial for Native people to be involved at the highest levels of production.

7. This relatively new and burgeoning Native film festival circuit may be seen as another "powwow trail" that opens up a space for the construction of solidarity and intertribal identity. For a thorough discussion of the role of film festivals as providing a social space for Native filmmakers to organize, see Pegi Vail, "Producing America," master's thesis, New York University, 1997; and Beverly Singer, *Wiping the War Paint Off the Lens* (Minneapolis: University of Minnesota Press, 2001).

8. Stuart Hall, "New Ethnicities," in *British Black Cultural Studies*, ed. Houston Baker, Manthia Diawara, and Ruth Lindeborg (Chicago: University of Chicago Press, 1994), 164.

9. Hulleah Tsinhnahjinnie, "Creating a Visual History: A Question of Ownership," *Strong Hearts: Native American Visions and Voices*, ed. Theresa Harlan (New York: Aperture, 1995), 20.

10. Robert Stam and Ella Shohat, *Unthinking Eurocentrism: Multiculturalism and the Media* (London: Routledge, 1994), 292.

11. Faye Ginsburg, "Indigenous Media: Faustian Contract or Global Village?" *Cultural Anthropology* 6, no. 1 (February 1991): 94.

12. Faye Ginsburg, "Embedded Aesthetics: Creating a Discursive Space for Indigenous Media," *Cultural Anthropology* 9, no. 3 (1994): 365–82.

13. Ibid., 368.

14. Troy Johnson, ed., *Contemporary Native American Political Issues* (London: Altamira, 1999), 16.

15. Jolene Rickard, "Sovereignty: A Line in the Sand," in *Strong Hearts: Native American Visions and Voices* (New York: Aperture, 1995), 51.

16. Lenore Keeshing-Tobias, "Trickster beyond 1992: Our Relationship," in *Indigena: Contemporary Native Perspectives*, ed. Gerald McMaster and Lee-Ann Martin (Hull: Canadian Museum of Civilization, 1992), 101.

17. For an example of the contemporary use of Trickster stories to educate Native youth, see *Stories from the Seventh Fire* (1998). This animated tale, produced by Gregory Coyes (Métis), illustrates a tale associated with Weesakejak, the Cree trickster figure. It was created for a Native children's television audience and has been screened on the Aboriginal Peoples Television Network (APTN).

18. Paul Radin, *The Trickster: A Study in American Indian Mythology* (New York: Schocken Books, 1972), 35.

19. Allan Ryan, *The Trickster Shift: Humour and Irony in Contemporary Native Art* (Vancouver: UBC Press, 1999), 5.

20. In this article I explore specific Native theories of aesthetics and therefore focus on "trickster aesthetics." However, I recognize that an excellent comparison could be made with other cultural practices and aesthetics of resistance, such as in the figure of Eshu-Elegbara in Yoruba traditions, practices of Haitian *voudon*, and carnivalesque.

21. Stam and Shohat, *Unthinking Eurocentrism*, 302.

22. Lawrence Sullivan, "Multiple Levels of Religious Meaning in Culture: A New Look at Winnebago Sacred Texts," *Canadian Journal of Native Studies* 2, no. 2 (1982): 231.

23. For a collection of trickster stories, see Alfonso Ortiz and Richard Erdoes, eds., *American Indian Trickster Tales* (New York: Penguin Books, 1998).

24. This is a term that Vizenor uses to identify himself as well as to theorize the colonial encounter and to discuss the experiences of "living in two worlds." For a thorough discussion of his theoretical framework, see Gerald Vizenor, *Earthdivers: Tribal Narratives on Mixed Descent* (Minneapolis: University of Minnesota Press, 1981).

25. Gerald Vizenor, "Trickster Discourse," *American Indian Quarterly* 14, no. 3 (1990): 282. For a cinematic example of Vizenor's use of the trickster figure, see *Harold of Orange*, written by Gerald Vizenor and directed by Richard Weise (1984, Film in the Cities).

26. For an in-depth analysis of Shelley Niro's work, see Audra Simpson, "The Empire Laughs Back: Tradition, Power and Play in the Work of Shelley Niro and Ryan Rice," in *IroquoisART: Visual Expressions of Contemporary Native American Artists*, ed. Sylvia S. Kasprycki with Doris Stambrau and Alexandra Roth (Aldendadt: European Review of Native American Studies Monographs,1998), vol. 1, 48–54.

27. Jennifer Skoda, "Image and Self in Contemporary Native Photoart: An Exhibition at the Hood Museum of Art," *American Indian Art Magazine* 1 (1996): 57.

28. Allan Ryan, "I Enjoy Being a Mohawk Girl," *American Indian Art Magazine* 4 (1994): 44.

29. Skoda, "Image and Self in Contemporary Native Photoart," 57.

30. Quoted in Lucy Lippard, "Independent Identities," in *Native American Art in the Twentieth Century: Makers, Meanings, Histories*, ed. W. Jackson Rushing (New York: Routledge, 1999), 146.

31. Shelley Niro, "Shelley Niro Speaks . . . ," in *Reservation X: The Power of Place in*

Aboriginal Contemporary Art, ed. Gerald McMaster (Seattle: University of Washington Press, 1998), 115.

32. "Two-spirit" is a term that is currently used by some Native Americans who identify as gay, lesbian, bisexual, and/or transgendered. Some Native American activists argue that their use of this term is a reappropriation too of the third or alternative gender ideology among many historic and traditional Native American communities. For additional scholarship on "two-spirit" identity, see Brian Joseph Gilley, *Becoming Two-Spirit: Gay Identity and Social Acceptance in Indian Country* (Lincoln: University of Nebraska Press, 2006); Sue-Ellen Jacobs, Wesley Thomas, and Sabine Lang, eds., *Two-Spirit People: Native American Gender Identity, Sexuality and Spirituality* (Champaign: University of Illinois Press, 1997); and Will Roscoe, *Changing Ones: Third and Fourth Genders in Native North America* (Hampshire: Palgrave Macmillan, 2000).

33. Paul Chaat Smith, "Home Alone," in *Reservation X: The Power of Place in Aboriginal Contemporary Art*, ed. Gerald McMaster (Seattle: University of Washington Press, 1998), 111.

34. Christopher E. Gittings, *Canadian National Cinema: Ideology, Difference and Representation* (London: Routledge, 2002), 229.

35. For more information on APTN, see Lorna Roth, *Something New in the Air: The Story of First Peoples Television Broadcasting in Canada* (Montreal: McGill-Queens University Press, 2005), and "The Delicate Acts of 'Colour Balancing': Multiculturalism and Canadian Television Policies and Practices," *Canadian Journal of Communication* 23, no. 4 (1998): 35–45; and Kathleen Buddle-Crowe, "From Birchbark Talk to Digital Dreamspeaking: A History of Aboriginal Media Activism in Canada," PhD diss., McMaster University, 2002. For more information on the history and current production schedule of the Aboriginal Peoples Television Network, see their website at www.aptn.ca.

36. Millie Knapp, "Shelley Niro: Seductive Humor," *Aboriginal Voices* (1998), 10.

37. Diana Taylor, The DNA of Performance, unpublished manuscript, 2000, 4.

38. Charlie Hill, *The Trickster Shift: Humour and Irony in Contemporary Native Art*, ed. Allan Ryan (Vancouver: UBC Press, 1999), 82.

39. Gerald McMaster, ed., *Reservation X: The Power of Place in Aboriginal Contemporary Art* (Seattle: University of Washington Press, 1998), 32.

40. Gerald Vizenor, *Survival This Way: Interviews with American Indian Poets*, ed. Joseph Bruchac (Tucson: Sun Tracks and University of Arizona Press, 1987), 295.

41. Niro, *It Starts with a Whisper*, 1993.

42. Ruth Phillips, *Trading Identities: The Souvenir in Native North American Art from the Northeast, 1700–1900* (Seattle: University of Washington Press, 1998), 277.

43. Smith, "Home Alone," 111.

Chapter 14. Speaking Lives, Filming Lives

1. Elaine Jahner, "A Critical Approach to American Indian Literature," *Studies in American Indian Literature: Critical Essays and Course Designs*, ed. Paula Gunn Allen (New York: Modern Language Association of America, 1983), 223.

2. Victor Masayesva, "Indigenous Experimentalism," in *Magnetic North*, ed. Jenny Lion (Minneapolis: University of Minnesota Press, 2000), 229, 237.

3. *The Real People Series*, dir. George Burdeau (1976, Office of Education, Department of Health, Education, and Welfare). Note that in 1966 members of the Navajo community at Pine Springs, Arizona, were given instruction in filmmaking techniques by non-Native researchers. The resulting films were analyzed from an anthropological perspective and the results published in Sol Worth and John Adair, *Through Navajo Eyes: An Exploration in Film Communication and Anthropology* (Albuquerque: University of New Mexico Press, 1997).

4. Select examples of well-known contemporary Native American filmmakers and videographers include George Burdeau (Blackfeet), Aaron Carr (Navajo/Laguna Pueblo), Lena Carr (Navajo), Shirley Cheechoo (Cree), Chris Eyre (Cheyenne-Arapaho), Phil Lucas (Choctaw), Shelley Niro (Mohawk), Victor Masayesva (Hopi), Malinda Maynor (Lumbee), Randy Redroad (Cherokee), and Diane Reyna (Taos/San Juan Pueblo). See Beverly R. Singer, *Wiping the War Paint Off the Lens* (Minneapolis and London: University of Minnesota Press, 2001), 44–55, for a more comprehensive list. Gerald Vizenor (Anishinaabe) has produced an original screenplay entitled *Harold of Orange* (1984), and writers such as Thomas King (Cherokee), N. Scott Momaday (Kiowa), Greg Sarris (Graton Rancheria), and Sherman Alexie (Spokane/Coeur d'Alene) have all been involved in adapting their fictional work for the big and small screens.

5. Steven Leuthold, *Indigenous Aesthetics: Native Art, Media and Identity* (Austin: University of Texas Press, 1998), 117.

6. Singer, *Wiping the War Paint Off the Lens*, 49.

7. Victor Masayesva, (quoted in) Leuthold, *Indigenous Aesthetics*, 1.

8. Victor Masayesva, "Kwikwilyaqa: Hopi Photography," *Hopi Photographers, Hopi Images*, comp. Victor Masayesva Jr. and Erin Younger (Tucson: University of Arizona Press, 1983), 10.

9. Elizabeth Weatherford, "To End and Begin Again: The Work of Victor Masayesva, Jr. (Video Artist)," *Art Journal* 54 (Dec. 1, 1995), http://elibrary.com.

10. *Itam Hakim, Hopiit*, dir. Victor Masayesva Jr. (1984, IS Productions).

11. Singer, *Wiping the Warpaint Off the Lens*, 64.

12. Ibid. Singer identifies the dancer as wearing a buffalo headdress.

13. Kathleen M. Sands and Allison Sekaquaptewa Lewis, "Seeing with a Native Eye: A Hopi Film on Hopi," *American Indian Quarterly* 14, no. 4 (fall 1990): 388, 395.

14. "Reviews of *Hopiit* by American Film Festival Panelists, Jurorists," http://www.infomagic.net/~isprods/FeatrsTx.html (accessed 11 August 2005; emphasis added).

15. *Itam Hakim, Hopiit*.

16. Weatherford, "To End and Begin Again," n.p.

17. Ibid. See also Singer, *Wiping the Warpaint Off the Lens*, 65, for a discussion of this point relating to *Hopiit* and Masayesva and Younger, *Hopi Photographers, Hopi Images*, 62, 67, which includes two still photographs of an eagle chained to a building. These photographs were taken by Freddie Honhongva, who worked as a media technician for Masayesva on the Ethnic Heritage Program from which *Hopiit* was created.

18. Sands and Sekaquaptewa Lewis, "Seeing with a Native Eye," 395.

19. Masayesva, "Indigenous Experimentalism," 230–31; see also Masayesva and Younger, *Hopi Photographers, Hopi Images*, 100. A complete version of Masayesva's short poem "Famine" appears here, accompanying his photographs of a room stacked with corn ears.

20. Masayesva, "Indigenous Experimentalism," 230–31.

21. Weatherford, "To End and Begin Again," n.p.; and Jacquelyn Kilpatrick, *Celluloid Indians: Native Americans and Film* (Lincoln and London: University of Nebraska Press, 1999), 208. See also Masayesva's own account in "Indigenous Experimentalism," 226–29. *Itam Hakim, Hopiit* was commissioned by the German television station ZDF and was originally produced entirely in Hopi with no English subtitles. When the film was broadcast on German television (retitled *The Legend of Lone Wolf*), it was with the addition of German subtitles from Masayesva's Hopi-to-English translation.

22. *Siskyavi: The Place of Chasms*, dir. Victor Masayesva Jr. (1989, IS Productions).

23. See Greg Sarris, *Keeping Slug Woman Alive: A Holistic Approach to American Indian Texts* (Berkeley and Los Angeles: University of California Press, 1993), 51–62, in which he discusses the decontextualized representation of Pomo baskets in museum exhibits and the unwillingness of Pomo basket weaver Mabel McKay to discuss her basket weaving in any context other than one deeply informed by her understanding and experience of Pomo culture.

24. Susan Berry Brill de Ramírez, *Contemporary American Indian Literatures and the Oral Tradition* (Tucson: University of Arizona Press, 1999), 145.

25. *Imagining Indians*, dir. Victor Masayesva Jr. (1993, IS Productions).

26. Subject, of course, to Masayesva's own editorial decisions.

27. Weatherford, "To Begin and End Again," n.p.

28. Masayesva, "Indigenous Experimentalism," 233–34.

29. Ibid.

30. Kilpatrick, *Celluloid Indians*, 221.

31. *A Season of Grandmothers*, in *The Real People Series*, dir. George Burdeau (1976, Office of Education, Department of Health, Education, and Welfare).

32. George Burdeau (quoted in Kilpatrick, *Celluloid Indians*, 220).

33. *The Pueblo Peoples: First Contact*, dir. George Burdeau (1990, KNME–TV, Albuquerque and the Institute of American Indian and Alaska Native Culture and Arts Development).

34. For a biographical sketch of Chino, see Joe S. Sando, *Pueblo Profiles: Cultural Identity through Centuries of Change* (Santa Fe: Clear Light, 1998), 281–85.

35. Leuthold, *Indigenous Aesthetics*, 111–12.

36. *Backbone of the World*, dir. George Burdeau (1997, Rattlesnake Productions).

37. Independent Television Service, "Backbone of the World," http://www.itvs.org/shows/ataglance.php?showID=7221.

38. Burdeau (quoted in Kilpatrick, *Celluloid Indians*, 221).

About the Contributors

SARAH BRYANT-BERTAIL is Associate Professor of Drama at the University of Washington in Seattle. She earned her PhD in comparative literature from the University of Minnesota and also studied at the Université de Paris III and the Akademie der Künste and Freie Universität in Berlin. Her essays on German, French, Scandinavian, and American theater have appeared in *Theater Journal*; *Theatre Research International*; *Journal of Dramatic Theory and Criticism*; *Assaph*; *Journal of Kafka Studies*; and *Theatre Studies*; and in the anthologies *Essays on Twentieth-Century German Drama and Theater*; *Brecht Yearbook*; *Strindberg's Dramaturgy*; *In Collaboration: le Théâtre du Soleil: A Sourcebook*; *The Performance of Power*; and *Germany in the Twenties: The Artist as Social Critic*. She is author of the book *Space and Time in Epic Theater: The Brechtian Legacy* (Camden House, 2000) and is now completing *Women of the Road: The Pícara in the Theater* with the University of Iowa Press. She has also taught at the University of South Carolina in Columbia, and at Trinity College in Dublin, Ireland.

JAYE T. DARBY, PHD, is cofounder and codirector with Hanay Geiogamah of Project HOOP (Honoring Our Origins and People through Native Theater). Project HOOP is a North American initiative based at the University of California, Los Angeles, that aims to advance Native performing arts academically, artistically, and professionally. In 2007, Darby's article "Broadway (Un)Bound: Lynn Riggs's *The Cherokee Night*" was published in a special issue of the *Baylor Journal of Theatre and Performance*, "Nations Speaking: Indigenous Performances across the Americas." Her chapter "Into the Sacred Circle, Out of the Melting Pot: Re/Locations and Homecomings in Native Women's Theater" appeared in *Unmaking Race, Remaking Soul: Transformative Aesthetics and the Practice of Freedom*, edited by Christa Davis Acampora and Angela L. Cotton. She is coeditor of the anthology *Keepers of the Morning Star: An Anthology of*

Native Women's Theater, with Stephanie Fitzgerald (2003). She and Hanay Geiogamah also coedited *Stories of Our Way: An Anthology of American Indian Plays* (1999) and *American Indian Theater in Performance: A Reader* (2000). They are also coeditors of a new collection entitled *American Indian Performing Arts: Critical Directions*, forthcoming 2009.

KRISTIN L. DOWELL is Assistant Professor in the Department of Anthropology at the University of Oklahoma. She received her PhD from New York University after completing her dissertation, Honoring Stories: Aboriginal Media, Art, and Activism in Vancouver, based on fieldwork with urban Aboriginal filmmakers, artists, and activists in Vancouver, British Columbia. She worked on several Native film festivals, including *First Nations/ First Features: A Showcase of World Indigenous Film and Media*, held in New York City and Washington, D.C., in 2005, and the *IMAGeNation Aboriginal Film and Video Festival* in Vancouver in 2004. She is a visual anthropologist who teaches ethnographic film history and video production and was the director of *Reel Steps: Irish Dance in America* (2002), a twenty-minute ethnographic video about Irish dancing and cultural identity in New York.

ANNE-CHRISTINE HORNBORG is Associate Professor at the Department of Culture and Communication, Linköping University, Sweden. In a number of articles and books, including *Mi'kmaq Landscapes: From Animism to Sacred Ecology* (Ashgate, 2008), she has documented the lifeworld of the Mi'kmaq; their traditions, rituals, and environmental engagements and the phenomenology of place. Hornborg has conducted fieldwork in Mi'kmaq reserves in Cape Breton, Nova Scotia (1992–93, 1996, 2000), on Tonga Island (1998, 2001), and recently in the Peruvian Andes and the Amazon (2004). She is currently developing the interdisciplinary field of ritual studies, which includes a study of the new ritualized practices of late modernity in Sweden, the indigenous traditions and issues concerning ecology and religion, and the environmental ethics and practices emanating from the green movement.

JORGE HUERTA holds the Chancellor's Associates Endowed Chair III as Professor of Theatre at the University of California, San Diego. In 2005 he was appointed associate chancellor and chief diversity officer by Chancellor Marye Anne Fox. He is a professional director and has directed for professional companies throughout the United States, including the Puerto Rican Traveling Theatre in New York City, Gala Hispanic Theatre in Washington, D.C., San Diego Repertory Theatre, and the Group Theatre, Seattle. Dr. Huerta has conducted workshops and lectured on Chicano theater throughout the United States, Latin America, and Europe. He has published many articles and reviews in journals and anthologies, including *Gestos, Latin American Theatre Review, TheatreForum*, and *Drama Review.* He has edited three anthologies of plays: *El Teatro de la Esperanza: An Anthology of Chicano Drama* (1973); *Nuevos Pasos: Chicano and Puerto Rican Drama* (1979, 1989), with Nicolas Kanellos; and *Necessary Theatre: Six Plays about the Chicano Experience* (1987, 2005). Huerta published the first book about Chicano theater, *Chicano Theatre: Themes and Forms* (1982), which is now in its second edition. His latest book, *Chicano Drama: Society, Performance and Myth*, was published by Cambridge University Press in late 2000. The Association for Theatre in Higher Education (ATHE) awarded Huerta "Lifetime Achievement in Educational Theatre" in 2007, and the American Society for Theatre Research honored him as "Distinguished Scholar for 2008."

DAYSTAR/ROSALIE JONES was born on the Blackfeet Reservation in Montana, of Pembina Chippewa ancestry on her mother's side. She holds a master's degree in dance from the University of Utah and studied at the Juilliard School in New York City under José Limón. In 1980, Jones founded her company DAYSTAR: Contemporary Dance-Drama of Indian America, which conceptualized a *native modern dance* repertoire including *Sacred Woman, Sacred Earth, Wolf: A Transformation*, and *Prayer of the First Dancer.* The all-native modern dance company has toured throughout the United States, as well as Canada, Ireland, Finland, Bulgaria, and Turkey. For over forty years, Daystar taught throughout the United States and Canada, encouraging and promoting Native American talent in the arts. In the early 1990s, Jones served as Chair of Performing Arts at the Institute of American Indian Art in Santa Fe, NM. In 1997 she received a prestigious two-year Individual Choreographer's Fellowship from the National Endowment for the Arts. Jones is a published author, notably of the scripted dance-drama "No Home but the Heart," in *Keepers of the Morning Star: An Anthology of Native Women's Theater* (2003). The Daystar Archive was created in 2004

274 ABOUT THE CONTRIBUTORS

at UC–Riverside Special Collections. Since 2005, Jones has taught and developed indigenous studies curricula for the Indigenous Studies Department, Trent University, Ontario, Canada. Currently, Daystar/Rosalie Jones continues as a dancer, teacher, choreographer, and writer.

ANNIE KIRBY-SINGH took her bachelor's degree in American studies at the University of Wales Swansea and her master's degree in creative writing at the University of East Anglia. In 2006 she received her PhD from the University of Wales Swansea for her dissertation, *Synthesising a Context-Specific Approach to Native American Narratives: An Analysis of Philosophies of Knowledge and Cross-Cultural Communication in Native American and Academic Contexts.* Her essay "Cultural Conversations and Tricky Naming in Thomas King's *Green Grass, Running Water* and the *Dead Dog Café Comedy Hour,*" appeared in *First Nations of North America: Politics and Representation*, edited by Hans Bak (Amsterdam: Vrije Universiteit, 2005). She is also a published writer of short fiction. In 2004, her story "Revelations of Divine Love" was published in *Bracket: A New Generation in Fiction* (Comma Press, 2004), and in the same year "Orchid, Cherry-Blossom" was broadcast on BBC Radio 4 as part of their *Ones to Watch* series. In 2005 her story "The Wing" won the Asham Award for women's writing and later appeared in *Don't Know a Good Thing: The Asham Award Short-Story Collection*, edited by Kate Pullinger (Bloomsbury, 2006).

RIC KNOWLES is Professor and former Chair of Theatre Studies at the University of Guelph, editor of *Canadian Theatre Review*, and former editor (1999–2005) of *Modern Drama*. He is author of *Reading the Material Theatre* (2004), *Shakespeare and Canada* (2004), and *The Theatre of Form and the Production of Meaning* (1999); coauthor (with the Cultural Memory Group) of *Remembering Women Murdered by Men* (2006); editor of *Theatre in Atlantic Canada* (1986), *Judith Thompson* (2005), and *The Masks of Judith Thompson* (2006); and coeditor (with Joanne Tompkins and W. B. Worthen) of *Modern Drama: Defining the Field* (2003) and (with Monique Mojica) of *Staging Coyote's Dream: An Anthology of First Nations Drama in English* (2003), a second volume of which is forthcoming in 2008. He is general editor of the book series *Critical Perspectives on Canadian Theatre in English*.

DAVID KRASNER is Associate Professor and Head of Acting at Emerson College. He is coeditor, with Rebecca Schneider, of the University of Michigan Press Theater series *Theory/Text/Performance*. He recently published *American Drama, 1945–2000* (Blackwell Press, 2006), and he is coeditor, with David Saltz, of *Staging Philosophy* (University of Michigan Press, 2006), and editor of *Theatre in Theory: An Anthology, 1900–2000* (Blackwell, 2007), an anthology of performance theory and criticism. He twice received the Errol Hill Award from the American Society for Theatre Research, and his book *A Beautiful Pageant* (Macmillan, 2002) was a finalist for the George Freeley Award.

MARIA LYYTINEN received her MA degree in English philology and North American studies from the University of Helsinki. She works as a translator and English teacher in Helsinki. Among her translations is Carol Shields's biography of Jane Austen.

BRUCE MCCONACHIE is Professor and Chair of Theatre Arts at the University of Pittsburgh. His major books include *Interpreting the Theatrical Past* (University of Iowa, 1989), with Thomas Postlewait; *Melodramatic Formations* (University of Iowa, 1992); and *American Theatre in the Culture of the Cold War* (University of Iowa, 2003). Recently, McConachie has coauthored *Theatre Histories: An Introduction* (Routledge, 2006) with three other historians, and coedited *Performance and Cognition* (Routledge, 2006) with H. Elizabeth Hart. He coedits *Cognitive Studies in Literature and Performance*, a book series for Palgrave Macmillan.

MONIQUE MOJICA is an actor and published playwright from the Kuna and Rappahannock nations. Based in Toronto since 1983, she began training at the age of three and belongs to the second generation spun directly from the web of New York's Spiderwoman Theater. Her play *Princess Pocahontas and the Blue Spots* was produced by Nightwood Theatre and Theatre Passe Muraille in 1990, and on radio by CBC, and was published by Women's Press in 1991. She is coeditor, with Ric Knowles, of *Staging Coyote's Dream: An Anthology of First Nations Drama in English*, vols. 1 and 2, published by Playwrights Canada Press. Mojica is a longtime collaborator with Floyd Favel on various research and performance projects investigating Native Performance Culture. Theater credits include premieres of: *The Rez Sisters* (Native Earth), *Red River* (Crow's Theatre), *The Adventures of a Black Girl in Search of God* (Nightwood Theatre/Obsidian/Mirvish), and *Home Is My Road* (Factory Theatre), as well as the one-woman show *Governor of the Dew*, by Floyd Favel (NAC/Globe Theatre). She received a Best Supporting Actress nomination from the First Americans in the Arts for her role as Grandma Builds-the-Fire in Sherman Alexie's film *Smoke Signals.* She is a cofounder of Turtle Gals Performance Ensemble, with whom she co-created *The Scrubbing Project, The Triple Truth*, and *The Only Good Indian.* Mojica was last seen in the role of Caesar in *Death of a Chief*, Native Earth's critically acclaimed adaptation of Shakespeare's *Julius Caesar* (Native Earth/NAC), and in the role of Martha on the series *Rabbit Fall* for APTN. She was the Artist in Residence for American Indian Studies at the University of Illinois in Spring 2008, and her upcoming projects include *Chocolate Woman Dreams the Milky Way*, a new interdisciplinary collaboration with Floyd Favel, visual artist Oswaldo DeLéon Kantule, textile artist Erika Iserhoff, and Gloria Miguel. She continues to explore art as healing, as an act of reclaiming historical/cultural memory, and as an act of resistance.

JULIE PEARSON-LITTLE THUNDER is Assistant Professor of Theater at Northeastern Oklahoma State University in Tahlequah, Oklahoma. She has worked in Native theater for over twenty years. She was cofounder and artistic director of Thunder Road Theater (formerly Tulsa Indian Actors' Workshop) and then taught at Haskell Indian Nations University, Lawrence, Kansas.

SHELLEY SCOTT is Associate Professor and Chair of the Department of Theatre and Dramatic Arts at the University of Lethbridge. She teaches theater history and Canadian theater and occasionally directs. Along with her colleagues Lisa Doolittle and Amethyst First Rider, Scott has been involved with bringing in guest artists to the University of Lethbridge, including Shirley Cheechoo and Daystar. She earned a PhD from the University of Toronto in 1997; her thesis was a study of Nightwood Theatre, the feminist company that premiered Monique Mojica's play *Princess Pocahontas and the Blue Spots.* Her first book, *The Violent Woman as a New Theatrical Character Type: Cases from Canadian Theatre*, was published in 2007. She is currently serving as president of the Canadian Association for Theatre Research.

S. E. WILMER is Associate Professor of Drama and a Fellow of Trinity College Dublin. He is the author of *Theatre, Society and the Nation: Staging American Identities* (Cambridge University Press, 2002) and coauthor (with Pirkko Koski) of *The Dynamic World of Finnish Theatre* (Like Press, 2006). He has edited *National Theatres in a Changing Europe* (Palgrave Macmillan, 2008), *Writing and Rewriting National Theatre Histories* (Iowa University Press, 2004), *Portraits of Courage: Plays by Finnish Women* (Helsinki University Press, 1997), and *Beckett in Dublin* (Lilliput, 1992). He has coedited *Humour and Humanity: Contemporary Plays from Finland* (Like Press, 2006), *Rebel Women: Staging Ancient Greek Drama Today* (Methuen, 2005), *Stages of Chaos: Post-war Finnish Drama* (SKS, 2005), *Theatre, History and National Identities* (Helsinki University Press, 2001), and *Theatre Worlds in Motion* (Rodopi, 1998).

Index